ROGER'S PROFANISAURUS

Nail Sweary

D0131684

Viz

Dennis

First published August 2013 by
Dennis Publishing Ltd.,
30 Cleveland Street,
London W1T 4JD.

Distributed by Pan Macmillan Ltd.

ISBN 978-1-781062-44-9

Copyright © 2013 Fulchester Industries/
Dennis Publishing.

The right of Fulchester Industries to
be identified as the authors of this
work has been asserted by them in
accordance with the Copyright, Designs
and Patents Act 1988.

Dearly beloved. All rights reserved.
No part of this publication may be
reproduced, stored in or introduced into
a retrieval system, or transmitted, in
any form, or by any means (electronic,
mechanical, photocopying, recording,
copied out longhand with a goose-quill
pen or otherwise) without the prior
written permission of the publisher.
Any person who does any unauthorised
act in relation to this publication may be
liable to criminal prosecution and civil
claims for damages in the name of the
Father, and of the Son, and of the Holy
Spirit. Amen.

A CIP catalogue record for this book
is available from the British Library.

Compiled, edited and illustrated
by Graham Dury, Davey Jones &
Simon Thorp.

Printed by Polestar Wheatons, Exeter

Contents

DESPITE WHAT the ScrewFix catalogue would have you believe, humankind's most useful and versatile tool is language. Words, when used correctly, can melt hearts or topple governments. Words can transport you to fantastical faraway worlds or whisper elegant wisdom in your mind's ear. They're also good for describing what happens when your bum does a shit. As this book proves.

Yes, this book contains descriptions of doing a shit so excruciatingly vivid, it feels as if the book itself is defecating directly into your head via a phantom ringpiece embedded in your brain, expanding and contracting as it pushes out a thick, slug-like bolus of excrement, which smears turdishly across your imagination cells, painting skidmarks down the walls of your memories like a dirty protest, before dangling pendulously down the back of your throat for a moment, before breaking off and landing in your lungs with a soft, mushy plop. That's what it's like. No exaggeration.

But it's not just endless shitting. There's endless farting and pissing too. And a fair amount of jizzing: this book also contains lots of sex. Not the kind of improbable fantasy fuckrobatics you get in pornography, but graphic descriptions of things filthier yet infinitely more disappointing than that. It's like standing by the bins at a dogging hotspot, your nostrils filled with the stench of stale cans and chip paper as you watch pale, anonymous sets of genitalia joylessly slapping and sliding against one another like the automated components of a meaningless flesh machine. This is the sort of sexual material it's impossible to masturbate to. You'd have more luck wanking in a train crash.

Taken as a whole, this book radiates detached, amused horror at the spluttering basics of human biology with such unrelenting intensely, it's hard to believe it was written by humans at all. In fact right now, the book itself is almost certainly revolted by your presence; by the needy way your greasy fingers clutch its covers. As your warm, sour breath wafts across its pages, the paper and ink within glares back at you with cold contempt. As far as this book is concerned, you are a risible slab of animated ham; a greasy cadaver that gobbles and snots and pisses and shits, and - if you're a man - occasionally splutters snot-like gobbets of idiot cum from its comically undersized hamspout. Let's face it, there's some truth in that.

And there's truth in this book. A lot of it. The Profanisaurus isn't some tossaway pamphlet. It puts its finger on something profound about the human condition, then pulls it out and sniffs it. As with many landmark works, it has been painstakingly compiled over many years, by many hands. From unassuming beginnings, it has now racked up over 16 ,000 entries - like your mum has. Although unlike her it wouldn't fuck a fisherman's dog in a shop doorway in exchange for ten pence and a ham roll. Sorry, but the truth hurts.

Now enjoy your book.

Charlie Brooker

abandoned shit farm, face like an *sim*. A poetic phrase describing one whom the good Lord has seen fit to bless with aesthetically unconventional features. *Ugly as a bag of slapped twats.*

Abba *1. n*. Erstwhile Swedish pop band with a cracking blonde in it. As well as two lady singers and a bloke with a beard who played the piano. *2. abbrev*. The *taint, tintis, notcher, great*. Area Between Balls and Arse.

Abba bladder *n*. A gentleman who, when out *on the pop, breaks the seal* early. From the lyrics of the eponymous group's 1980 chart-topper *Super Trouper, viz*. One who is constantly "feeling like a number one".

Abi habit *euph*. A married man's compulsion to fire up his computer and search out the buxom Miss Titmuss's famous video the moment his missus toddles off to bed.

accstellarate *n*. To greatly increase your rate of *wifebeater* consumption in order to catch up with drinking companions who got to the pub before you did.

ACNB *abbrev*. Moderately ample in the *snake stakes*, but with little or nothing to offer in the *clockweights* department. All Cock No Bollocks.

Action Man syndrome *n. medic*. A condition suffered by male cyclists who find that, following a long bike journey, their genitalias have gone all numb in the style of the popular *fruitbowl*-free boys' dolls.

Adam Ant shit *n*. An act of defecation performed when the seat is broken, *viz*. When one is forced to "stand and deliver". A *muddy two-shoes*. See also *angry cossack*.

Adam Richman's chod bin, as full as *sim*. Said of anything that is comprehensively packed to the gunwales. A reference to the state of the eponymous *Man vs Food* presenter's *bum sink* following one of his frequent televised gustatory challenges. A *fat bird's shoe, parson's sack*.

address the Nuremberg rally *n*. To excitably perform *cumulonimbus* on a *bird* with a *Hitler tash*, whilst simultaneously fondling her left *churn* and *nip-nop* with one's extended right hand; the overall effect calling to mind the erstwhile Führer's infamous pose whilst addressing the masses in 1938, albeit rotated through about 90°.

adultery tax *n*. The exorbitant cost of buying breakfast in a Little Chef handily located adjacent to a discreet rural Travelodge. *'I'm afraid you can't claim your adultery tax back as a legitimate business expense, Mr Giggs.'*

aerosoil *n*. The fine faecal spray which typically accompanies a blast that is, frankly, unlikely to freshen the air.

after eight mince *1. n*. The exaggeratedly flamboyant gait affected by one who has recently taken a gallon of booze on board and is concentrating extremely hard on not falling over. *'Where the hell are Andrew, Michael and Diane? The Question Time end credits are rolling and they're supposed to be on air in two minutes.' 'Don't worry, I just saw them all doing the after eight mince out of the BBC bar.' 2. n*. The uncomfortable filling of a drinker's *tackle hammock* as a consequence of his unwise decision to have *one for the road. 'Fancy another pint, Dr Williams?' 'Better not, Dr Sentamu. I'm doing a royal wedding in the morning and I've already got a full serving of after eight mince here.'*

air biscuit guitar *n*. When suffering from flatulence, using one's cupped right hand to "pluck" pockets of one's gaseous foulage out of the air and propel it nosewards, whilst holding one's left arm outstretched as if fingering an ear-shredding solo on an imaginary fretboard.

air of the dog *n*. A noisome stink that follows you about *the morning after*, and cannot be shaken off. Also *air of the log.*

air tattoo *n.* A *shit* image of a *cabbage brown* butterfly stencilled onto the *fairy hammock* of the *dunghampers*. A *wind sketch.*

Ajax, like *sim.* Descriptive of a large *Simon Cowell* movement which disappears, in the words of the late Molly Weir, "clean around the S-bend" Usually followed by a *glory wipe*. Without scratching. Actually, come to think of it, Molly Weir did the Flash ads, not Ajax, didn't she.

AK farty-seven *n.* A loud and powerful fusillade of *shite*, caused by pockets of *sulphur dibaxide* becoming trapped between the *faceeshusses* in one's *back body*, which sounds and feels not unlike the discharge of a crudely-constructed Albanian assault rifle. *'I crouched down and took out my underpants with an AK farty-seven.'*

alco-Popeye *n.* A gentleman who, after imbibing one too many WKDs, takes on the persona of the famously incoherent maritime cartoon mentalist and wants to fight everyone in sight.

aliens, abducted by *euph.* Excuse proffered by one who finds himself afflicted with terrible, unexplained anal injuries the morning after an evening that he is unable to recall.

Alabama hot pocket *n.* An act so vile that, in the unlikely event that it exists and anybody's ever done it, it makes a *Boston pancake* look like a vicarage tea party. *'Welcome to the Yellowhammer State, Home of the Alabama Hot Pocket'.*

alarm plop *n.* An early morning wake up call courtesy of the previous night's tea.

Alaskan pipeline *n. Ice docking. Ninety-nine flake.*

Albany Street phone box, as busy as *sim.* Descriptive of any person or establishment that is particularly over-active or rushed off its feet. Named in honour of the popular public telephone kiosk at the top of the eponymous Hull Street, which is famous for the freelance herb and spice merchants who ply their trade there. *'That Phil Schofield's never off the telly these days is he? He's as busy as Albany Street phone box, him.'*

Alfgarnetstan *n. geog.* Hostile zone in the *Middle East End* which is populated by intolerant, violent people who dress strangely and talk funny.

Al Jizzera *n.* Any of a number of satellite television channels whose monodextrously-inclined viewers' interests are focused principally around issues related to the *gulf. Kebab TV. 'You coming to bed, love?' 'In a minute, dear. I'll just sit up and watch Al Jizzera for a bit.'*

alkie seltzer *n.* An effervescent drink taken to settle the stomach following a night *on the lash*. The hair of the dog. *'Christ, my guts are fucking rotten this morning, but I'll be right as rain after a few cans of alkie seltzer. You seen my pilot's cap anywhere, love?'*

all inclusive *n.* An unfeasibly large holiday *Thora Hird* comprising the remnants of an array of exotic and unfamiliar foodstuffs.

all stand for the French national anthem *phr.* A humorous introduction to be declaimed before performing a rousing fanfare on the *botty bugle.*

all you can shit buffet *n.* The unfortunate consequence of gluttonous over-indulgence at a favoured oriental eatery.

alright, put your cock away *exclam.* A useful put-down phrase when someone has been hogging the limelight for too long, *eg.* By going on about his car, his salary or an international sporting event he has successfully organised. *'Alright Seb, put your cock away, there's a good lad.'*

alter birthday *1. n.* The fictional birth date two years after their actual birth date that a teenager has to memorise in order to get a half fare on the train. *2. n.* The fictional birth date two years prior to their actual birth date that a teenager has to memorise in order to buy white cider.

altitude thickness *n. milit.* Helicopter pilot's airborne equivalent to the more earth-bound condition of *convoy cock*.

amber gambler *1. n.* An impatient motorist who takes the opportunity to drive through the lights even as they turn to red or just before they turn to green, thus leaving themselves open to prosecution. *2. n.* Likewise, any male who *cops off* with a young *goer* of dubious vintage. *'Todays birthdays: Fran Zwitter, Slovenian historian and rhyming slang, 1905; Robin Day, phlegmatic British political interviewer and television presenter, 1923; (name, type of guitar played and identity of former rock band removed on legal advice) and amber gambler, 1936.'*

Amsterdam uppercut *n.* The "wrist deep" action employed by one skilled in the art of *fisting*. *'Palmolivia was powerless to resist. The oily mechanic's eyes burnt into hers like sapphires. She felt muscular arms enfolding her softly yielding body as she was literally swept away in a whirlwind of passion behind a pile of old tyres. Yearning for his manly touch, she lay down and yielded her most precious womanly treasure to him. 'Do it now, Swarfego,' she breathed. 'Give me an Amsterdam uppercut.''* (from *The Lady and the Exhaust Fitter* by Barbara Cartland).

amuse bush *n.* Sophisticated term for foreplay; a fiddly entrée prior to the main course of *pork in cider*, typically finishing with a yoghurt-themed dessert. *Frigmarole.*

anal bleaching *1. n.* Having the skin around one's *nipsy* lightened to improve its aesthetic appearance, although to be frank, the words "silk purse" and sow's ear" spring to mind. *2. n.* A *Neptune's kiss* from a *jobby engine* which has recently been cleaned and

still contains a strong solution of Harpic.

and if you listen ... that sounds like a golf *exclam.* A carefully-timed two part gnomic epigram to be delivered with a solid, German-engineered *backfire* in the middle.

Andrex puppy nose *n.* An unexpectedly moist, brown finger end which one finds protruding through a square of toilet tissue after inadvertently *shaking hands with the French* whilst dandifying the *rear deck*.

and the dirt is gone! *exclam.* What Barry Scott probably says after he *steps on a frog*.

and tonight's lottery numbers are *exclam.* Something to announce before *dropping a bonus ball*.

angry birds *1. n.* A popular "app" for mobile telephones, to be played whilst ensconced on the *chod pan*. (Mind, it's not as good as our *Profanisaurus - Das Krapital* one. Check it out at *www.profanisaurusapp.com*). *2. n.* A group of disgruntled women, reacting badly to a humorous gentleman playfully dipping his *knackers* into their drinks whilst he is *heavily refreshed*. *3. n.* Any hardcore dominatrix-based pornography viewed on a smartphone or similar device. *'Why don't you switch that thing off for a minute and come down and watch television with me?' 'I'll be with you in a minute, love. I can't help it if I'm addicted to angry birds.'*

angry cossack *n.* Upon sitting down for a *tom tit* when the *bog* seat is missing, the exuberant and energetic folk dance that must be performed in order to prevent one's *bum cheeks* accidentally touching the porcelain.

angry turds *n.* A frustrating game enjoyed opportunistically on the *shit pot*.

animal crackers *rhym. slang.* The male *clockweights*. From the Shirley Temple song of the same name, but you wouldn't necessarily want them in your soup.

Annie and Clarabel *n.* The sort of thing you see on *Jeremy Kyle*; two subservient girlfriends of a domineering male, who live in full knowledge of each other's existence and are indeed happy to engage in regular three-way activities.

anointing the faithful *1. n.* In a church, where the vicar drops holy water onto the faces of his kneeling congregation. *2. n.* In a *grumble flick*, where the leading male thespian drops *spaff* onto the faces of his kneeling co-stars. *3. n.* In church, where the vicar drops *spaff* onto the faces of his kneeling congregation. Admittedly, not in many churches, but it probably does happen.

another man's gravy *n.* Whilst *dining at the Y*, an inadvertent taste of a previous customer's *special sauce*.

ant burners *n.* Powerful, jam-jar-style spectacles. *'Your majesty, I'd like to introduce you to Sir Mervyn King, the Governor of the Bank of England.' 'Bugger me, Lord Chancellor. Check out the ant burners on this fucker.'*

anteater's gasmasks, pair of *n.* A brassiere of the sort worn by women whose *wombles' noses* have migrated south over the years.

antflaccid *n.* Viagra. *Bongo Bill's banjo pills.*

antiques scroteshow *n.* Any car-boot-sale-quality heirloom-valuation-based daytime television programme, *eg. Flog It!, Dickinson's Real Deal, Cash in the Attic etc.*

anusthetic *n.* The feeling of numbness in the lower body experienced following a protracted period spent sat on the *porcelain throne* reading the *Autotrader*.

any old pork in a storm *n.* The "last resort" chap that a desperate lady brings home after suffering a prolonged *sausage* drought.

AONB *abbrev.* A view that takes one's breath away. A UNESCO World Heritage Sight. Arse of Outstanding Natural Beauty.

apollo 13 *euph.* A rapid release of gas in a confined space that causes the occupants to retreat to a safer place. *'Houston, we have a problem. Fred's done an Apollo 13.'*

apple *n.* A Special Constable or Police Community Support Officer. Because they're "not a PC". A *Happy Shopper copper, potted plant.*

approach shot *1. n.* In golf, a pitch from fairway to green. *2. n.* In sex, an unfortunate premature ejaculation just as you are getting near the *hole*. *Spending your money before you get to the shop.*

Arabian goggles *n.* The saucy act of sitting on a woman's forehead and resting your *bollocks* in her eyes whilst being noshed off. Possibly anatomically impossible, but might be worth a try nevertheless. *Eggcupping.*

areola borealis *n.* An enchanting, ethereal phenomenon, occasionally glimpsed around the poles on a *bird's northern hemispheres.*

aris tweed *n.* Tough, hard-wearing, matted anal hair from which you could weave a pair of gamekeeper's trousers. Also *glarsefibre.*

armadillo *n.* The characteristic shape formed by the rolls of adipose tissue around a lardy lass's shoulders, hips and back while she is being *scuttled* from behind.

armed knobbery *n.* Any manual manipulation of the *single-barrelled snotgun* performed with a view to making a sudden withdrawal from the *wank bank*.

arse-and-a-half of full cream milk *phr.* A gentlemanly exclamation of approbation upon seeing a comely female backside. *'Anneka! The clue is in the windmill! It's somewhere in the windmill! Get out of the helicopter and run up the ... Wow! That's an arse-and-a-half of full cream milk!'*

arse balm *n. milit.* Any emollient skin preparation applied to a squaddie's *south mouth* to avoid chaffing prior to a 20-mile route march in full kit.

arsebidextrous *adj.* Gifted with the ability to

lean over onto either *bum cheek* in order to *let one rip*. *'What very few people realise is that the Princess Royal is also arsebidextrous, as this clip of her elegantly dropping a gut during the dressage section of the Badminton Horse Trials shows.'* (Nicholas Witchell, narrating *Princess Anne - Sixty Years of Being Absolutely Marvellous*, BBC TV).

arse gasket *n.* One of those paper *bog seat* covers that you get in the USA to stop you getting germs on your *nipsy.*

arse gout *n. medic.* High class flatulence fuelled by rich foodstuffs. *'Another helping of venison and port trifle, Sir Terry?' 'I shouldn't really, Heston. It gives me terrible arse gout.'*

arsemageddon *n.* An apocalyptic rectal meltdown that feels like the end of the world as we know it. An *arse like a broken ice cream machine, three pile island.*

arsenal *n.* The public toilet fixture that isn't the urinal. The *bum sink, jobby engine.*

arse-patcho n. A thin anal soup; a delicately-balanced consommé of partially-digested *catbab* meat, exotic spices, crisps, pork scratchings and farmhouse cider.

arseterity measures *n.* Taking all your *dumps* whilst at work to save on the expense of buying your own *brown shield stamps.*

arse tobacco *n.* The unpleasant collection of colonic detritus, anal effluvium, faecal flotsam and pubic jetsam left on the *bog seat* after wiping. So called because it is "a mixture of ready-rubbed and flake".

arse-whipped *adj.* Said of a bloke who'd do anything for a sniff of *back door action* off his missus. *Under the bum.*

arsewife *n.* A *bag for life* who's not averse to letting her hubby have the odd rummage round her *chutney locker.*

art room sink, face like an *sim.* Said of a lucky lady who has been the more or less simultaneous recipient of the romantic at-tentions of several generous gentlemen. Also *plasterer's radio, quattro formaggio.*

Arthur Fowler's allotment *euph.* An un-kempt, overgrown *ladygarden* which looks like it has not been tended since May 1996. Also full Belgian, Ken Dodd's hairbrush.

artistic spectrum, on the *euph.* Said of a chap who *bakes a light cake, knows what's in his flowerbeds* and likes *bumming.*

asboranto *n.* Grunt-based language used by those of low breeding when communicating with each other. *'What's happening on Jeremy Kyle?' 'Search me. I don't speak asboranto.'*

ascertain *1. v.* To determine or discover con-clusively. *2. v.* To entertain with one's anus. *'Phwooarr!!! Frumpy Kate's nipsylicious sister Pippa certainly puts the "hot" into patri-hot-ic as she ascertains the horny crowds outside Westminster Abbey.'* (picture caption from The Daily Telegraph, April 30th 2011).

Asda price *euph.* Without any disrespect to the quite excellent supermarket chain, said of a lady who looks particularly *cheap,* and worthy of a good slap on the *arse.*

Ashford and Simpson euph. A *motion* that is, in the words of the eponymous Motown duo's 1984 single, "solid as a rock".

assquatch *n.* An abominable cryptozoologi-cal monster that is occasionally spotted emerging from its dark cave with a great deal of moaning. A post-constipation *Meat Loaf's daughter.*

Astra map pocket, fanny like a *sim.* Large but surprisingly tight.

athlete's foot *n.* A twelve-inch erection brought about by illegal performance-en-hancing pharmaceuticals.

athlete's fud *n. medic.* A yeasty infection of the *minnie moo.* Thrush, *gash rash, Lady Chalk of Bilingsgate.*

at lagerheads *euph.* Said of a couple having a lively exchange of philosophical opinions whilst *heavily refreshed.*

atomic punch *n.* A harmless, yet borderline unethical/illegal practice during a bout of *the other* with the *bird* on top, whereby a sneaky clout to the base of the *veiny bang stick* effects a lightning-quick transition from entering through the *front door* to the *back passage.*

a touch of the vapours *1. phr.* An excuse offered by any Victorian maiden aunt who found herself light-headed and in need of a sit down on a *chaise longue. 2. n.* A sprout-some *arse biscuit* which is so foul that it has to be blamed on the dog, whether or not you own one.

Audi driver *n.* Someone who appears desperate to get up your *arse.* From the customary tail-gating road manners exhibited by drivers of the stupid-fairy-light-bedecked German motor cars.

Augustus poop *euph.* A huge blockage of the *pipes* in one's *chocolate factory* that causes a dangerous build-up of back pressure until it is eventually forced out at speed.

auntie freeze *n.* During an act of *gentlemanly relaxation*, a involuntary suspension of erotic inspiration engendered by an unbidden mental image of an elderly female relative. *Nanaphylactic shock.*

austerity night *n.* A curtains-closed evening in with a pot noodle and a *wank. 'You coming down the Pugin Room for a few jars of Chateau d'Yquem 1787 with me and a few of the other Buller boys, Gideon?' 'No thanks, Dave. It's another austerity night at number eleven for me, I'm afraid.'*

auto-bography *n.* A memoir of negligible literary merit kept for reading on the toilet. *'I'm halfway through Jeremy Clarkson's auto-bography, vicar.' 'Well can you hurry up? I'm dying for a piss out here.'*

Axminster spinster *n.* A single *lady in comfortable shoes, ie.* One who has not done a great deal of *rug munching* lately. A *Wilton widow, les-been, hasbian.*

babnride *n.* Colloquial contraction/elision of the words "kebab" and "taxi-ride", used when referring to certain late-opening establishments where food and a cab may be simultaneously requisitioned. *'And that completes the shipping forecast. Ace, that's me finished for the night. I'm off for a babnride at the Trojan takeout.'*

babooning *n.* In *dogging* circles, inadvertently breaking the windscreen wipers off a car whilst engaging in vigorous sexual congress across the bonnet. Also known as *doing a Whipsnade.*

baby drowners *n.* Unfeasibly humungous *assets* that could prove hazardous to a neonate.

baby gap *n.* A vagina.

bachelor's arm *n. medic.* Temporary condition experienced following a quick bout of unexpected exercise. *Penis elbow.*

bachelor's goodnight kiss *n.* The touching, smooching sound of an uncircumcised *five-skin* being squeezed clean after a pre-slumber *prong-throttle.*

bachelor's heft *n.* Involuntary tumescence experienced by a single fellow who isn't getting *any.* Not entirely dissimilar to *middle-aged heft*; which is involuntary tumescence experienced by a married man whose missus has "had enough of that sort of thing".

bachelor's lifestyle *euph.* A foetid, woe-filled dwelling piled high with empty pizza boxes, discarded lager cans and pornographic magazines, not to mention a lavatory that has been blocked with *bangers and mash* since shortly after the householder's last girlfriend left him, several years ago.

back catalogue *n.* A list of people you have of had, or would like to have of had, *done up the dirtbox.* Also *A-list.*

Back Door *n. prop.* Notional middle name of any female celebrity who might be deemed worthy of *getting her back doors smashed in, eg.* Kelly "Back Door" Rowland, Kylie "Back Door" Minogue or the late Kathy "Back Door" Staff.

back forest gateau *n.* A well-baked *chocolate cake* from the *bum oven,* served up on a pan of white porcelain with a Guinness glaze, following a good evening out. May be accompanied by cherries.

back teeth are floating, my *phr.* An expression of a person's urgent need to pass water. *'You couldn't point me towards the nearest gurgler, could you, Carson? Only I've had six cups of Earl Grey this morning and my back teeth are floating.'*

back to bed Peppa! *exclam.* An amusing thing for a chap to say after *stepping on a duck.* Also *a thank-you for the music; a bit more choke and she would have started; better an eviction than a bad tenant; ease springs.*

backdraft *n.* The rousing fanfare that precedes a good *shit.* The *Bakerloo breeze.*

backside disaster *1. n.* A radical skate/snowboarding trick performed on the lip of a gnarly half-pipe, whatever the fuck that's supposed to mean. *2. n.* The result of *gambling and losing.*

bad blood *n.* The feeling of resentment felt by a bloke who has organised a romantic getaway only to find that his inamorata's *pussy* is devouring *cunt mice* at a rate of knots.

badge *n.* One's coital colours. *'I went to Brian's house-warming party last night. Pinned my badge on his sister.'*

badger baiting *n.* Deliberately tormenting one's better half whilst she's *up on blocks* by doing things that will cause her to go into a *blob strop, eg.* Leaving the bog seat up, placing a dirty cup on the floor, breathing too much.

badger gas *n.* Noxiously toxic fumes experienced whilst evacuating the *Simons* the morning after a surfeit of rough cider and *catbabs.*

bagged salad breathe for a while, likes to let his *euph.* Said of one who *eats fancy cakes.*

bagging area *n.* The dance floor of any club or bar whenceforth a gentleman may find himself leaving with an "unexpected item".

bag of beef *n.* A capacious *butcher's dustbin* which is not suitable for vegetarians. See also *box of cow tongues.*

bag of knickers *n.* Scampi fries. *'Two pints of cooking and a bag of knickers, please.'*

bag of Lego *euph.* Descriptive of the experience of intimacy with a lady devoid of womanly curves. *eg. 'Fuck me, I wouldn't fancy fucking that Kate Moss much. It would be like humping a bag of Lego.'*

BAIB/baib *acronym.* Notional accolade awarded by male office workers to the female colleague whom they consider to be in possession of the most aesthetically pleasing anterior elevation. Best Arse In Building.

bakes a light cake *euph.* Said of a chap who *likes to let his bagged salad breathe for a while. 'It's no good. I can't keep living this lie any longer. I'm going to just come out and say it. Mum, dad, I bake a light cake.'*

ball butter *n.* Oleaginous, cheesy spread produced after giving one's *man milk* a good old churn.

ballcuzzi *n.* An improvised whirlpool bath for the testicles, apparently consisting of a teapot filled with warm (not boiling) water, to which bath oil and/or salts are added. The gentleman then lowers his *chicken skin handbag* into the water whilst his partner blows gently down the spout to create a swirl of soothing bubbles. That could work, but probably best not try it in the café at Wetherby Services.

ballfro *n.* A cool 70s-style halo of hair around the *happy sack.*

ballroom clitz *n.* A bulbous *vajazzled vajay-jay* that looks not unlike a glitterball in a 1970s discotheque.

ballshoop alley *n.* The *gooch, tintis, taint, notcher.*

ball snorkel *n.* The male penis.

ball soup, sitting in *euph.* A polite way of saying that someone has very *sweaty bollocks.* Also *scrotum soup. 'By the end of his cross-examination at the hands of the Home Affairs Select Committee, Mr Buckles appeared to be sitting in ball soup.'*

balls think my cock's been cut, my *phr.* Exclamation bemoaning a protracted period of celibacy. *'Look, your holiness I've not had a wank since the fifties. My balls think my cock's been cut.' 'Tell me about it, Cliff.'*

Balotelli's fireworks *n.* A particularly explosive burst of *tommy tits* that wreck the bathroom.

banana steamer *1. n.* A speciality coffee-based beverage. *2. n.* A large, crescent-shaped and pungent *Douglas.*

banal sex *n.* Pedestrian lovemaking in the missionary position. *'Sorry love, I don't do banal.'*

B & poo *euph.* A sturdily-constructed *log cabin*, such that the person responsible can look upon it and proudly state: "I did that", in a manner reminiscent of an actor in one of the popular semi-eponymous DIY empire's current batch of adverts, standing in front of something that has been built by a team of professional carpenters.

bandsome *adj.* Said of an aesthetically ill-favoured fellow who is rendered inexplicably attractive by his proximity to a microphone, electric guitar *etc. 'Eeh, that Mick Hucknall's bandsome, isn't he.'*

bangaroo *n.* A *scuttle* exhibiting an elevated coefficient of restitution. A bouncy *space-clopper.*

bangers and gash *n.* A filling portion of *tits* and *fanny.*

banging the cutlery drawer, like *sim.* A delightful trope describing sexual intercourse with an unacceptably scrawny woman, with all her knobbly knees, sharp elbows and jutting hips and that.

Bangkok handbag *n.* Dubious hotel-wardrobe-based solitary sexual practice enjoyed by many now-deceased celebrities.

Bangkok 2am rule *n.* Unwritten legal statute that anything that happens in the family holiday resort after two in the morning doesn't count. Also *Wanchai goggles, Blok M fever*. *'Was that a ladyboy you ended up with last night, then?' 'Yeah, but I was completely rat-arsed, so I invoked the Bangkok 2am rule.'*

banjo pie *n.* Any food product whereby the first bite causes debris to fall down your front, so you hold the pie at a safe distance whilst brushing pastry crumbs from your shirt front with a strumming motion.

bank *exclam.* Monosyllabic ejaculation said in the style of a *Weakest Link* contestant when a bloke spots an attractive lady and wishes to store the image in his *mammary banks* for later use. Also *file under W*.

baptop *n.* A portable computing device maintained for the purpose of accessing the *binternet*. A *filth machine, faptop, dirty mac*.

barbecue alone *v.* To engage in a solitary bout of *meat manipulation* whilst drinking lager in the garden.

barbepoo *n.* The unmistakeable excrement that results from the standard British summer diet of charred, half-cooked sausages, ketchup and lager, consumed whilst experiencing the early stages of drizzle-induced hypothermia.

barber of Savile *n.* A gents' hairdresser who typically purveys the sort of *sex case* coiffures favoured by *philanrapists*, trainspotters and 1970s television personalities.

Barbie gap *n.* The alluring aperture between the tops of a woman's legs. Also *Toblerone tunnel, Cumberland gap, Foyston gap*.

bare-arsed boxing *n.* The s*xual act.

barely got the smell off one's fingers *phr.* Said of a chap who moves swiftly from one ladyfriend to the next. *'Rolling Stone Ronnie Wood certainly wasn't allowing the moss to gather under his feet last night as he stepped out with new girlfriend Brazilian supermodel Macarena Parasol, 21, just days after being dumped by his previous girlfriend, Brazilian supermodel Copacabana Maracas, 21. A close pal of the wrinkly rocker, 62, commented: "This is the real thing. Ronnie's head over heels about Macarena, even though he's barely got the smell off his fingers from Copacabana."'* (from *The Daily Mail*, every day).

bare that in mind, I'll *exclam.* Said by a cheeky chap when he espies an attractive lady about whom he intends to later fantasise whilst manually stimulating his penis.

bariatric buggy *n.* Chariot of choice for the *big-boned* when trundling to the shops for pasties, pies and diet pop.

barnacle *n.* An inconsiderate pub-goer who prevents others from replenishing their drinks by obstinately guarding his position at the bar all night, nursing a single pint of the cheapest lager available. From bar + nacle.

Barnacle's nosh box *1. n.* A world-famous £2.40 variety "meal deal" at the eponymous Stockton-on-Tees fish & chip shop. *2. n.* A manky *muff* licked out behind a Teeside fish & chip shop, for about £2.40.

Barnsley caviar *n.* Mushy peas. Also *Geordie hummus, Scouse guacamole*.

barrel fever *n. medic.* The shakes, whereby the first pint of the day has to be held with both hands to prevent spillage. Also *hatties*.

barsicle *n.* A *stalacshite*.

barter in the fish market *euph.* Of a lady, to *play the invisible banjo*.

BAs *n. rhym. slang.* The testicles. From the name of the aviophobic *A-Team* character played by Mr T (real name Mysterious Teapot) who, notwithstanding his fierce appearance, was famously compassionate towards the imbecilic, *viz.* Bosco "Bad Attitude" Baracus = knackers.

Basildon bidet *n.* A cold, wet smacker on the *trumpeter's lips* that fortuitously obviates the need for wiping. *Neptune's kiss.*

BAST/bast *acronym.* Big Arse Small Tits.

bath jack *n.* In the bath, putting a clenched fist at the bottom of the spine, to allow you to *grip the lather* without making splashes.

bathtub bathyscaphe *n.* Following a bout of *waxing the dolphin*, an hermetically-sealed, clasped hand which is used to transport recently-shot *man fat* down to the bubbly depths of the plughole in order to dispose of it cleanly via a swirling vortex which is then re-plugged. This facilitates further bathing/soaking/*wanking* without running the risk of being attacked by the *cock mess monster.*

batmanning *1. n.* In the world of rock-climbing, cheating by using the belay rope to hoist oneself up. It says here. *2. n.* Superheroic act performed by those returning home from the pub, *ie.* Crawling along on all fours in a manner reminiscent of the not-very-special effect used to make Adam West and Burt Ward appear to climb up a vertical wall in the eponymous television series of the 1960s.

bat signal *n.* A warning of imminent *evil-doings* that calls for immediate action. *'Excuse me, ambassador, I have to run. I've just had the bat signal.'*

battleships, just like playing *sim.* Trying to engage genitals with a lardsome *piabetic,* on account of her repeatedly informing you of your progress by saying "Missed ... Missed ... Missed".

Baumgartner's balloon, more air than *sim.* Suffering from an excess of *carbon dibaxide*; a reference to fizzy-pop-fuelled Aus-

trian daredevil Felix and his supersonic parachuting shenanigans.

Bay of Pigs *1. n.* Some sort of Cuban shenanigans in the 1960s involving Russian missiles and President Kennedy. *2. n.* A humorous reference to the state of Hornsea beach in the summer; a harmless quip which will nonetheless no doubt fall foul of the so-called "politically correct" lobby.

BBQ *n.* A Bodleian Beauty Queen. A woman in a workplace populated by socially inadequate males (*eg.* A monastery, trainspotter's clubhouse, a university library), who becomes an object of lust for the habitués of said establishment notwithstanding her limited appeal in the wider world.

bead in your bellend, have a *euph.* To be grumpy. *'And now we head over to Ambridge for tonight's episode of the Archers, where Jack's got a bead in his bellend after finding a pair of Nigel Pargetter's spunked underpants in Peggy's handbag.'*

Beadle *n.* A small drinks can of the sort given out on planes. *'Can I have six Beadles of tomato juice and three vodkas, please?' 'Of course, Captain.'*

beadleboobs *n. medic.* Unfortunate condition of the female, (or male former Home Secretary and founder of the SDP), whereby one of the *churns* is noticeably larger than the other. And vice versa. Named after the respective handfuls that the late asymmetrically-mitted entertainer would have been able to comfortably support.

bean buddies *n.* Ladies who are wont to stash their *comfortable slippers* under the same bed.

beanis *n.* A confusing, fleshy protuberance found in some underpants that is, one might think, too big to be a *clematis*, whilst paradoxically being too small to be a *cock.*

bearded ninja *n.* A frustratingly fleeting glimpse of a *fuzzy peach* in a film, *eg.* Sharon Stone's in *Basic Instinct,* Jenny Agutter's in *Logan's Run* or Doris Hare's in *Mutiny on the Buses.*

Bear Grylls pills *n.* Any drink or drugs taken on board by a man which may cause him to act in a more courageous and/or foolhardily fisticuffsome manner than might be good for his health. *'Please pay no attention to my companion, Mr Doorman. He's been on the Bear Grylls pills.'*

beast of chodbin *n.* A massive black *turd.*

beast with two sacks *n.* A visually off-putting *chicken skin handbag*-based *Newton's cradle* typically experienced by a pair of professional footballers engaged in a spot of *Dorothy Perkins.*

beatifying the cardinal *n.* A more extreme version of *bashing the bishop. 'Cup of tea, your holiness?' 'Give me ten minutes, will you? I'm just beatifying the cardinal.'*

beaver cheese *n.* Stale *man milk* fermenting on a woman's *badger. Chuffdruff, gusset sugar, blick.*

be bog *n.* Free-form atonal public lavatory jazz, improvised on *brass eye* instruments. *Pan pipes, pot music, acrapella.*

Bechamel bullet *n.* A high velocity, savoury slug of *gentleman's spendings* which could be used to garnish a parmo.

Becks ray specs *n. Beer goggles* with expensive German optics.

bed & buckfast *n.* A sojourn in Glasgow during which one samples the local culture and has a fight in the park.

bedroom tax *1. n.* Welfare reform intended to cut the amount of benefit that people can claim if they are considered to have a spare bedroom that could, conceivably, be let out to a paying lodger. Whose rent would presumably then count as income, so they wouldn't be able to claim any other benefits either. *2 n.* The cost of a meal in a fancy restaurant that paves the way to the bedroom.

beef curtain, the *n. geopol.* The imaginary line running along the borders of European countries of Holland, Germany, Austria and Hungary where *knocking shops* are legal, dividing them from their more prudish counterparts. *'A beef curtain has descended over Europe. Can anyone change me this ten bob note into Guilders?'* (Winston Churchill addressing the Hague Congress, 1948).

beef olive *n.* A *sausage* wrapped in *beef.*

beeory *n.* A ludicrously ill-informed hypothesis on any subject that is formulated under the influence of brown booze.

beerby *n.* What a gent acquires after years of *refreshment, viz.* An enormous gut that makes him look pregnant. See also *kebabby. 'Eeh, have you seen Ricky lately? He's blooming. He looks as if he's having a beerby.'*

beer gas *n.* An extremely potent odour that can be used to disperse crowds.

beergasm *n.* The moment of pure pleasure experienced upon taking the first sip of bitter at the end of a hard day at work or watching television, marked by a tingly sensation all over and the release of a low moan.

beer googles *n.* Recognition of the fact that, throughout the course of an evening, the quality and tone of the *grumble* being searched out by a web user is inversely proportional to the amount of alcohol he has consumed.

beermuda triangle *n.* The triangulated geographical space defined at its vertices by three public houses, within the boundaries of which Euclidean polygon a drinker may be lost for days, if not indefinitely. In Sydney, Australia, there is a particularly potent *beermuda triangle* between The Lord Nelson, The Palisades and The Hero of Waterloo.

beer trumpet *n.* Primitive, alcohol-powered hearing aid which causes users to laugh uproariously at a statement which, in the cold light of day, is seen to contain no trace of humour whatsoever.

Beijing traffic jam *n*. A particularly intractable bout of constipation lasting several days, and resulting in high levels of noxious pollution.

bellendrical *adj*. Shaped like the end of a chap's generative member. *'How would you like your hair done this week, Miss Widdecombe?' 'Bellendrical please, Sandra.'*

bellendsleydale *n*. Full fat, matured Yorkshire *knob cheese*.

bell mop *n*. A chap's intimate wipe.

Bells *n*. A child of questionable parental lineage, that is to say one who is descended from a blend of various manly liquors. *'Well, he's got the coalman's nose, the postman's eyes, the gas man's ears and the 1992-1993 Division Two Premiership-winning Featherstone Rovers squad's hair. He's definitely a Bells.'*

belt-tightener *n*. A *shit* of such epic magnitude that the cincture must afterwards be pulled in by a notch to prevent the trousers declevitating.

belvita *n*. An early morning *trump* that completely puts you off food until at least lunchtime.

BEMHO/bemho *n*. A standard issue *boner*. Basic Early Morning Hard On.

Bengal tiger *n*. An Indian beast that growls ominously in one's guts. *'Fuck me, what the fucking fuck was that?' 'Pardon me, your holiness. My Bengal tiger has awoken.'*

Benghazi *1. n*. Beleaguered town in Libya. *2. n. rhym. slang.* The lavatory. From Beng hazi = khazi. *'How much longer you going to be in that Benghazi, Esther?'*

Benjamin Button *n*. A *one pump chump* who is *up and over like a pan of milk*. A fellow who, like the character in the eponymous Brad Pitt film, "finishes right at the start".

Bensham tuxedo *n*. The pyjamas. Smart/casual wear for exclusive soirées in the salubrious Gateshead garden suburb.

Bernie Clifton, the *euph*. The naked, *cock*-bobbing walk to answer a knock on one's door when in a state of "comedy-ostrich-neck"-style arousal.

bespoke poke *n*. An act of sexual congress enjoyed in relatively refined surroundings, such as in a posh hotel bedroom with en-suite bathroom facilities on hand for post-coital ablutions. As distinct from, say, in a Glasgow phonebox with vomit on the floor or the bonnet of a Ford Focus in the Hog's Back layby just off the A31.

better an empty house than a bad tenant *exclam*. A gnomic apothegm following the eviction of a tenacious rectal squatter.

better than a wank in Heaven *phr*. An amusing exclamatory rejoinder to be uttered, possibly whilst winking and elbowing the nearest person in the ribs, after someone else says "Fuckin' Hell".

Bieber's ballbag, like *sim*. Something hairless and empty. Justin Bieber's *scrotum*, for example.

big bluey storage *n*. A reliable bachelor friend with whom a man can deposit his lifetime's accumulation of *grot mags, stick vids*, *split kipper* Polaroids of his ex and other items of sentimental value, when he is about to commence cohabiting with a new *bird*.

big in Japan *1. euph*. Said of niche musical acts who barely manage to scrape into the UK charts but somehow shift *shitloads* of records in the Land of the Rising Sun. *2. n. A clearing of the nether throat* which has little impact in the immediate vicinity of its progenitor but inscrutably matures to eye-watering rankness at the farthest end of the office, church, Houses of Parliament *etc*.

Biggles's scarf *n*. Unusually long *Keith Burtons*.

biker foreplay *n*. The romantic practice of

kick-starting the motorbike next to one's significant other, and then holding her head under the covers so that the potent *exhaust fumes* can get her in the mood. A *Dutch oven*.

Bilbo Baggins' sock drawer *euph.* A particularly commodious *clout*.

Bill Oddie *n. onomat.* A short, sharp *Edward Woodward* in the bath.

billy goat's chin *n.* A gruff *muff under the bridge* with a distinctly coarse beard of pubic hair.

Billy Joel *1. n. prop.* Scrotum-faced New York singer/songwriter who, bizarrely, is friends with opinionated Fitzwilliam-born bat-swinger Geoffrey Boycott. *2. n.* A *Boris Johnson*.

bimbo bakery *n.* The tanning salon.

binterruption *n.* An unwarranted wifely reminder to keep one's counsel.

bin tumescence *n.* The way a full black bag becomes sexually excited and swells up to an unlikely and disturbing volume as it is removed from its container.

bingo doors *n.* An old, well-battered set of *cat flaps*. *'My next guest needs no introduction, except to say that even well into her seventh decade her bingo doors would be well worth bashing in. Ladies and gentlemen, Dame Helen Mirren.'*

bingo wing commander *n.* A chap with a penchant for the company of more mature females. *'Today's birthdays: 1923, Robin Day, erstwhile political interviewer; 1936, Bill Wyman, Rolling Stones bass player and (removed on legal advice); 1985, Wayne Rooney, Premiership footballer and bingo wing commander.'*

binter *n.* The pointless, shrill and inconsequential gossip about *The X-Factor, Strictly Come Dancing* or *Big Brother* that passes for conversation on programmes such as *Loose Women. Fanny banter.*

bird feeder *n.* A hard cylinder full of *seed*, around which *birds* flock. *'There were a couple of swallows on my bird feeder this morning. And I also got my nuts nibbled by a cheap whore behind a skip, which was nice.'*

bird table *n.* Unpleasantly sexist term for an otherwise attractive lady who is spoiled by a dearth of *knockers*. From the fact that "it would look great with a couple of tits on it."

Birmingham booty call *n.* The West Midlands hobby of setting one's mobile phone to vibrate before inserting it up a bird's *fundament* and ringing it. The *Birmingham booty call* became even more popular when the original 1983 Motorola 8000 "brick" was superseded by more modern, streamlined units.

Bishop's minger *n.* A woman so plain that she has to marry a vicar.

Bisto kids *n.* The products of *comfortably shod* couples' judicious use of the gravy baster.

black forest gateau *n.* A luxuriant and filling *knicker pudding.* £3.95.

Black Magic box, I bet she knows the secrets of the *exclam.* Said of a woman *with a lovely personality.*

Blackpool cocktail bar *euph.* Any drinking establishment whose clientelle, it could be argued, might be somewhat lacking in poise, refinement and sophistication, *eg.* Sneaky Pete's in Edinburgh before it got shut down due to one too many murders.

blartifacts *n.* Items of used ladies' *intimate apparel* stolen from washing lines in, to pick an example entirely at random, the town of Barnoldswick, Lancashire or bought from vending machines by *bespectable* Japanese businessmen.

blast from the past *1. n.* In disc jockey *hyperbole*, any record that is not currently in the charts. *2. n.* A not particularly appetising whiff of last night's supper. *3. n.* A senior citizen's *dropped gut,* still bearing vestigial traces of their quondam wartime diet of powdered egg, Woolton pie and snoek. *'Ooh, I definitely got a sniff of steamed mutton there, nan. It was a real blast from the past.'* 4. *n.* A crafty *one off the wrist* fuelled by saucy recollections of an erstwhile conquest.

blat splatter *n.* Female ejaculate. *'Persil Bio simply lifts stains out of clothes, even on the cold water cycle. Mud, ketchup, red wine or dried-on blat splatter are no match for Persil, which leaves your clothes lemon fresh and with a new, bluey-whiteness you'll love.'*

blazing saddle *n.* A severe case of the *Adrians.*

BLBP *abbrev.* A ring of *bumwad* wrapped around the front rim of a public *crapper* seat to ensure that a well-endowed fellow's *pride and joy* does not accidentally come into contact with the danger zone. Big Lad Buffer Pad.

blobseekers allowance 1. *n.* Loose change frantically excavated from the depths of his pockets by a drunk man swaying optimistically in front of the *jubber ray* machine in a pub *shitter.* 2. *n.* Permission to *plough* his *bird's back forty* granted to a man after he has proved his *boner fides* by gallantly scrambling the streets to locate a *Jimmy hat* after closing time.

block of flaps *n.* A multi-storey pile of *lady golfers.* With a broken lift. For example, the fondly-remembered "Razzle Stack" that was regularly featured in the hedge-dwelling *bongo pamphlet* of the same name.

Blofeld *n.* A *biddy fiddler, mothball diver, tomb raider, OAP-dophile* or *granny magnet.* Named after the erstwhile James Bond villain in honour of his habit of "stroking a white pussy."

blood diamond jubilee *n.* A dense, semi-precious *Fabergé dog egg* which takes a sphincter-splitting hour of agony to force out. An inglorious sixty minutes *on the throne.*

blood diamonds *n.* The testicles. An unpre-

possessing bag of *dirty stones* that is handed over into a young lady's care in the middle of the night.

blotto voce *adv. Ital.* As spoken indiscreetly by one who has imbibed an excess of *brown sauce.* It's just the beer talking. *'(A burly builder MR O'SHAUGHNESSY exits the pub and finds TOM in his car, throwing toys into the street). MR O'SHAUGHNESSY: Oi. What the fuck do you think you're doing in the back of my fucking car? TOM: I'm the Bishop of Southwark. It's what I do.'* (extract from unfilmed screenplay for biopic entitled *Tom Butler Did It*).

blotty *n. coll. Pissed-up tussage, wankered crumpet, soused mackerel.* From blotto + totty. *'There's a nice bit of blotty at the bar, Sid.'*

blouse lifter *n.* A female in *comfortable shoes.* Also *skirt lifter, Victorian photographer, lady golfer.*

blow diddley *n.* An unsuccessful conclusion to an evening of wooing; a familiar experience, you would imagine, for Ernie Bishop when he started going out with Emily.

blow job tickets *n.* Cash.

blow on the ragman's trumpet, a *euph.* A long and tuneless blast on the *botty bugle.*

blow the bogpipes *v.* To produce a howling, eardrum-shattering drone from the vicinity of one's sporran whilst *crapping* in the *but'n'ben.*

blowtox *n.* Simple cosmetic procedure, usually performed by a female, which plumps up one's *old man*, temporarily removing his visible lines by up to 100%.

blubber johnny *n.* One who *lives life in the vast lane*; whose sheer bulk effectively prevents copulation.

blue ball *n.* The *taint.* Because it is "between the pink and the brown".

Bluto's beard *n.* The dark ring of fluff found festooned around the *aardvark's nose* after wearing black *undercrackers.*

BNB *abbrev.* A *one night stand* whereby the chap sneaks out the bed and *fucks off* out of it before his slumbering coital partner awakes. Bed Not Breakfast.

boabie lard *n. Scots. Population paste.* '*Och, maw. Gran'paw's bin surfin' yon internet on ma wee laptoppie again, and he's left boabie lard a' awa the keyboard.*'

BOAT/boat *acronym.* Someone who is a Bit Of A Twat. Also *boater.*

Boba Fett's hat *n.* A *helmet* that has seen plenty of action. From the legendary *Star Wars* bounty hunter's battle-scarred *titfer.*

bob a job *euph.* The gentlemanly art of urinating onto a *floater* left by a previous visitor, such that it "bobs" about, charmingly, like something out of *Swallows and Amazons.*

bobbing for apples *n.* Alternately applying and relaxing light pressure to the back of a lucky fellatrix's head whilst giving her a *drink on a stick,* thus allowing her the opportunity to take a short gasp for air between noshes.

boghogger *n.* One who spends an inordinate amount of time ensconced in the smallest room.

bog's jellyfish *n.* Dangerous yet passive aquatic creature found floating in the *bum sink* when an excess of *arsewipe* traps an air bubble. Rolls around in the murky water after the first flush only to be discovered hours later by unsuspecting bathers. A *Welsh man o'war.*

bog treacle *n.* The utterly predictable result of eating a whole bag of Pontefract cakes in a single sitting.

bogzilla *n.* An unfeasibly large and frightening monster that emerges from the water to terrorise the populace.

bollock ballast *n. Man custard.*

bollock boiler *n.* A hot bath. '*So, you've been in the jungle for the best part of two weeks. What's the first thing you're going to do when you get back to the hotel, Nadine?' 'I'm going to have a shit on a proper toilet and run meself a nice bollock boiler, Ant. Or are you Dec?'*

bollock in each pocket, a *exclam.* Said of a fellow whose trouser frontage might be considered somewhat too well-fitted. *Squirrel cheeks.* '*Jesus, them jeans are a bit tight. You look like you're carrying a bollock in each pocket, if you don't mind me saying so, Mr Plant.*'

bollocks in a sack *phr.* A crude variant of "peas in a pod". '*Have you seen them Jedward twins? They're like two bollocks in a sack.*'

bollockules *n.* Microscopic *clockweights.* '*Okay, Mr Straw, I'd like you to cough for me whilst I've got my hand under your bollockules.*'

bollonary *n. medic.* A sort of mild heart attack suffered whilst emptying an over-full *pod purse.* A *hardiac arrest.*

bolloquialism *n.* A particularly irritating figure of speech, *eg.* "Touch base", "Know what I mean?", "Does what it says on the tin", "Simples" *etc.*

Bolly odour *n.* The spicy aroma one's *back body* develops following a night on the *Ruby Murrays.*

bollywood *n.* Penile tumescence achieved whilst watching a sexy screen starlet who hails from the Indian subcontinent, such as Priyanka Chopra, Padma Lakshmi or Barbar Bhatti.

bolt from the brown *n.* A sudden an unexpected appearance made by a *bum cigar.* A *break for the border* or *charge of the shite brigade.*

bolt on *1. n.* A large bore exhaust pipe strapped to the rear of an *estate car. 2. n.* A *boner* that is achieved with seemingly impossible speed, but which appears to soften up just before the end.

bomb-bay mix-up *n.* Accidentally licking the wrong hole during an amorous encounter and getting an unexpected taste of the previous evening's takeaway.

Bonanza, arse like the start of *sim.* A reference to the title sequence of the popular American cowboy-based television show, which featured a ring of fire repeatedly burning through a paper map. *'Fuck me. That's the last time I order a Chinese curry from the kebab van out the back of Matalan. I've got an arse like the start of fucking Bonanza here, Evan. And now Thought for the Day with Anne Atkins.'*

bonekickers *1. n.* Extraordinarily well-researched, realistic and popular drama starring that fat bloke out of *Downton Abbey. 2. n.* Extraordinarily grotesque harpies whose appearance in a nightclub, bar, Agora amusement arcade *etc.,* may have a somewhat adverse effect on any latent priapism.

boner bus *n.* A particular public transport route whereby one's omnibus driver is forced to navigate several cobbled streets, the vibrations thus experienced furnishing male passengers with *half a teacake* on their daily commute. Also *double dicker, Coronation treat.*

boobery *n.* A place where *boobs* are kept.

bookie's favourite *n.* A surefire *ride*, even when *the going is soft.*

borderline Frenchman *adj.* Politically incorrect and unacceptably xenophobic expression descriptive of terrible body odour. *'Fair enough, it's a hot day and everyone in the coach is sweating. But that bird is borderline Frenchman.'*

bored dog's balls, cleaner than a *sim. 'In order to avoid the transmission of puerperal fever between patients, it is important that, before making examinations, doctors ensure that their hands are cleaner than a bored dog's balls.'* (from *Etiology, Concept and Prophylaxis of Childbed Fever* by Ignaz Semmelweis).

Boris Johnson cycling down the South Bank, like *sim.* Descriptive of a windswept blonde *mingepiece*, a reference to London's Gerard Hoffnung-channelling comedy mayor.

born again pissed-ian *n.* One who has recovered from a bout of temperance and rediscovered the joys of the malted hop and the fermented grain.

borp *n.* A *dropped hat.* From bottom + burp.

Bose shit *n.* Named in honour of the compact-yet-expensive speakers, a small *turd* that nevertheless produces a rich, room-filling smell. With plenty of trouser-flapping bass.

BOTBLATRIT/botblatrit *acronym.* A woman whose impressive *busty substances* are her only redeeming feature. Big Old Tits But Look At The Rest (of) It.

bot-holing *n.* Weekend pursuit of mud-covered chaps who don't mind getting trapped in narrow crevices.

bot noodle *n.* A lipsmacking mixture of boiling water, savoury sludge and spicy sauce that stops thankfully short of a *pan*'s "fill level".

Botson strangler *n.* A *poo* that is half in and half out of the *nipsy* at the moment the *cigar cutter* reflex kicks in.

bottanical garden *n.* Any place popular with *al fresco fruit-feelers.*

bottom of a ratcatcher's mallet, fanny like a *sim.* A poetic turn of phrase which can be used to describe a particularly messy *snatch* when in polite company, for example on Radio 4's *Midweek* programme, whilst sitting on the Booker Prize judging panel or when taking afternoon tea with the Dowager Duchess of Grantham.

bounce that on your cock a few times and see how it feels *exclam.* Offensively sexist phrase for use when pointing out a tasty bit of *blart* to a mate. Can be accompanied by the qualifier *Phoar!* for greater emphasis, if required.

bouquet of beans *n.* A *fart, borp.*

bovvercraft *n.* A vehicle that slews across in front of you in traffic but you resist the temptation to remonstrate because it is driven by a bald, thick-necked hard case.

bowl winder *n.* A long, unbroken, helical *potty python.* Often requires disassembly with a coat hanger or other improvised *poo horn* in order to facilitate disposal. A *coil pot.*

bowling ball *n.* A woman who loves nothing more than getting *fingered* down an alley.

boxcar willy *n.* Involuntary priapism occasioned by the steady, low-frequency throb of a large diesel-engined vehicle. Also known as *bus driver's knob, travel fat, traveller's marrow, diesel dick, routemaster* or a *Varney teacake.* Named after the erstwhile, dead country & western singer of the same name who always got a *hard-on* whilst sat on his tour bus.

box of cow tongues *n.* An unpleasantly graphic *snapper.* A *butcher's dustbin.*

box office *1. n.* A brothel, *rub-a-tug shop. 2. n.* A *good time girl's bodily treasure* with a £3 handling fee. *3. n.* A *porn* shop.

box on standby *1. phr.* Statement that one's televisual receiving apparatus is more or less powered up although inactive. *2. phr.* Said of a lady who is more or less permanently *up for it.*

boxpok *1. n.* A steam locomotive wheel made using box sections instead of solid spokes, it says here. *2. n.* An infectious condition afflicting a lady's *front bottom. 'Hang on, what's this?' 'It's a boxpok, love. Can you just work round it?'*

boy scout's penknife *n.* The tell-tale bulge in an adolescent's pocket that gives away the location of his favourite whittling implement.

box to box action *1. n.* Football commentator speak for an exciting match that is, if you will, "end to end stuff". *2. n.* Something that is always a welcome sight in any half decent *lezzer* vid.

brabarian *n.* A fellow who finds the tricky act of unfastening the catches on a lady's *titpants* overly cerebral and tiresome, and prefers to simply pull the *knockers* out of their cups and go at them like that, a bit like how you'd imagine Brian Blessed would.

brake fade *n.* Whilst *touching cloth*, that fear that you may not make the last corner to the toilet without suffering a nasty accident.

Brando butter *n.* Any handy substance, such as margarine, baby oil, lard or a Barry White LP on the radiogram, pressed into service to assist the *smashing in* of a lady's *back doors.* As popularised by gargantuan actor Marlon in classy *scruff* movie *Last Tango in Paris.*

branstorming *n.* Taking a little time out of the day to *paint the porcelain* courtesy of yesterday's high fibre breakfast cereal.

bra snack *n.* A nourishing, opportunistic ogle of the barmaid's *knockers* whilst ordering drinks. *Nork scratchings.*

bread knife *rhym. slang.* The *bag for life. 'Quick. In the wardrobe. It's the fucking bread knife.'*

break a cock *v.* Hardcore *grumble* actor's pre-performance version of "break a leg".

breakfast at stiffany's *euph.* Early morning *horatio.*

breakfast at wiffany's *euph.* An all-you-can-eat *seafood smorgasbord* served when *dining at the Y.*

breastaurant *n.* One of those eateries where the waitresses are hired based on their *impressive qualifications, eg.* Hooters, Mugs'n'Jugs and the Honey Shack. But not necessarily Betty's Tea Rooms in Harrogate.

breastimate *v.* To assess the size of a woman's *shirt potatoes* using one's skill and judgement.

brewnami *n.* A disastrous spillage of tea or similar hot beverage which causes devastation out of all proportion to the amount of liquid in the cup.

Brian *n*. A cockney lady's *bits*, named in honour of erstwhile *Playschool* presenter Cant. The *twat-shaped window*.

brickie's wrist, thick as a *sim*. A girthwise measurement of a man's penile endowment.

bride & gloom *n*. A matrimonial couple, one of whom is not necessarily quite as happy at the prospect of getting hitched as the other.

bride frightener *n*. A *mighty Wurlitzer*, such as that sported by Stephen Pound MP.

Brideshead *n*. A second trip to the lavatory for a *dump*, named - as all students of classic English literature ought to know - after Evelyn Waugh's famous novel *Brideshead Revisited*, in which she wrote about someone posh going for two *shits*.

bridge of doom *n*. The female *perineum*. Also *carse, tinter, taint, biffon, butfer, gooch*.

Bridlington tan *euph*. A measure of extreme improbability. *'A Windows Vista computer still running at full speed more than a fortnight after being purchased? It's like a Bridlington tan. Technically, it could happen, I suppose, but I've been an IT professional for thirty years and I've never seen it.'*

Brightlingsea bidet *n*. The act of depositing a wet wad of *hockle* onto a square of bathroom tissue before wiping one's *freckle*, as an aid to personal daintiness. Named in honour of the notorious dearth of functioning toilet facilities in the delightful Essex seaside resort.

bring home the bacon *1. v*. Of a heavily *refreshed* fellow, to return to his domicile with a *right pig* after a night out. *2. v*. To perform the selfless, yet pointless, unnecessarily fiddly and time-consuming act of enabling a female companion to achieve an *organism*.

Bristol cream *n*. A warming splash of *man milk across* the missus's *fat rascals*.

Bristol meth *n*. Incredibly strong scrumpy that transports the drinker into *ciderspace*.

Electric lemonade, Tone Vale tonic.

Bristols rover *n*. A man with wandering hands who is fond of fondling *norks*. *'Watch out for the Archbishop when you're in the vestry signing the register, Kate. he's a right Bristols rover, that one.'*

broboe *n*. The male member. *'Entering the room very softly, I had a view of Mr Rochester before he discovered my presence. He sat in his chair leafing through his mam's Grattan Catalogue - his countenance downcast as he tugged listlessly at his broboe.'* (from *Jane Eyre* by Charlotte Brontë).

brokeback breakfast *n*. Any non-fried, continental-style, vegetarian-friendly foodstuff, such as yoghurt, fruit, muesli or brown bread with seeds, tomatoes or olives, such as might be nibbled in the morning by a man who *throws a light dart*.

broken catflap *n*. A damaged *nipsy*. A term apparently coined by cheeky Scotch funnyman Frankie Boyle in his humorous routine at last year's Royal Variety Performance. *'A German married to a Greek for sixty years? You must have an arse like a broken catflap, ma'am.'*

broken deckchair, fanny like a *sim*. A lady's *bower of bliss* with which proves very difficult, if not impossible, to successfully sort out. *'Sorry, love. I did me best, but in the end I just had to give up. You've got a fanny like a broken deckchair.'*

Bromley tickle *n*. Digital titivation of a lady's *undercarriage* to gauge whether congress is on the cards or what. Named after the South London high street in which the technique was perfected, the *Bromley tickle* often precedes a *Bolton dip test*.

brown baubles *n*. The tightly-knotted bags of *dog eggs* with which thoughtful pet owners decorate the trees in the countryside whilst out walking their *shit machines. Fairy shites*.

brown bobsleigh *n*. A term used to describe

the speedy downhill movement of a *digestive transit* that involves impossibly tight turns and feelings of terror and impending disaster. A *brown knuckle ride.*

brown candle, light a *v.* To go for a *number two*. '*I'm just going to light a brown candle. Here's Alex Deakin with the weather.*'

brown derby *1. n.* Epithet of an ultimately unsuccessful Wimpy's restaurant dessert from the 1970s, named for some unfathomable reason after a stiff-brimmed felt hat. *2. n.* A mass *bumfest,* involving a multitude of muddy runners and riders. *3. n.* A sprint to the lavatory whilst suffering from a *farmer's protest.*

browned zero *n.* The epicentre of a particularly catastrophic anal detonation. '*I'd avoid trap two if I was you, Bamber. That's browned zero.*'

browneye points *n.* Nominal credits awarded by a fellow's ladyfriend which he may - in the fullness of time - redeem against *wrong'un*-based shenanigans. '*There was another dead pigeon in the water tank this week, so I went up and fished it out to earn myself a few browneye points.*'

brownloading *n.* Surfing the internet on a smartphone whilst taking a *dump. Cable and wireless, poogling.*

brown peacock *n. medic.* A serious case of the *Brads* whereby one small twitch of the *back body* produces an impressive rooster tail of sepia plumage from the *rusty sheriff's badge.*

buffer *v.* To pause, motionless, for 10-15 seconds during coitus to delay the inevitable and thus prolong sexual pleasure. From the message that often appears onscreen when watching *grumble* online *via* a low bandwidth internet connection. Apparently.

buffers *n.* A pair of large, solidly-sprung buttocks. '*Sorry Kim. I can't get it any further in from here. I've hit the buffers.*'

buggeralls *n.* Your birthday suit. '*How was I to know the missus had planned a surprise party for me? In she bursts with all my friends, my mother, the vicar and all the girls from my class at school, and there's me sat watching Television X in me buggeralls.*'

buggy balm *n.* Spooge, heir gel.

Bugner's clinch *n.* The dance performed by a pair of knackered heavyweights at the end of the evening in a nightclub, where they lumber sweatily about in a circle whilst clinging to each other for support. Named after Hungarian/British/Australian ex-boxer Joe.

builder's airbag *n.* The 6-inch-thick layer of tabloids, empty crisp packets, pork pie wrappers and other assorted detritus perched on a white van's dashboard.

builder's wink *n.* A *brickie's crack* that's frankly gone too far. '*The plasterer was bent over when I walked in and I got a full-on builder's wink.*'

build up some charge on the Van de Graaff generator *v.* In an action familiar to anyone who has studied physics beyond O-Level, to rub up and down on a piece of equipment that consists of a long pole with a shiny dome on the top.

bukkake labrador *n.* A dalmatian.

bull bars *n.* The type of hostelries frequented by *carpet munchers.*

bull fiddle *1. n.* What Jack Lemmon calls his double bass in *Some Like it Hot. 2. n.* A spot of *firkyfoodling* on a hefty *cow* with *a lovely personality.*

bulling *1. n. milit.* The act of a new recruit who is forced to spend endless hours adding layers of polish to his boots in order to achieve an almost mirror-like shine he can see his face in, and thus *2. n.* the act of a new recruit to the world of hardcore *grumble* who feels compelled to invest great effort attempting to get a similar glossy finish on his *little soldier's helmet.*

bulljob *n.* An aggressive, drunken *nosh* off

an aggressive, drunken lady, possibly with a ring through her nose.

bum bees *n.* Anal discomfort suffered after a mild curry, for example a Bhuna. *'Rest assured you'll never get bum bees if you eat at the Rupali Restaurant (formerly the Curry Capital (formerly the Rupali Restaurant)), Bigg Market, Newcastle upon Tyne. It's arse wasps every time or your money back.'*

bum bhaji *n.* A deep-fried, spicy rectal *fritter.*

bumble bee pants *n.* Nethergarments which have been worn for so long that they are "yellow at the front and brown at the back".

bum boulder *n.* A giant, exit-blocking *chod* that rolls down your large intestine sending all screaming before it, like that one off of *Indiana Jones.*

bumclutter *n.* The rubble, dreck and general spoilage that must be cleared from the back passage before taking the missus *up the chip shop.*

bumfit *1. n.* "Fifteen" in the bizarre counting system operated by Cumbrians, where counting on the fingers isn't an option unless you want to use base 12. *'Forty bumfit. Federer only has to hold this serve to take the tethera set.' 2. n.* A spectacular and unheralded attack of the *tom tits* that leaves the victim shaking on the floor.

bum grenade *n.* Small post-*cuzza* incendiary bomb which is lobbed into the *pan,* causing the grenadier to beat the retreat with the greatest possible alacrity.

bum gum *n.* The nose of a feculant *motion* that gets chewed when *cable-laying* is delayed for any reason.

bumjela *n. Pile* cream.

bummer's toe *n. medic.* Fungal infection of a *good listener's* cuticle caused by the his foot getting trodden on repeatedly during vigorous *uphill gardening.*

bummery *n. coll.* A rather pleasing collective term for all things anus-related, *viz. Bottery,*

fisting, felching, grapeshot, rimming etc.

bum pasty *n.* A steaming, crusty *arse pie,* fresh out of the *mud oven.* May be liable to VAT.

bumper *n.* A *Richard the third* of such firmness, solidity and density that one can hear it bumping about through the digestive tract whilst making its way to freedom, occasionally setting off bells like a pinball machine.

bum scum *n.* The unpleasant residue on an improperly-wiped *fifties tea towel holder.*

bum soup *n. Ad hoc* savoury consommé cooked up between the *mudflaps* of catering staff working in hot kitchens. *'Another bowl of bum soup for Mr Winner on table six.'*

bum yawn *1. n.* A putrid early morning utterance to greet the new day. *2. n.* A frequently glimpsed phenomenon in certain high quality *grumble flicks.*

bunch *n.* A mid-day session of *uphill gardening.* A *nooner* for those who *know what's in their flowerbeds.* From bumming + lunch.

bunga bunga *adj.* Type of party enjoyed by fun-loving former/future Italian Prime Minister/convict Silvio Berlusconi during which, in preference to playing pass the parcel and musical chairs or bobbing for apples, the guests are invited to *have it off* with teenage prostitutes.

Bungle fever *n. psych.* An attraction to hairy women. *'My husband suffers from chronic bungle fever, so he makes a point of never missing an episode of the Weakest Link.'*

bunglefuck *n.* An act of coitus enjoyed whilst dressed as an animal.

Bungle's wallet *n.* An untidily hirsute *steak purse.*

bunt *n.* The bit between a female's stomach and her *blurtch.* Derivation unknown. The *fupa, poond, fat hat* or *blubber beret.*

burger nips *n.* Large aereolae that are similar in size, shape, texture (and possibly flavour) to the comestibles typically found in a tin of Goblin-brand beef patties. Quarter pounder-style *tit pizzas*. With a bit of relish on for good measure.

burning dufflecoat, pull me through with a *exclam.* A jocular cry uttered upon producing a particularly malodorous *air biscuit* whilst in company, for example when appearing on Radio 4's *Law in Action* or *Newsnight Late Review*.

burn off a digestive *v.* To use up approximately the same number of calories as there are in a wheaten sweetmeal biscuit by *having one off the wrist*.

burn the bacon *v.* To *go at* one's ladyfriend so enthusiastically that her *gammon flaps* chafe, and you have to open a window and waft her *fanny* with a newspaper in case the smoke alarm goes off.

burnt picket fence, teeth like a *sim.* A poetic evocation of the sort of quirky, charming and characterful half-timbered pearlies typically found in British mouths.

burst crate of tomatoes, arse like a *sim.* A phrase illustrative of the state of a traumatised ringpiece. *'I wish I could tell you that Andy fought the good fight, and the Sisters let him be. I wish I could tell you that - but prison is no fairy-tale world. The Sisters kept at him - sometimes he was able to fight 'em off, sometimes not. Every so often, Andy would show up with an arse like a burst crate of tomatoes.'*

burst sausage *n.* A female *salad dodger* who has somehow squeezed her porky frame into a frock which is several sizes too small to accommodate it.

bury a king *v.* To surreptitiously deposit a *Richard the Third* in a car park.

bus door *n.* An *airbrake* released with a satisfying hiss.

busdriver's chair, like a *sim.* A beautiful, poetic expression used to describe a well-used

and stinking *clopper* which has had all the stuffing knocked out of it.

bushey troughs *1. n.* Whence locomotives scooped up water into their tenders during the days of steam power. *2. n.* The deep, wet *bowers of pleasure* to be found on larger lasses.

bush pilot *1. n.* A lugubrious Australian aviator who delivers canned lager to sweating, pithily monosyllabic, outback-dwelling, cork-hatted men in television adverts. *2. n.* A fellow gifted with the almost uncanny ability to instinctively navigate his way round a *fat lass* and find her *minge*.

bushtugger challenge *n.* A trial of manliness undertaken whilst out on a morning constitutional whereby a fellow attempts to *pull himself off* over a *bongo book* found discarded in the undergrowth without being detected by passers-by, parkies, clergy *etc*.

bushtugger man *n.* A gentleman of the road *relaxing* himself daft amidst the municipal shrubbery.

bus lane bollards *n.* Unexpectedly prominent *nip-nops* which, one might fondly imagine, sound a warning klaxon whilst becoming erect. *Pygmies' cocks, Scammel wheel nuts, chapel hat-pegs, fighter pilot's thumbs.*

bushwrinkle *n. Mummy's toolshed*. The *vaginis horribilis*.

busker's hat, doormat like a *sim.* The coin-bestrewed state of a chap's porch following a difficult navigation home from the pub using the popular *fancy walking* method.

butcher's fist *n.* The male equivalent of the *camel's toe,* as regularly spotted at the Tower Ballroom in Edgbaston, Birmingham's premier over-sixties nitespot. Also *hamster's mouthful, packet, Darcy Bussell's footrest, munge.*

butler sauce *n.* A rich *man gravy*. *'"I say, Jeeves," I expostulated. "What's this bally sticky custard stuff all over my kedgeree?*

Dash it all, it's all over my toast, and floating in my Earl Grey too!" The sage retainer barely looked up from ironing my spats. 'It is butler's sauce, sir," he replied. "I just wanked on your breakfast."' (from *Stick It Up Your Arse, Jeeves!* by PG Wodehouse).

butta blockers *n.* As beta blockers regulate blood flow, so *butta blockers* regulate *arse* flow. *'I've been on the butta blockers all day after the trip to the Rupali Restaurant, Bigg Market, Newcastle upon Tyne and 15 pints of Guinness last night.'*

butt butter *n.* The grease left in the *hob* after a good *grill-rattler. Satan's prune juice.*

butterfly effect *n.* A disastrous *Bakewell* encased in a cocoon of hot liquid that forms a lepidopterous brown smudge between the *buttock* cheeks. A blast of wind so chaotic and unpredictable in its effects that it may well change the course of events for the rest of your day.

buttery *n.* A bar frequented by men who *know what's in their flowerbeds.*

buttonhole *v.* To *shag* a *RFHTFH* right in the belly button. Or thereabouts.

button mushroom resting on a spacehopper, like a *sim.* Descriptive of a gent whose relative lower proportions are somewhat out of whack. A *cheese wagon*; the opposite of *ACNB.* '*Ooh, Cliff. It's like a button mushroom resting on a spacehopper.'*

button on a fur coat *n.* A less-than-impressive *endowment.* A tiny *knob.* '*What do you make of that then, doctor?' 'Bloody nora, the Right Honourable Mr Straw MP. It's like a button on a fur coat.'*

butt tumbler *n.* A *fruit feeler* or *mudflapper.*

butt wood, chop some *v.* To *hack off* a large, knotty *log,* possibly whilst shouting "Timber!" *'Those were lean years on Walton's Mountain. Work was hard to find, and we often went hungry. But throughout that harsh and bitter time we were sustained by the love, warmth and laughter that filled our family home. The house in which we were born and raised is still there, and on the winds that sigh along those misted Blue Ridge Mountains, the sound of Grandma chopping her morning butt wood echoes still.'*

Buzz lightbeer *1. n.* A mate who drinks *vicar's piss* rather than proper beer like a real man, thereby remaining relatively sober instead of going to "incapacity and beyond". *2. n.* A *two pot screamer* or *half-pint Harry* who gets *banjoed* after a pitifully small amount of *booze.*

cabbage brown *n.* The delicately traced sepia image of a rare butterfly found stencilled into the gusset after one has absentmindedly *got engaged*.

CAB/cab *acronym.* The male genitalias, *viz.* Cock And Balls. Alternatively, in cold weather, after swimming or when Bobby Davro, *minicab*.

cable & wireless *euph.* Browsing the internet whilst *on the throne. Poogling, brownloading*.

cackaccino *n.* An invigorating brown potful topped with a "froth" of unflushed *bumwad*, often found upon entering the *Rick Witter* on a train.

cack-ack/cack-ak *n. onomat.* Repeated volleys of hot excrement that pepper one's *chod-bin* bowl with smoking shrapnel. *Cack-ak* fire can be particularly intense following a meal of vegetarian food that is rich in peas, beans and pulses.

cack-in-the-box *n.* A large, unflushed *railway sleeper* which startles you when you lift the lid.

cackophony *n.* The jarring, discordant sound of a really noisy *German Bight. Musique concrète*.

Cadbury *n.* One that can't handle his beer. A *two pot screamer, half pint Harry, almond, one can Van Damme*. From the fact that he can only accommodate "a glass and a half".

caesar salad *euph.* A messily carnal combination, whereby the gentleman brings the *cheese* and *salad dressing* whilst the woman is responsible for providing *lettuce* and a hint of *anchovy*.

CAFOD/cafod *acronym.* Said of a *bad thrower.* Clearly A Friend Of Dorothy.

Cain & Abel *n. rhym. slang.* A *Vince* of biblical proportions, ironically not named after the hugely *shite* Jeffrey Archer potboiler.

cakebowling *n.* The act of *licking someone out* with more enthusiasm than usual.

call the midwife *exclam.* Cry of alarm reserved for the most severe cases of flatulence, when there is a genuine risk of one's *brown waters* breaking.

calamari ring *n.* An unappetisingly rubbery, battered *nipsy*.

Callum Plank *1. n. prop.* Founder of Scotland's leading auto-salvage haulage company. *2. rhym. slang.* An act of auto-erotic delight. *'I'm just off for a Callum Plank over the bra pages of your catalogue, nan.'*

Cambridge Smith! *exclam.* A mildly amusing response to a *starter for ten*. Spoken urgently in the style of the excitable voiceover on BBC2 boffin quiz *University Challenge*. Also *there's no taste like Hovis; Congratulations, it's a boy*.

camouflush *n.* In a public *crapper,* the act of concealing the embarrassing sound of plops, splashes and *Lionel Barts* from your fellow cubicle-dwellers by pulling the chain.

canaraderie *n. Fr.* Alcohol-induced bonhomie.

candy twist *1. n.* A term local to the potteries of Stoke-on-Trent; a stylish flourish when pulling a handle for a cup, beaker or jug. *2. n.* A deft twist of the *helmet* when *pulling yourself off*.

canned laughter *n.* The bouncing *enbonpoint* of a tittersome female.

cannon trousers *n.* An amusing epithet bestowed upon one who is suffering from high-calibre flatulence.

Captain Birdseye *n.* A fellow who doesn't seem to have too much trouble getting *fish fingers. 'Today's birthdays: Linda Lovelace, late movie knob gobbler, 63; Eddie Cheever, US racing driver, 54; Rod Stewart, gravel-voiced Captain Birdseye, 67.'*

Captain Birdseye's chin *n.* Something hairy and haddocky. *'Fucking hell, love. It's like Captain Birdseye's chin down here.'*

Captain Scott's last morning stiffy, as hard as *sim. Nails.* From the intrepid Antarctic explorer's final, frost-bitten night under canvas. *'Careful, Phil. I wouldn't flick any more peanuts at that nutter by the bar if I was you. he's as hard as Captain Scott's last morning stiffy.'*

Caravaggio *1. n. prop.* Hell-raising Oliver Reed-style painter of the Italian Renaissance. *2. n.* It. The act of *copping a swift feel* in the back seat of an Italian car just before the doors fall off and it rusts away.

car bar *n.* Whilst attending, for example, a wedding reception, sneaking your empty glass out into the car park to fill it up with your own beer; a practice that is expressly forbidden at Judge's Hotel in Yarm. Although, just possibly, it might not be quite so prevalent amongst their clientele if they weren't charging £4.75 for a fucking can of Guinness.

car door khazi *n.* A discreet, improvised roadside toilet created by opening the nearside front and rear doors of one's landaulette in a layby - the doors thus conveniently forming the sides of a vehicular *pissoir,* if you will.

cargo pants *n.* A *bird* who *beeps while reversing*. *'Today's birthdays: Pete Burns, rubber-faced funnyman, 52; Anthony Cotton, soap star, 36; Lisa Riley, You've Been Framed cargo pants, 35.'*

Carlsberg colonic *n.* A full rectal auto-irrigation carried out conveniently whilst one sleeps off a fair few cans of what is probably the best super-strength *wreck the hoose juice* in the world.

Carlsberg expert *n.* A philanthropically didactic bar-dwelling gentleman who, having consumed more than a few pints of the eponymous Danish lager, becomes a generous fount of knowledge & wisdom. See also *gintellectual.*

carpentry *euph.* Lesbism, *viz.* "A spot of tongue & groove".

carpet bagger *n.* A voracious *woman in com-* fortable shoes, who has a lusty appetite for *munching rugs.* A *KD lady* who is at the *box biter* - as opposed to the *lettuce licker* - end of the lesbidatory spectrum.

carrot sorbet *n.* A refreshing, palate-cleansing *chunder* enjoyed in the middle of a drinking session.

carte brune *n. Fr.* The nominal licence afforded one who enters a cubicle in an otherwise empty public lavatory, to *release the chocolate hostage* with as much noise, fury and gusto as he sees fit, protected as he is by the cloak of anonymity.

case of the creaks *n.* An excuse typically made by those suffering from loud flatulence. *'Fetch the WD40, dear. The kitchen door's got a case of the creaks. And even that hasn't covered up the sound of my horrendous trumps.'*

cashier number two please *exclam.* An amusing utterance to warn the denizens of neighbouring traps about the impending splash as a length of *dirty spine* hits the water.

cast a bronze *n.* To drop forge a *copper bolt* using the lost wax method. *'Stay stood like that, Mademoiselle Claudet. Don't move. I'm just off to the crapper to cast a bronze. I'll not be gone more than half an hour.' 'Right you are, Monsieur Rodin.'*

catalob *n.* The involuntary semi-erection which pops up whilst innocently browsing the *funderwear* section of a mail order catalogue.

catcher's mitt, the *n.* The use of one's spare hand to catch the *jitler* when *pulling the Pope's cap off.*

caterer's tribute *euph. Spunk.* From the touching, little-known ceremony to mark the passing of the late Michael Winner, when *masturchefs* across the country gravely ejaculated into whatever they were cooking in honour of the *jizz*-necking "film" director, gourmand and bon viveur.

CAT F/cat F *abbrev.* Rating of the severity of

a traffic jam where there is no good reason for it to have formed, so that one is forced to blame the tailback on "(some) Cunt At The Front".

cath-arse-is *n.* A dramatic bowel movement of such magnitude that it triggers a vicarious emotional purgation (see Aristotle's *Poetics* for further details).

Catholic condom *n.* An elastic band around the base of the *pope's hat* and both sets of fingers and toes tightly crossed.

cat one incident *1. n.* Term used by employees of the Environment Agency to describe pollution that kills loads of fish and stuff. *2. n.* Term used to describe a really big *Eartha* that blocks the *bogs* at the Environment Agency offices. *'I wouldn't go in there if I was you, Paul. There's a cat one incident in trap two.'*

Cat's call *n.* A five second warning issued to those in one's immediate vicinity that an *air biscuit* is about to be released. From the lyrics to Cat Stevens's 1972 hit *Can't Keep It In, viz.* "Oh I can't keep it in / I can't keep it in / I've got to let it out".

cat's cradle *n.* The globulous, sticky spoils strung between the fingertips of a *crane driver*.

caveman knickers *n.* A large and unruly *muff*, not unlike a mammoth fur undergarment.

C-biscuit *n.* An *air cookie* which inadvertently slips off the front of a lady's *plate*. Also *queef, Lawley kazoo, flap raspberry, a hat dropped forwards*. Recently made into a moving film about a champion racehorse suffering from chronic vaginal flatulence.

cement the relationship *v.* To *tip your filthy concrete* up a lady's crevice. *'Kate caught William's eye at a St Andrews student fashion show, but the young Prince didn't cement the relationship until several weeks later, behind a skip outside the university Geography Department.'*

cesar geezer *n.* A gent who cultivates a close relationship with his pet hound, by the simple expedient of smearing the eponymous dog food upon his *bone* and inviting said canine to partake. *'Born on this day in history: George Washington, wooden-toothed first president of the United States, 1732; Heinrich Rudolf Hertz, German physicist and car hire entrepreneur, 1857; Eric Gill, British sculptor, typographer, wood engraver, and cesar geezer, 1882.'*

CFCs *n. 1.* Chloroflourocarbons; the greenhouse gases which used to damage the environment. 2. *n.* Huge 4-wheel-drive vehicles required by people in Chelsea and Wilmslow when shopping and collecting the kids from school. Cars For Cunts.

chag *n.* A *chav* who is also a *slag*. Someone who would probably *do it* with anyone in return for a swig of Frosty Jack.

chamber of commerce *n.* Any orifice which is leased to the public for financial gain.

Champion the wonder log *n.* An heroic, thoroughbred *feeshus* that leaves its begetter walking like they've just ridden Red Rum up and down Southport sands for an hour.

chap rag *n.* A baby wipe used to clean the *balls*.

charge the Rolex *euph.* To *knock yourself about a bit*. From the rapid wristular oscillations that are required to wind the kinetic mainspring of an exclusive Swiss timepiece.

Charlie and the Chocolate Factory *1. n.* A well known children's book by Roald Dahl. *2. euph.* Sex up the *cocoa channel*. *'Oh, Go on, June. It's my birthday tomorrow. How about showing Charlie round the chocolate factory?' 'But I've already got you a socket set, Terry.'*

Charlie foxtrot *1. exclam. milit.* In the radio operators' phonetic alphabet, an abbreviation for an unfortunate sequence of events, *viz.* "CF" - a *clusterfuck*. *2. n.* The ludicrous nightclub dancefloor gyrations of a children's television presenter who is under the influence of a conkful of *bacon powder.*

Charlton Heston *n. prop.* An inveterate *wanker.* One whose cold dead hands have to be peeled from around his *fouling piece.*

Chas'n'Dave, do a *euph.* Of a saucy strumpet, to "get her knees up".

Chatham pocket *n.* A prisoner's rectum, where contraband goods, such as Class A drugs, lighters, tobacco and mobile telephones may be deposited.

chav cans *n.* Big, gaudy headphones with inferior sound quality.

chav cockerel *n.* The raucous dawn chorus of banging, shouting and swearing that rouses estate dwellers at 4am on a Sunday as their *scrattulent* neighbours return home after a heavy night on the *Nelson.*

chav coffee *n.* A can of energy drink. *Baseball cappuccino, nedscafe.*

chavelodge *n.* Budget accommodation for young folk vacationing at her majesty's pleasure.

chavian flu *n. medic.* Any of a range of difficult-to-disprove ailments which are fortuitously contracted by a long term jobseeker, entitling the sufferer to graduate from the dole to sickness benefit. *'I would go out to work, Jeremy, only I've been struck down with chavian flu for the last eight years. Some days I've barely been able to muster enough energy to sit on the sofa and watch your programme.'*

chavs' VIP lounge *n.* The back seat upstairs on a double decker bus.

chav tapas *n.* A selection of savoury morsels hurriedly purchased from a petrol station chiller cabinet by a member of the urban underclass who is suffering from a hangover, *eg.* Dairylea Dunkers, Peperami and Matteson's Chicken Bites. Best enjoyed with a carafe of blue Powerade and a Nurofen chaser.

chav truffle *n.* A pork pie.

check *n.* On a person with a *lovely personality,* where the chin is indistinguishable from the neck. From chiropodist + poopdeck.

checkmate *n.* The abrupt ending of a *wank* due to one's laptop battery running out of juice at a critical moment.

checkout trauma *n.* Whilst carrying out a *Bolton diptest* on a new ladyfriend, finding an *unexpected item in the bagging area.* An unsettling experience typically suffered by western males whilst sojourning in far-eastern fleshpots, when they accidentally cop off with *flippers.*

check the house for moles *euph.* When in company, to vanish for an extended period of time in order to rid the premises of burrowing brown creatures. *'You haven't seen the Autotrader or my glasses anywhere, have you? I'm just off to check the house for moles.'*

Cheddar gorge *n.* A malodourous, *cheesy twotsit.* A curdled *cream pie.*

Cheddar ledge *n.* The ripe collar of the *bell piece.* The *brim, cheese ridge, wank stop* or sulcus.

cheeky caravan club *n.* That happy, permanently-vacationing section of society who supply pegs and tarmac to the locals whilst on their holidays.

cheese board *n.* In a public convenience, the inside front rim of the toilet bowl against which your *bellend* brushes while you perch uncomfortably on the lavatory seat.

cheese wagon *n.* The phenomenon of a huge *ballsack* and a tiny penis. Also *button mushroom sitting on a spacehopper.*

cheeto *n.* Descriptive of the withered, Judith Chalmers-hued state of a *self-employed* fellow's *privates* following an apathetic act of *self flagellation* essayed whilst listlessly eating a family-sized bag of Wotsits or similar. As they do.

chef d'emission *n. Fr.* Any disgruntled employee in a catering establishment who takes the opportunity to add his own *secret ingredient* to, picking an example entirely at random, the late Michael Winner's soup. A *masturchef.*

Chelsea physio *n.* A right *hottie* who turns up in a place where you'd never expect it, such as a *Star Wars* convention, the opening ceremony at a tram museum or a railway memorabilia auction in Sheffield. A reference to the rather fetching wielder of the magic sponge at Stamford Bridge, Dr Eva Carneiro.

Chelyabinsk Oblast *n.* A huge flash and bang that shatters windows and panics citizens over a wide area.

cherries *n.* The hanging male testicles of a man, which resemble nothing so much as a pair of the eponymous items on a fruit machine.

cherubimical *adj. Wankered*; an expression noted by Enlightenment polymath Benjamin Franklin in a treatise of 1737. *'Leave him, Mifflin. He's cherubimical as a fucking newt.'*

chest freezer *n.* A sports bra.

chest measles *n.* Flat *tits*.

Chewbacca's knackers *sim.* An area of notably unkempt and overgrown *gorilla salad*. Named after Han Solo's badly-coiffed pet dog in the *Star Wars* films. *'Bloody hell. I bet that Lorraine Kelly's clout's hairier than Chewbacca's knackers.'*

chewing a Revel *n.* The sensation upon finishing an unsatisfactory, or otherwise incomplete, *sit down lavatory adventure.*

chicken lickin' *n.* A bout of *horatio* performed in the exuberant, strutting style of erstwhile cartoon rooster Foghorn Leghorn. A *throatbanger.*

chicktionary *n.* A fellow's *little black book*, containing the telephone numbers of his past inamoratae. *'Hi Shaz, it's Baz. I hope you don't mind me phoning you up, only I found your number in my chicktionary. Anyway, my missus is in a coma so I was wondering if you fancied meeting up for a fuck some time later this week.'*

Chilean miner *n.* An impotent fellow. From the fact that he "has trouble with his shaft".

Chilean mineshaft *n.* A dark, narrow, dirty tunnel; the *trap two* version of a *mouse's ear.*

chilistytis *n. medic.* A chance to experience all the fun and games of a serious urinary tract infection by forgetting to wash your hands after preparing a habanero chili and going for a *gypsy's kiss.* Also *jalapenis.*

chimp grooming for ticks, like a *sim.* Reminiscent of a person rummaging through the *gorilla salad* looking for croutons.

CHIMPS/chimps *acronym.* Police Community Support Officers. Can't Help In Most Police Situations. Also *potted plants, apples.*

chinge *n.* An unsightly beard. From chin + minge. *'It's about time Lewis Hamilton shaved that fucking stupid chinge off.'*

chinny merkin *n.* A sexy old lady's wispy beard.

chin omelette *n.* A concoction of briskly whisked *man-egg-white* served warm onto a lucky recipient's lower mandible. A *cumbeard, St Bernard's chin.*

chip pan winkle *n.* A somnolent, heavily-*refreshed* fellow whose kitchen catches fire at about 2 am.

chipolata *n.* A Mexican lady *con los huesos grandes.* A *greedy Gonzales.*

chip-panzee *n. Scratter, ned, pog, Kyley.* A lower primate with a penchant for deep-fried spuds.

chippy's toolbag, piss flaps like a *sim.* A reference to a set of female *pudenders* that are heading south. And east and west. *'Mary was powerless to resist. Bert the Sweep's eyes burnt into hers like sapphires. His muscular arms enfolded her softly yielding body as she felt herself being swept away by an um-*

brella of passion. Tenderly, his sooty hands tugged down her silken bloomers to reveal the womanly treasure he had so long longed to behold. 'Fuck me, missus,' he cried in his authentic cockney voice. 'No offence, but you've got piss flaps like a chippy's toolbag.'' (from *The Edwardian Sweep and the Nanny* by Barbara Cartland).

chip shop back gate, bangs like a *sim.* A rhetorical reference to the performance of an enthusiastic sexual partner. Also *bangs like a belt-fed mortar* or *bangs like a shit-house door in a gale.*

chlorine cock *n. medic.* When visiting the public baths, a stiffening of the male member which is caused by the chemicals in the water.

chobe *n.* A *choad.* A *giggle stick* that is wider than it is long.

chocolate porridge *1. n. milit.* A tasty and energy-giving mixture of rolled oats and chocolate powder cooked up from an old ration pack. *2. n.* The result of eating a surfeit of salad and a pack of cheese & onion rolls before knocking back a lot of cheap cider.

chocolate swirl *1. n.* Soft-centred confection usually offered out of guilt. *2. n.* An unimpressive and ultimately ineffective flush on a train *chodbin.*

chocolate workshop *n.* An intense session of *doing* a loved one up the *wrong 'un.*

choddbins *n.* Cistern-based can storage solution.

chodzilla *n.* A *Douglas* of such gargantuan proportions that it could snap a Tokyo bus.

chollocks *n.* On a lettuce-averse male, where the double chin and gut merge seamlessly into a single continuous surface down to his *clockweights.*

chomit *v.* Following a *refreshing* evening *on the sauce*, to stand up whilst on the *Rick Witter* in order to *shout soup* onto a freshly-laid *cable.* From chod + vomit.

choosing a horse *n.* The act of taking a news-paper to peruse at length whilst ensconced on the *jobby engine.* '*Why does dad always take the Daily Mirror to the bathroom, mummy?*' '*He's just choosing a horse, dear. And he also likes to wipe his arse on Tony Parsons' column.*'

choreplay *n.* Frigmarole.

Christmas vegetables *n.* The *trouser department*; that is to say, "two sprouts and a parsnip".

chuckle grapes *n.* Adrians, farmers, ceramics. '*The LORD will smite thee with the botch of Egypt, and with the chuckle grapes, and with the scab, and with the itch, whereof thou canst not be healed.*' (from *Deuteronomy* 28:27).

chud *n.* A short, easily-dealt-with length of *dirty back* that is accidentally dropped into the *undercrackers* whilst mismanaging a *heart to heart.* A neatly-severed *rat's nose, geetle* or *bumbob.*

chum fart *n.* A foul, meaty stench that manifests whilst a fellow is relaxing in his armchair after Sunday lunch, whether or not he owns a dog.

chumhole *n.* The bit of a *bottee* that gets *botted* by a *botter.* The *freckle, dot* or *nipsy.*

chunder and lightning *n.* Drinking oneself sick on white cider in a park, aged thirteen.

chunderwear *n.* Lingerie that has an emetic, rather than an erotic, effect on the viewer, *eg.* A size 48 *throng* on a size 52 *arse.*

chunt *n.* A more-than-usually-aggressive *chugger*, who refuses to take no for an answer. From charity + cunt. '*You off down Greggs again, Susan?*' '*No, too many chunts on the high street today. I'll order a pizza in instead.*'

ciderfects *n.* The unpleasant results of a night drinking fermented apple juice. Symptoms may vary from mild headache or nausea to permanent blindness, insanity and death.

city trader *n.* A fellow who is adept at studying multiple screens concurrently, *eg.* Watching *Match of the Day* on his television whilst simultaneously viewing *grumble* on his laptop.

clad the impaler *v.* To put on a *jubber ray, dress for dinner.*

clamdestine *adj.* Of sex, surreptitiously stolen whilst the wife is drunk, asleep or otherwise unaware/preoccupied.

clampage *n.* A night out spent in frenzied pursuit of a *seafood supper.*

Clams Casino *1. n.* American hippity-hop producer best known for his use of unorthodox female vocal samples and work with Lil B and A$ap Rocky. Yes, him. *2. n.* A *lesbidaceous* niterie.

claque *n.* The unsightly residue formed on the banks of a single man's *brown trout pond.* Very difficult to shift, even with vigorous brushing. From cack + plaque.

clarse-hole *n.* A posh person who behaves like a *ringpiece.* An *aristo-twat.* *'Today's birthdays: Smokey Robinson, American singer and songwriter, 71; Ray Winstone, roly-poly cockney thespian, 54; Andrew Albert Christian Edward, Prince Andrew, Duke of York, golfing clarse-hole, 51.'*

cleanis *n.* The pristine, hygienic state of the male member which, on average, lasts for about a minute a day.

clean your golf clubs *v.* To buff up your *one wood* in the garage. *'Where are you going, darling?' 'I'm just off to clean my golf clubs, dear. I'm going to do it over this brand new issue of Razzle I've just brought back from the newsagent so none of the polish goes on the floor.'*

clear smear *n.* Perseverance soup, guardsman's gloss, knuckle varnish, ball glaze.

cleavadge/cleavag *1. n.* The gap between the knuckles in a *camel's foot.* *2. n.* Not to put too fine a point on it, when a *bird*'s top is cut so low you can almost see her *twat.*

cleftal horizon *n.* Technical term for the *crack* of the arse. *'ROY: Just to the left of the cleftal horizon. BARRISTER: In layman's*

terms please Mr. Tenneman. ROY: Just to the left of the bumline.' (from *The IT Crowd* by Graham Linehan).

Clegg *n. S. Yorks.* A short length of *hound cable* pushed through the letterbox of an unpopular person. Derivation unknown.

Clegged *adj.* Caught out by your own dissemblement. Suffering the inevitable, disastrous consequences of a catalogue of previous falsehoods. Named after Thaddeus von Clegg, the German inventor of the kazoo who, in the 1840s, was famous for being a fucking lying bastard.

clegma *n.* A tenaciously noisome deposit lurking under a *bell end.*

Cleopatra's needle *n.* A huge, pock-marked, veiny, granite-hard phallus that tapers towards the top.

click and drag *euph.* The act of *farting* and then walking to another location whilst "dragging" the aroma behind you for everyone you pass in between to enjoy.

Clio lane *n.* The inside lane of a motorway or dual carriageway.

clippage *n.* The brown mark at the back of the *chod bin* seat caused by inept *arsal* positioning when dropping the shopping. *'Lot 345. A rhinestone-encrusted lavatory seat removed from the Graceland Mansion, Memphis, Tennessee, formerly the personal property of Elvis Presley (1935-77). Signs of use. Some clippage. Est. $50,000 – $75,000.'*

clip the cigar *v.* To dextrously use one's *nipsy* to cut short a thick, brown, smoking object.

clit lit *n.* Any book which is taken up and read by a bloke with the sole purpose of instigating conversation with members of the opposite sex, with the ultimate aim of getting into their knickers, *eg. A Short History of Tractors in Ukranian, Girl with the Dragon Tattoo* or anything by Jane Austen.

clitmitten *n.* The non-string bit on a particularly small G-string. Presumably the G.

clittybashing *n.* Whilst pleasuring a lady doggy-style, the 180 degree longitudinal oscillation of the *clockweights* along the axis of motion that rattles her *clematis*.

clock *n.* Something that is smaller than a *cock* but larger than a *clit*.

clocker *n.* A lady who has done a somewhat higher mileage than advertised.

clock off *v.* To *wank* yourself to sleep. To have a *knuckle nightcap*.

cloppercino *n.* A foaming *furry cup*. A bit more frothy than a *twatte*. *Twattuccino*.

cloppicing *n.* The clearing of overgrown *twat thatch* for lumber.

close, but no bum cigar *exclam.* A consolatory retort to a noisy *parp*, in the style of *another turn and I'm sure she would have started.*

closing ceremony *euph.* A disappointing or embarrassing end to an otherwise enjoyable experience, *eg.* A failure to achieve *organism* or a non-existent or tiny *Thora* at the end of a prolonged bout of hearty *guffing.* Derivation unknown.

clot hammock *n.* A feminine hygiene requisite for the management of *women's things.* *'And get us some extra-large clot hammocks while you're out, will you? I'm bleeding like a fucking stuck pig here.'*

clothes horse *euph.* When copulating with a lady who is blessed with an aesthetically unconventional appearance, to drape a towel, bed sheet or dust mat over her back so that you can only see the *back doors.*

clout atlas *n.* A particularly graphic *bongo book.* *'Eeh, look at all those pink bits in the clout atlas.'*

clown's car *n.* A short, violent anal expulsion which sounds like a troop of comical circus entertainers has arrived in a small, backfiring automobile.

club sandwich *n.* The practice of discreetly secreting a *fine art pamphlet* between two high brow journals whilst making one's way to the *throne room.*

cluck off *exclam.* Parting words to a *one night stand* whom you don't wish to see again but would ideally like to do a spot of washing up and push the hoover around a bit before she leaves. An amalgamation of "clean up" and "fuck off".

clunge sponge *1. n.* Any handy textile item pressed hastily into service post *coitus* by one's ladyfriend to stop the *Harry Monk* leaking out of her *James Hunt. 2. n.* A beard. *'There was an old man with a beard, who said, "It is just as I feared! Two owls and a hen, four larks and a wren, have all built their nests in my clunge sponge."'* (from *Edward Lear's Book of Fucking Nonsense*).

clutch Bungle *v.* To be in dire need of a *tom tit.* *'Honest, I'd love to come on the pitch and play, only I'm clutching Bungle at the moment, Mr Mancini.'*

Cock and Can, the *n.* The perfect evening in for a single gent. *'You fancy coming to the Red Lion, Baz?' 'Nah, it's the Cock and Can for me tonight, Dave.'*

cockasins *n.* Uncomfortable *applecatchers* that are not fit for purpose.

cockforest *n.* A pub with plenty of *wood* but not enough *bushes.*

cockfoster *n.* A warm and welcome, albeit temporary, home for one's *baby's arm.*

cock monkey *n.* A *loose* woman who mimics her simian namesake by swinging from *giggle-twig* to *giggle-twig* in the style of a gibbon, making sure she has established a firm hold of the next one before releasing her grip on the last.

cock Ness monster *n.* A *lazy lob on* in the bath that is reminiscent of a Scottish plesiosaur poking its head out of the water and having a bit of a look about.

cock off *n.* Of a *grumble* actor, to leave work at the end of a hard day at the orifice. Having *cocked on* in the morning, obviously.

'You're home early, Ben.' 'Yeah. I fancied getting a round of golf in before me tea, so I cocked off early.'

cock on the block, put your *phr.* Figure of speech comparable to "put your neck on the line". *'Earlier on today, apparently, a woman rang the BBC and said she heard there was a hurricane on the way. Well, if you're watching, I'm going to put my cock on the block and say don't worry, there isn't.'* (Michael Fish, BBC weather forecast, October 15th 1987).

cock pocket *n.* Any orifice frequented by the excitable *sausage man.*

cocks orange pippin *n.* A massive *herman jelmet* that is guaranteed to keep the doctor away.

cock star *n.* A virtuoso performer on that most challenging of instruments - the *pink oboe.*

cockupational therapy *n.* Repetitive exercises that ease stiffness, aid relaxation and can help restful sleep. That'll be *wanking*, then.

cock witch *n.* The hideous mental crone summoned into the mind's eye of a fellow when he wishes to *keep the wolf from the door*, for want of a better expression for *not spunk up.*

cocoa pops, doing *n.* The act of having a shower when in possession of a *shitter* which is "so chocolatey it turns the water brown".

codel *n.* To *break wind* sufficiently loudly that one risks setting off an avalanche. From colon + yodel.

codpiece yoghurt *n.* Soured, semi-solid *man milk. 'Fancy a bowl of codpiece yoghurt, Una?' 'I'll go and get me spoon, Cliff.'*

cogging *n.* It's like *dogging*, but on your push-iron.

cointreauception *n.* Middle class *brewer's droop* caused by over-indulgence on orange-flavoured triple-sec apéritif.

coldplay *1. n.* Sexual practice whereby the saucy participants smear each other with cold human excrement. *2. n.* A pop group. *'Fancy a bit of Coldplay?' 'Unless you mean the sexual practice whereby the saucy participants smear each other with cold human excrement, then no. I do have my standards.'*

collie's ear, fanny like a *sim.* Descriptive of a battered old *minge* that the vet might poke a torch inside whilst tutting.

Colonel's breath, the *euph. Dropped* approximately 25 minutes after consuming a portion of food from the popular high street fried chicken franchise, a pungent *trouser cough* that is redolent of ex-military man Sanders's secret blend of herbs and spices.

come-atose/cumatose *adj.* Of a male, unconscious shortly following the *shooting* of *his wad.*

come to bathroom eyes *euph.* A seductive Teutonic metaphor. *'Achtung, Eva's giving me them come to bathroom eyes again, Heinrich.'*

comfortable *adj.* Of shoes, having "lesbian" written all over them.

commode dragon *n.* A venomous species of unflushable U-bend-dwelling monster, characterised by its giant size and mottled, angry appearance.

competent at ironing *euph. Sensitive. 'You know that bloke off that thing on the telly? He's as competent at ironing as a nine-bob note.'*

compost mentis *adj. Lat.* Descriptive of a person of limited mental capacity; a *shit-for-brains.*

conjaculations *n.* Mutual expressions of appreciation following a satisfactory conclusion to a bout of genital intercourse.

consonant dodger *n.* Disparaging term for a member of the lower orders who eschews stops, fricatives, nasals, bilabial articulants, pulmonic egressives, ejectives and implosives whilst speaking.

consult Clarkson *v.* To adjourn to the bathroom for a sit-down perusal of yet another *shite*-sized chapter of the *Top Gear* petrol-mouth's cistern-worthy literary *oeuvre*.

contemplation pit *n.* The *khazi*. *'Jesus Christ, archbishop. Was you the last in the contemplation pit? It fucking stinks in there.'*

controlled explosion *n.* Detonating your *suspicious package* in advance of a date in order to avoid a *schoolboy error. Taking the edge off, putting a wank in the bank.*

controlled explosion in the number two reactor *euph.* An unexpectedly lively *dump* of toxic material, which may occasion the imposition of an exclusion zone.

cool down a transformer *v.* An old Southern Electric Board term; to have a crafty *piss* in an electricity sub station, usually altruistically performed against the side of an overheating piece of voltage conversion equipment.

copper's knock *n.* An unnecessarily brusque *back-scuttling* which is abruptly initiated at 6.00am, while the missus is still half asleep.

coq au vag *n. Fr.* The main course after an evening spent warming up a saucy *bird* of Gallic extraction.

corned beef gash *n.* A well-pounded *school dinner.*

Cornish nosebleed *euph.* The consequences of a young lady suffering a coughing fit at a critical moment whilst having a *drink on a stick.*

coronal mass ejection *1. n.* In astrophysics, a huge burst of solar wind, plasma and electromagnetic radiation which is periodically released into space by the sun. *2. n.* A spectacular forward blast caused by the consumption of an excess of Mexican lager. *'Thanks for lending me your suit, Dave. I had a bit of a coronal mass ejection down the front of it, but I reckon that'll just sponge out.'*

corpse in a carpet *n.* A *Sir Douglas* of such huge dimensions that it resembles a lorry driver's victim, rolled up in a length of Axminster with all flies buzzing round it.

corridor of uncertainty *euph.* As a rude lady lowers herself towards a bloke's erectivitated member, the few seconds whereby, were you to enquire of him whether he is expecting to be *potting the pink* or *the brown,* he really couldn't answer you with any degree of confidence.

cottager's waddle *1. n.* The tell-tale gait of a man who has just, successfully, been *looking for badgers. 2. n.* A small village in Dorset. Possibly.

cottaging bag *n.* A *puddle jumper*'s public *cludgie* portmanteau, in which he and/or his chum discreetly stand whilst they get up to their saucy antics, to avoid being spotted under the door by a nosy *tit-head.*

cottaging tax *n.* The 20p entry fee for the *bogs* at large railway stations.

coughart *v.* To attempt to disguise a loud *exchange & mart* with a theatrical clearing of the throat. Or vice versa, for that matter.

cough drop *1. n.* Technique used by a woman to empty her *front bottom* of *cock hockle.* *2. n.* Throat-clearing technique used, usually unsuccessfully, in a public lavatory cubicle to mask the sound of a *load of old shoes falling out of the loft.*

coughy morning *n.* The first full tar *Harry Wragg* of the day, which creates a refreshing wave of nausea before setting off an invigorating fit of violent hemoptysis.

couldn't hit his own cock with a slipper *euph.* Said of a footballer whose kicking has lately exhibited a marked lack of accuracy. *'Why the fuck didn't he let Carroll take that penalty?' 'Because Carroll couldn't hit his own cock with a slipper, your highness.'*

could you repeat that in English, please? *exclam.* A humorous quip to be uttered after someone drops a *windy pop.*

council estate landmine *n.* A *dirty bomb* left not particularly covertly on the pavement in an area with a high *SPSM* quotient.

council facial *n.* The steamy blast that greets you when opening the dishwasher at the end of its cycle.

council go-kart *n.* A mobility scooter. Also known as a *Belfast taxi, Disneyworld dragster, Frinton Ferrari, Mansfield motorcycle* or *nanbretta*.

country supper *n.* Something regularly enjoyed in Chipping Norton by David Cameron and Rebekkah Brooks.

crabitat *n.* Pubic hair.

crack addict *n.* A fellow who has a penchant for the *wrong'un*.

crackaratti *n.* The luminaries that make up the cream of the Glaswegian narcotics community, who convene their daily *salons philiosophiques* outside the Renfield Centre at around 5.30pm to take advantage of the free soup.

crack the pan *v.* To lay a massive *egg*. To *chip the china*.

crafty *n.* A discreet act of *self pollution*. *'The inspector completely over-reacted when he caught our Steve having a crafty on the bus. He says they might take his PSV licence off him.'*

crankenstein *n.* A *Charlie* with all bolts stuck through its neck. *'What's the matter, Justin? You're white as a sheet.' 'I was just stood next to Evan in the bogs having a piss and I accidentally caught a glimpse of his crankenstein out the corner of my eye, Rabbi.'*

crapaplegic *n.* One who finds himself unable to walk after spending far too long reading *auto-bographies* on the *shitter*. A *crapple*.

crappetiser *n.* A *pony & trap* taken to make a bit of space for your tea.

crapture *n.* The semi-ecstatic afterglow of a successful *sit down toilet adventure*.

creaking gate *n. medic.* Doctors' terminology for a person who has been in bad health for some time but who *refuses to buy the farm*.

cream egg *n.* A rather sickly treat for a *felcher*; a *snowdrop* with a chocolate coating.

cream tea *n.* A deliciously nourishing afternoon treat that a thoughtful gentleman might provide for a ladyfriend.

credit cunt *n.* Anyone who has come out of the present worldwide economic meltdown in markedly better circumstances than when they went into it.

cri de curry *n. Fr.* The plaintive, anguished howl (*eg.* "Fire in the hole!") of a person who has over-indulged in the culinary delights of the Orient the previous evening, and whose *fundament* is now paying the inevitable bill. Plus tips.

Cringer & Battle-Cat *1. n.* Something off *Masters of the Universe*; He-Man's tiger horse thing that he rides round on and its alter-ego, or something, probably the other way round. *2. n.* The two extreme states of male genitalias.

crinkles *n. Cock* wrinkles. *'Q: What's the first thing to come out of a man's penis when he gets an erection? A: The crinkles?'* (from The *Jim'll Fix It Joke Book*, BBC Publications 1975).

cripple shit *n.* A desperate urge to *drop off the shopping* that leaves one physically challenged.

crips and bloods *1. n.* Rival Los Angeles-based street gangs. True dat. *2. n.* A post-curry *shite* that combines the twin qualities of galloping *squits* and a bleeding *nipsy*.

crisping *n.* The result of being so distracted whilst ensconced on the *jobbie engine* that any residual ordure remaining around the *marmite pot* dries to such a consistency that wiping is no longer required and a brisk brush off should suffice.

crofting *n.* Rugged, tweedy, north Scottish form of *cottaging*, possibly taking place in a granite but'n'ben.

cronk *v. rhym. slang.* To do a *shite*. Named after the late US broadcaster Walter "and that's the way it is" Cronkshite.

crotch opera *n. Aus.* Classy *grumble*.

Cruft's jellies *n.* The uniquely bouncing *shirt potatoes* of the well-nourished matrons who canter around the show ring of the famous *shit machine* festival.

cruise at periscope depth *n.* To walk about in the morning with your twitching *Kilroy* poking over the waistband of your *grundies*.

crumpee *n.* A non-gender-specific affliction affecting those in the autumn years of their lives, whereby they cough, *trump* and *pee* almost simultaneously. *'Fetch a mop, Carol. She's done another crumpee.'*

crystal skull *1. n.* A Damien Hirst masterpiece consisting of a human cranium adorned with over eight billion pounds' worth of Swarovski crystals. *2. n.* A young lady's head encrusted with several *pods'* worth of *jelly jewellery*.

CSI *abbrev.* The post-crime damage surveillance done in a room where a violent act of *self harm* has occurred. Cum Scene Investigation.

cubicle grin *n.* A sly smirk on one's face whilst standing at the public lavatory hand basin as an unsuspecting victim walks in and enters one's recently-vacated defecatory paralleliped where he will encounter the full, foetid stench of the recent *porcelain massacre* that has occurred therein.

cuckoo clock *n.* A *cottage* where the patrons pop out from the door every quarter of an hour in the hope of drumming up a bit of business. *'Where are you off to, George?' 'I'm just off down the cuckoo clock in the park, Andrew.'*

cuckoo nest *n.* Stuffing loads of *bog roll* into a public *crapper* in order to construct a cosy roost for one's *bum eggs*, where they can be admired *in situ* by the next lucky occupant.

cuddle the monkey *n.* After a bout of *chimping*, when a fellow falls asleep whilst still grasping *half a teacake*.

cumber-queue *n.* A fresh selection of vaguely-cylindrical groceries lined up on a table, waiting to be pressed into use in a nightmarish, home-made *grumble-flick*.

Cumbledore *n.* A *plasterer's radio* whose chin is adorned with a long, white beard in the fashion of the late Hogwarts headmaster. Although his was made out of hair rather than *jitler*.

cum/fart zone *n.* A *boomerang-socked* bachelor's olid bedroom or, even worse, his *Dutch oven*.

cumoflage *n.* Putting one's crusty *Womble's toboggan* at the bottom of the laundry pile in the hope that it blends in with the respectable washing and one's mum/wife doesn't notice.

cunnilingual *n.* Sufficiently fluent in a foreign tongue that one can seduce that country's women. Not all of them, obviously.

cunny money *n.* The cash equivalent of the *hairy cheque book*.

cuntage *n.* Acts of profound idiocy. *'There's a lot of cuntage going on out there on the M25 today.'*

cuntan *n.* The pale complexion sported when returning from a holiday abroad by a lucky gentleman who has been unavoidably detained in his hotel bedroom throughout his sojourn.

cuntankerous *adj.* Of a *splitarse*, *showing off* whilst the *tomato boat is docked in tuna town*.

cunt envelope, pushing the *euph.* Used to describe someone whose behaviour is frankly testing the bounds of *twattishness to destruction and beyond*. *'Do we have to invite Uncle Andrew to the reception? Only he's really been pushing the cunt envelope recently.'*

cuntestant *n.* A type whose chance to grab their allotted fifteen minutes of fame consists of an appearance on *Bargain Hunt, Deal or No Deal* or any one of a number of similar shows that make relatively few demands on their participants' intellect.

cunt hair *n.* An Imperial unit of measurement used in carpentry, equal to about three sixteenths of a whiff-waff. *'Just take a cunt hair off that door, Steve, and it'll fit like a finger up an arsehole.'*

cunting *n.* The bits of general paper effluvium and detritus decorating a woman's *minge.*

cuntlery *n.* Delicate ironmongery in a bird's *drawers.*

cunt of Monte Cristo *n.* Someone who gets *pissed* on cheap sherry and makes a *twat* of theirself at a family occasion. *'Don't take any notice of your Uncle Gerald, children. He's the cunt of Monte Cristo.'*

cuntourage *n.* The cohort of *twats* who accompany a radio DJ on his metropolitan peregrinations.

cuntpany *n.* Any business that falls into disfavour for any reason.

cunt rope *n.* A polite term for pubic hair. *'I say, your majesty. I just found some cunt rope in my vol-au-vent.'*

cuntsultant *n.* In business, an expert who is hired at huge expense by one's boss to evaluate working practices from an outsider's

perspective. Invariably a complete *cunt.*

cuntylinctus *n. Milp, blip, fanny batter.*

cup-a-poop *n.* The art of catching a *guff* in the palm of the hand and then passing it on to an unsuspecting victim so he/she can share its wholesome, warming, hopefully crouton-free goodness.

curious otter *n.* An elongated *Peter O'Toole* lying contentedly with its nose just above the waterline.

currant in my tooth, I've a *exclam. euph.* Phrase used by one who is suffering from *sweetcorn itch.*

curry morning *euph.* A day when it is "wet and windy".

custard *n.* A contumelious epithet. From cunt + bastard.

custardy battle *n.* A fight to resist the temptation to push one's *bellend* into a trifle.

custurd *n.* A *feeshus* that is the same colour, temperature and consistency as the popular dessert topping.

cut on a bear's arm *n.* A particularly hairy *growler.* A *ripped sofa.*

cybernating *n.* Socially dormant due to a preoccupation with visiting certain seedy domains along the information superhighway.

DA *abbrev.* 1950s "Teddy boy"-style haircut, so-called because of its supposed resemblance to an American District Attorney.

daddy longlegs *n.* A particularly firmly-anchored, stubborn *winnet* that, when extracted, takes a bunch of uprooted *coil springs* with it, thus resembling the eponymous lampshade-dwelling household pest.

Dagenham *adj.* Mad as a lorry. "Two stops past Barking".

Dahl-on *n. Half-a-teacake* that could suddenly rise up into a firm *French stick* at a moment's notice whilst watching Sophie Dahl's cookery programme. A *Dahl-on* is significantly less rigid than a *Nigella horse-on*, and can thus be pleasantly enjoyed in the company of one's missus without her attention being drawn to it unnecessarily.

Dalai Larga *n.* In a public house, a man who, when suitably *bitten by the brewer's horse*, spouts endless words of wisdom.

Daley *n.* Named after teenage Olympic diving sensation Tom, a streamlined *Douglas* which leaves the *wrinkled penny* and enters the water without making a splash, possibly fitting in a triple somersault and a half-pike during its graceful descent.

Dalton *n.* A small, unimpressive *Douglas* that, judging from the immense straining it took to produce, you might have expected to be an absolute *dreadnought*. From the bouncer character played by Patrick Swayze in the 1989 film *Road House*, who is constantly told by other characters: "I thought you'd be bigger".

Dannii Minogue *n.* The pointless bit of flesh that sits between a *cock* and an *arsehole*; from Kylie's sister's job sitting between Brian McFadden and Kyle Sandilands (no, us neither) on *Australia's Got Talent*. Also *tintis, taint, BBBA, scrincter, stinker's bridge, scran, gisp, barse, great, notcher, ABC, gooch, Finsbury bridge, isnae, scruttock, Per-*

ry Como's lip, tornado alley, scranus, smelly bridge, Brick Lane or *crunk*.

dart blart *n. coll.* The attractive females who escort overweight tungsten ticklers to the stage during high profile televised events.

dashing white sergeant, the *1. n.* A traditional ballroom dance that is popular with old people. *2. n.* Hot beads of *love piss* fired at high velocity across the face and *churns*. Not necessarily quite so popular with old people.

datebomb *n.* A revelation uttered during the course of a romantic evening that instantly blows a burgeoning relationship out of the water. Something that, on reflection, would probably have been better left unsaid.

dating *euph. Aus.* Indulging in *bum games*. *'Yeah, Sheila and I were dating last year. But then I got hepatitis C.'*

dawn star *n.* The desirable lady who is currently taking a leading role in the somnolent erotic reveries of a tumescent fellow at the time his morning alarm goes off. Also *pole star.*

day-nighter *1. n.* In limited-overs cricket, a match started mid-afternoon and completed under floodlights well into the evening. *2. n.* A less-than-attractive *good time girl* who nonetheless offers very reasonable hourly rates.

dead man's handle *1. n.* Safety cut-out switch on a piece of machinery, such as a train, which must be depressed in order for it to operate. *2. n.* A cheeky - not to mention borderline illegal - use of one's partner's *wanking spanner* whilst they are asleep in order to *make the bald man cry.*

dead midget *n.* Politically incorrect term for a dimensionally-challenged, pathetic-looking *lob on*. A *French horn* that couldn't even be used to clear ear wax. From the fact that it is "Just a little stiff".

dead possum with its tongue hanging out, like a *sim. Aus.* A poetic Antipodean turn of phrase describing a badly-maintained and unsightly *stamped bat.*

dead rubber *1. n.* In cricket, when a series is won but there is still one nothing-at-stake match remaining. *2. n.* A used *dunky.*

deal with the queue at the trade counter *v.* To excuse oneself in order to sort out *the shopping.*

decant sediment *v.* To inadvertently *follow through. 'Could you fetch me a clean pair of plus fours please, Carson? I appear to have decanted sediment into these fuckers.'*

decent chippy *euph.* Something that is open most nights, and where one is certain of getting a tasty *fish supper* with plenty of *batter.*

decompression guff *n.* A small *Bakewell* let out in order to create a little breathing space whilst desperate for the *crapper.*

deep vein thronebosis *n. medic.* Loss of feeling and temporary paralysis in the lower legs due to extended periods spent ensconced on the *shit pan* reading this.

defrost the freezer *v.* To go through the tiresome twice-yearly *frigmarole* of performing foreplay on the missus.

delete your wristory *v.* To purge one's *filth machine* of all incriminating evidence.

Delia *n.* Following excessive alcohol intake, a floppy male member at which its owner may be reduced to shouting "Where are you? Let's be having you!" in a style reminiscent of the famously emotional television cook's heavily *refreshed* half-time outburst at Carrow Road on February 28th 2005.

demilitarized zone *euph.* Another name for the *no glans land* which sits between the *pudenders* and the *freckle.* Also known, variously, as the *Dutch canal, scrincter, stinker's bridge, scran, gisp, barse, tintis, great, notcher, ABC, gooch, Finsbury bridge, isnae, scruttock, Perry Como's lip, tornado alley, scranus, smelly bridge, Brick Lane* and *crunk.*

dentally handicapped *adj.* Blessed with *Eng-*

lish teeth. 'My cousin's dentally handicapped, you know. He's got a gob like a burnt fence.'

depoomidifier *n.* The air-freshening act of opening the bathroom window after *making room for seconds.*

deputy dog *n.* Unacceptably sexist term to describe the *hound* who is typically seen shadowing a *fox.*

Dermot O'Leary's shirt, as wet as *sim.* Sopping. From the cuddly presenter's unfailing willingness to offer his shoulder as a tear-sponge to blubbing, over-emotional *X-Factor* hopefuls who've just had their dreams stamped into the dust by Simon Cowell.

despatch master *n.* One who has achieved a high level of expertise in the art of loud and/or noxious *trouser coughage.*

Detroit Cities *n. rhym. slang. US.* Big softly-sprung *headlamps* that soak up the bumps like a 1970s Cadillac Fleetwood Eldorado.

devil's thumbprints *n.* The intriguing dimples usually found on the lower backs of erotically-inclined women.

diamond dogs *1. n.* Title of an album by formerly *half-rice half-chips* rocker David Bowie. *2. n.* An offensively sexist and unacceptably misogynistic expression describing a gaggle of *fugly munters* with *vajazzled hoo-has.*

dick doc *n.* The bloke's equivalent of his missus's *snatch dentist. 'Excuse me, nurse, I've caught my bellend in my zip. I'd prefer to see a man dick doc, if that is at all possible, as I am uncomfortable about the idea of a woman getting excited at the sight of my bleeding, septic prepuce.'*

dick frost *n.* The sparkly residue found on the *pizzle shaft* the morning after a night of *frottage.*

dickie light *n. Aus.* In a brothel bedroom, a fluorescent bulb at crotch level which allows a shrewd *good time girl* to examine her prospective customer's *fruit bowl* for any untoward boils, warts, rashes or *cockrots.*

dick mist *n.* At the end of a *grumble* marathon, the white foam that gathers around the *brim* of a chap's *helmet* like the graveyard fog on the front of *Bat Out of Hell.*

dickram yoga *n.* The subtle art of *pissing* whilst balancing on one leg in a *bog* with a broken lock, with one's other leg fully extended behind in order to hold the door shut.

dicksy chicks *n.* Ladyboys. Also *bobby dazzlers, rotten peaches, Gwendolens, flippers, shims, tiptops* and *trolley dollies.*

dick tits *1. n. Top bollocks* which are eminently suitable for the provision of *diddyrides. 2. n. Headlamps* which *hang down like copper's torches. Knee shooters, sock tits.*

Dierdre's specs *n.* Large *aereolae,* named in honour of the generously-proportioned eyewear worn by the gravel-voiced screen wife of Ken Barlow. Also *saucepan lids, waggon wheels.*

difficunt *n.* A difficult *cunt.* From difficult + cunt. *'Blimey, have you been watching this series of I'm a Celebrity? That Anthony Cotton's a bit of a difficunt, isn't he?' 'Yeah, and he always seems so nice on Corrie.'*

dig for victory *v.* To deliver a two-fingered Churchillian salute up a lady's *front* and *back gardens.*

digital Coventry *n.* A roomful of ignorant *twunts* all staring at their fancy phones.

digitally enhanced *adj. Fingered.*

digitoflatal reflex *n. medic.* A primitive physiological response whereby the release of flatus through the anal sphincter is initiated by a small force applied by a third party longitudinally to the extensor indicus proprius.

dignity curtain *n.* When having an hirsute male dog's coat clipped, a lower abdominal pelmet of hair which discreetly obscures any dangling bits, thus sparing his blushes.

diminishing returns *n.* The series of about twenty *wanks* that a fellow must have after his vasectomy operation before he eventually begins to produce 100% *decaff spaff.*

dining at the eye *n.* Enjoying a *drink on a stick.*

dino-whore *n.* A *good time girl* who hasn't been a girl for a good long time. A *pro-AP.*

dinosaur's ball bag, face like a *sim.* Said of a person with a particularly haggard, careworn physiognomy. *'That Keith Richards. Fuck me, he's got a face like a dinosaur's ball bag, him.'* Or indeed *'That Tyrannosaurus. Fuck me, he's got a face like Keith Richards's ball bag.'*

dip the clutch *v.* To elongate or otherwise flex the left leg whilst in one's motor car, in order to lift the corresponding buttock cheek off the driver's seat and thus ease the release of *brownhouse gases* from the *exhaust pipe.*

Dirk Diggler's thumbprints *n.* Them dimples on a *bird's* lumbar region.

dirt penny *n.* An unwiped freckle. *'It's a very simple, straightforward procedure. I'm just going to put a glove on and pop my finger up your dirt penny, Paul. Then, after the break, Gino d'Acampo will be here to bake a chocolate and jam cake with almond sauce and we'll be talking to TOWIE's Gemma Collins about her battle with piles.'*

dirty air *1. n.* The region behind a Formula One racing car which is affected by aerodynamic turbulence, thus making it difficult to overtake. *2. n.* The region behind a flatulent person which is affected by *arseodynamic burbulence,* thus making it difficult to breathe.

dirty Groucho *n.* Like a *dirty Sanchez,* but including a pair of dark-rimmed spectacles. And probably a cigar.

dirty scarecrow *n.* When roped in by your significant other to help change the bedsheets, the charming, amusing and affectionate act of *dropping a gut* into an empty pillowcase, forcing it over her head and gathering it around the neck. It is estimated that *dirty scarecrows* are the cause of more than 40% of marriage failures in Britain.

disabler *n.* Very obvious and prolonged penile tumescence acquired during office hours that more or less permanently prevents one from getting out of one's chair.

disappinted *adj.* Descriptive of the emotional state of one who has inadvertently been left out of a round at the pub. *'I'm not upset, your royal highness. I'm just disappinted, that's all.'*

discovery channel *n.* Any satellite television station used by teenagers in the pursuit of *self improvement. Al Jizzera.*

disturbance in the force *1. n.* An uneasy feeling experienced after unleashing the destructive power of your *death star. 2. n.* Horrible gut pains you get before having a massive *tom tit. 'What's the matter, Obi-Wan?' 'It's nothing, Luke. Just a disturbance in the force. I'll be right as rain after I've dropped me shopping.'*

divine wind *1. n.* Usual translation of the Japanese word *Kamikaze,* used to describe the typhoon which destroyed a Mongol invasion fleet in the 13th Century and which was later applied to suicide pilots in WWII. *2. n.* Tuneful and fragrant *botty pops* released by highly-skilled geishas during the final stage of congress.

DMJ *abbrev.* A smart sportscoat or blazer bought in a charity shop. Dead Man's Jacket. *"You'll never get into the Royal Enclosure dressed like that.' 'Not a problem. I'll nip into Action Cancer and get a DMJ.'*

DNAisse *n.* Male generative condiment. *Baby gravy.*

DNF *1. abbrev.* In Formula 1, a form of letters which denotes a car that failed to successfully complete the full distance of a grand prix. Did Not Finish. *2. abbrev.* Following a date, a form of letters which denotes that a gentle-man failed to bring his evening to a successful conclusion. *'How did you get on with all them stewardesses in the hotel last night, James?' 'Not so well, Murray. Twenty-three DNFs and only eighteen pole positions.'*

dock fairy *n. E. Yorks.* A mysterious siren who flits about the cosmopolitan harbour-sides of Goole, guiding the inebriated matelots of Vladivostok and Murmansk to warmer quarters.

doctopussy *n.* A consultant gynaecologist. Also *fanny mechanic, snatch doc, box doc, cunt dentist. 'I'm having a bit of bother with me clopper, love, so I'm off to see doctopussy for a scrape.'*

Doctor Doom *n. coll.* Any online medical self-diagnosis website.

dodgy corner *n.* Anal sex. "He's taken it, and it's gone behind".

doesn't skip like a boxer *euph. S*aid of a chap who *bakes a moist sponge.*

doff one's cap *1. v.* To exhibit due deference to one of a higher social rank as a mark of respect. *2. v.* To ejaculate one's filthy *man-muck* onto a posh *tart's tits.*

dog coffin *n.* An unwanted jumper, worn once at Christmas and then put aside until a shroud is required for a deceased best friend.

dog eat dog *n.* Poor quality lesbidaceous *soixante-neuf.*

dogger bank *n.* A receptacle found in lay-bys along quiet rural roads, containing *jipper-*filled tissues and *jubber rays.*

dogging in Dubai *sim.* The rhetorical *ne plus ultra* of unlikelihoods. *'I tell you, mate. You've about as much chance of getting in her knickers as you have of going dogging in Dubai.'*

dog in the fog, like a *sim.* Descriptive of one who vanishes unexpectedly at some point during a all-day drinking session. *'Where's Dr Williams gone? He just disappeared like a dog in the fog.'*

dog left in the kennel *euph.* An unimpressive

single *Douglas* discovered in the *pan* after what felt like a serious session on the *bum sink*.

dog shagging a football, rumped up like a *sim*. Said of someone with notably poor posture. *'Okay, cut. That was great, Sister Wendy, really good. Absolutely perfect. But can we just try it once more, please, and this time could you try not to be all rumped up like a dog shagging a football?'*

dog shit on toast *euph. milit*. A bad situation. Also *dog shit on toast with ginger hairs on top* - A bad situation that is deteriorating.

dog toffee liqueur *n*. A length of *hound rope* that looks firm and solid until trodden on, when it reveals its rich, liquid filling that can ruin any trainer.

dollar up a sweep's arse, as clean as a *sim*. Something that is very clean indeed. *'The Armstrong-Rockwell P1600 Superatmospheric Autoclave uses high pressure steam super-heated to 121C to sterilize surgical instruments, leaving scalpels, retractors and forceps as clean as a dollar up a sweep's arse.'*

dolphin pods *n*. An immaculately-presented, glossily hairless scrotal sac, as sported by the likes of Richard O'Brien, Duncan Goodhew and R Kelly. It says here.

Donald *n*. A *trump* that could blow the hair on the back of your *noggin* up and forward over your forehead.

donk bin *n*. The metal waste receptacle typically found in the viewing area cubicles of peep-show booths for the convenience of sneezing patrons. Named after the noise that heavily-laden tissues make when hitting the sides.

donner meat *n*. Sundry lumps and slices of greasy flesh hanging from the *clunge* of a dumpy *piece*.

door handle biter *n*. A large and painful stool.

doorknob *n*. Humorous epithet for a nightclub bouncer which one would do well to keep to oneself, all things considered.

doorstep darts *n*. The vain and laborious process of repeatedly trying to find the keyhole at the conclusion of a serious night *on the sauce*.

doosra *1. n. Urdu*. In cricket, a particular type of offspin delivery that "turns the other way", and hence *2. n*. A fellow who is *fond of shopping, doesn't skip like a boxer,* and *bowls from the pavilion end*.

doppelginger *n*. The red-headed offspring of an otherwise normally *barnetted* couple. Yes, him for example.

doppling *n*. The act of a member of a superannuated rock group who *spoffs up* onto an unsuspecting member of the public from an upper-storey window, multi-storey car park or hotel balcony. Also *seagulling*. *'What shall we do after the concert, Rick?' 'I fancy a couple of pints and then a spot of doppling, Francis.'*

dossier *n. Fr*. A Parisian vagrant. *'Zut alors. Un dossier a fait un grand merde sur la chaise d'autobus. Donc je dois m'asseoir sur le siège à côté.'*

double deluxe *n*. The right royal act of simultaneously *shouting soup* and *shitting* oneself.

double flusher *n*. A recalcitrant *re-offender* that refuses to leave until one has pulled the chain at least twice.

double jeopardy *n*. Unexpected secondary *stoolage*.

double-yolked eggs, balls like *sim*. Of testicles, wrecked by over-exertion. *'Careful there, Precious. If you try to lift that fucker, you'll end up with balls like double-yolked eggs.'* (John Noakes, *Blue Peter* on BBCTV 1970).

dove's chest *n*. A plump *front lump* or *beetle bonnet*. Also *monkey's chin, monkey's forehead, grassy knoll* or *proud Mary*.

downstairs filter *1. n*. Something essential that must be wired into your satellite system in order for shopping channels, Teachers' TV and Bloomberg to reappear on your television screen. *2. n.* A pair of ragged underpants. *'They're barely a downstairs filter, them.'*

dragon's claw *n.* A Welsh *camel's hoof*. *'Look you, Mrs Llwwyydd, that's some dragon's claw you got there in your jeggings, isn't it?'*

drag strip *n.* A damp track on the toilet seat left by *well hung* lady who has went and got up without having a wipe first.

drambo *n. Scots.* Someone who will fight anyone in the room after a few shandies. Also *two can Van Damme, half pint Harry, tinny mallet.*

draughtsman *n.* A fellow whose only skill is the ability to regularly *tread on ducks*. A *backsmith.*

draw a map of the Bakerloo Line *v.* To leave a long, thin tube-shaped *motion* across the lavatory bowl. Substitute Northern Line if a Guinness drinker or Central Line if suffering from chronic *Adrians.*

drawing with a brown crayon *n.* An extended and frustrating session of *nipsy*-wiping, whereby one inscribes a sepia line across fifty sheets of *bumwad* before finally achieving an acceptably clean sheet. Or giving up. See also *arse like a marmite pot*. *'Sorry I was in there so long, your holiness. I was drawing with a brown crayon.'*

dream cream *n.* That which is frequently to be found spread across the inside of a young gent's jim-jam bottoms.

dredge *v.* To slowly and systematically trawl through the furthest, murky, Stygian recesses of nightclubs in search of female companionship.

drink straight from the tap *v.* To perform a *Boris Johnson.*

drinking hamster, like a *sim.* Descriptive of a thirsty fellow who goes at his missus's *snatch* like a stumpy-*arsed* rodent licking its water bottle.

drip mat *n.* Three sheets of *bum wad* used to soak up *dew from the lily* during a sordid act of *self pollution.*

dripping like an egg sandwich *sim.* Of a lady, *frothing at the oysters.*

drive in the slipstream *euph.* To be the *botter* rather than the *bottee*. To *bring up the rear* in the style of an *Audi driver*. *'Have you met David? He drives in Elton's slipstream. Or is it the other way round?'*

driving test *n.* The act of seeing how far it is possible to wind up one's missus. Often ends in an *emergency strop*. See *badger baiting.*

drop a cork *n.* To launch a remarkably buoyant *dreadnought*. To excrete a *jack-in-the-box, brown ping-pong ball, poomerang* or *repeat offender*. *'What are you doing in there, Mr Smith? Shouldn't you be up on the bridge, steering the boat?' 'I just dropped a cork, Mrs Ismay. I've flushed it six times, but ninety gallons of Atlantic seawater haven't been enough to see it off yet. God himself could not sink this shit.'*

drop anchor *v.* To become aroused in the *trunks department* whilst doing the breast stroke. See *chlorine cock.*

drop box *1. n.* A cyber portal for uploading and downloading large files. *2. n.* The *crapper.*

drop off a calling card *n.* To politely deposit an *air biscuit* on a silver tray whilst visiting an acquaintance in their home.

drop shot *n.* An expertly-executed *hockle*, neatly nutmegged between the thighs, the rim of the *shit-pan* and the *Autotrader* whilst sat on the *Rick Witter.*

drop the competitors off at the Aquatic Centre *euph.* To go for a *dump* of Olympian proportions. To pass a *digestive transit* so impressive you could hang a medal round its neck and give it a bunch of flowers.

drop the hymn book *v.* To *guff* in church.

drout *n.* A dried-up *fanny*. From drought-ridden + clout.

DRS enabled *1. phr.* In Formula 1, a reference to some sort of flaps that open up. *2. phr.* When *feeding the pony*, a reference to some sort of *flaps* that open up.

dry lining *n.* Workmanlike use of *shit tickets* laid around the *bum sink* to ameliorate *acid splashback* when *releasing the chocolate hostage.*

dryrrhoea *n. medic.* An uncontrollable and alarming-sounding - yet ultimately harmless - bout of flatulence.

Duckhams, do a *v.* To *tip your filthy concrete* after just a couple of pushes. Wittily named after the popular "two stroke" engine oil.

duckles *n.* The indentations in the back of a fatty's hands where their knuckles should be. From dimples + knuckles.

Duke of Kunt *n.* A proper aristocrat amongst *cunts, eg.* Jeremy Kyle, Piers Morgan.

dukes *n. rhym. slang. Charms, shirt potatoes, headlamps.* From Grand old Duke of Yorks = norks. *'I see the Duchess has went and got her Dukes out in the paper, then.'*

Dumbo's ears *n.* The large, sometimes grey, flaps of meat found in a lady's *dunghampers*.

dump grump *n.* Depression brought on by constipation or the lack of an opportunity to defecate. *'I'm sorry Mr Dee. The toilets in the dressing room are out of order.'*

Dundee suitcase *euph. Scots.* A bin bag.

dungsten carbide *n.* The material from which the leading end of certain, particularly firm stools appears to be forged, with which they could drill their way through the most tightly-pursed *fifties teatowel*

holder, like the Mole out of Thunderbird 2. *'Bloody hell, mother. That one had a tip of pure dungsten carbide on it. It's completely de-burred me nipsy.'*

dung trumpet *n.* A melodic refrain on the *botty bugle* which brings to mind nothing so much as the opening bars to the signature tune of *Johnny Briggs.*

dust sucker *n.* A woman who prefers to take her romantic pleasures with a more mature gentleman caller.

Dutch brogues *n.* A pair of plain suede shoes decorated with delicate traceries of *piss* spots. *Flush puppies. 'Hey, I like the Dutch brogues, Ken.'*

Dutch jellyfish *n.* The free-swimming result of a *five knuckle shuffle* in the bath.

Dutch look *n.* An uncomfortably detailed examination of the range of unappetising products produced by the *dirt bakery.*

Dutch timeout *n.* Two fingers up the *chocolate windmill.*

Dutch traffic *n.* The *wanking* queue of gentlemen at a *gang bang. 'I would've come earlier, only the Dutch traffic was terrible.'*

duvet charming *n.* The mythical eastern art of consuming *musical vegetables,* then falling asleep and causing the counterpane to rise mystically to the plangent whinnying of your *arse flute.*

duvet dive *n.* The act of a fellow who rapidly heaves up the bedclothes and pretends to be fast asleep when he hears his wife approaching the bedroom door halfway through his morning *hand shandy.*

earth wind & fire *1. n.* Critically-acclaimed US disco/funk band, founded in Chicago in 1969, whose hits include *Got To Get You Into My Life, September* and *Fantasy. 2. n.* The truly woeful digestive after-effects of an evening spent drinking copious amounts of real ale, topped off with a vindaloo. And some lager. And a kebab on the way home.

ease springs *1. exclam. milit.* In the armed forces, an order to move the working parts of a weapon forwards into a safe position after firing. *2. exclam.* An amusing announcement to make after a particularly mechanical-sounding burst of flatulence. Also *back to bed Peppa; a confident appeal by the Australians there; an excellent theory, Dr Watson; anybody injured?; fer-fetch a cloth, Granville.*

Eastbourne, on the way to *euph.* Of an ageing lady's *Davy Jones's lockers*, heading south for a well-earned retirement.

Easter egg on legs, like a *sim.* Unpleasantly judgemental phrase which nevertheless perfectly describes the red-faced woman in glasses who appeared to be the principal dancer in Les Dawson's Roly Polys. You know the one, she used to be the Mighty Atom out of the Mighty Atom and Roy.

East Hull loan *euph.* A short term financial advance arranged by altering and kindly cashing other people's benefits cheques. *'How did you pay off the fine you got for that War Widows Pension fraud, Dave?' 'I took out an East Hull loan.'*

Eastwood *n.* A *clit* which is a real fistful.

easyjet eardrum *n. medic.* Severe tympanic pressure felt when returning from the pub *shitfaced* and *her indoors* starts *giving it this*.

easy now *exclam.* Humorous post-flatal shout-out, delivered in a drum'n'bass stylee. Also *ET phone home; you were only supposed to blow the bloody doors off; be not afeard, the isle is full of noises; move along, nothing to see here; I second that motion and add a turd.*

eBaids *n.* The virulently infectious, deadly germs that must be scrubbed off the disease-ridden things bought on online auction sites before they can be used. From eBay + Aids. *'I like your new china tea service, Audrey.' 'Yes, it's Crown Derby. But we're not using it yet because I haven't cleaned the eBaids off it.'*

e-chimping *n.* Hurling *shit* at people electronically, *eg.* Via emailed corporate newsletters, press announcements, endless fucking reminders to leave "feedback" *etc.*

Edinburgh fringe *n. Scots. rhym. slang. Minge.* *'Demerara was powerless to resist. His eye burned into hers like a sapphire. His muscular tentacles enfolded her softly-yielding body as she felt herself being swept away in a tempest of passion. "It's no good, I can't hold on any longer," Fernando whispered urgently, as he shot his thick black ink up her Edinburgh fringe.'* (from *The Lady Deep-sea Diver and the Octopus* by Barbara Cartland).

egg banjo *n.* The characteristic pose adoopted when hot yolk spills out the bottom of an egg sandwich, with one hand holding the sandwich and the other making a strumming motion to cool it down.

egg hole *n.* The *fanny, quim, blurtch, clunge* or *clopper.* *'Artist Gustave Courbet scandalised the French art world in 1866 when he unveiled his controversial painting The Origin of the World. The canvas, which is now on display at the Musée d'Orsay in Paris, is a graphic, close-up depiction of his muse and lover Joanna Hiffernan's egg hole.'* (from *Civilisation* by Kenneth Clark).

eggycentre *n.* The source of a cataclysmic posterior detonation. *Browned zero.*

eggy pop *n.* A brief, yet pungently sulphurous, *air omelette* that could seriously vitiate a bystander's lust for life.

e-jaculate *v.* To discharge the *mutton musket* over some form of computerised *grumble.*

ejaculatte *n.* A hot, milky serving from the *jerkolator.* Also *fappuccino.*

ejaculee *n.* He whom has *spoff offed.*

elephant's eyelashes *n.* The vigorous, jumbo-sized nasal hairs which Mother Nature inexplicably deems an essential *bird*-pulling accoutrement for males once they reach the age of thirty or so.

elephant's toenails *n.* Big, brown, crusty nipples on a *bird* who, one might reasonably surmise, has been round the block a few times.

Elsie Tanner Montana *n.* Another phrase for an ageing woman who adopts the fashions of someone much younger. Also *atomic mutton, nana Kournikova, Thora bird.*

emergency stop button *n.* The *bollocks*. From the fact that a sharp blow to the *knackers* will instantly render any man into a state of agonised immobility, whatever he happens to be doing. *'Welcome to Fight Club. The first rule of Fight Club is: you do not talk about Fight Club. The second rule of Fight Club is: you DO NOT talk about Fight Club! Third rule of Fight Club: don't kick anyone in the emergency stop button. It's just not nice.'*

Emily Mateless *n.* The female equivalent of *Billy No-mates,* named for no discernible reason after the occasional *Newsnight* presenter.

emission control *n.* Any deliberately unerotic mental countdown practised in order to prevent a premature *blast off. 'Why do you keep muttering that list of the various team sheets and scores from Celtic's 1970 European Cup run, Rod?' 'It's just a bit of emission control, Penny.'*

Emperor Minge *euph.* One who is a wow with the ladies, *eg.* Hugh Hefner, Peter Stringfellow, Rod Stewart, Ken Barlow. A man who seems to *have a chocolate knob.*

empire of dirt *n.* A lifetime's accumulation of *mucky books, eg.* The contents of Philip Larkin's attic.

empty the brown bin *v.* To perform an dolphin-unfriendly act of waste disposal.

encore une fois! *exclam.* A rousing francophone announcement in the style of the famous sample featured in the 1997 song of the same name by *twattish* German band Sash, to be uttered after a healthy *René Descartes.*

encyclopaedo *n.* A childless adult with a suspiciously comprehensive knowledge of the *High School Musical* films, *Glee*, the life and works of Justin Bieber, or any other bollocks that you really shouldn't know anything about if you're more than twelve.

Ennis elbow *n. medic.* Type of repetitive strain injury suffered by a male who has been closely following the Olympic women's heptathlon competition.

Ennis, have a *v.* To relax in a gentleman's way in seven different styles during the course of a single day's viewing of female athletics.

enough to make one's blood run beige *phr.* A nonplussed reaction to something deeply dull or bland. *'This exhibition of watercolour landscapes by the Prince of Wales is enough to make my blood run beige, it really is.'*

ensure the juices are running clear *v.* On a game *bird,* to perform a handy check that her *meat* is ready for *eating.*

enthusiagasm *n.* An expression of overly-effusive ardor. *'Did you see Great British Bake-Off? Paul Hollywood had an enthusiagasm over a lemon meringue pie.'*

e-rection *n.* Tumescence achieved via the medium of internet *Frankie.*

eskiho *n.* An unacceptably sexist and offensive term for a girl who wears *pugg boots* and a mini-skirt, which we would never print in a respectable publication such as this.

Esther *n.* The one amongst any group of fellows engaged in simultaneous onanism who is first to *lose his deposit.* Derivation unknown. But it might be a reference to Esther Rantzen only getting 4.4% of the votes when she stood for Luton South in the 2010 General Election, and forfeiting her £500 deposit.

ET *euph.* When your *earthing cable* hits the water while still connected to your *fifties tea towel holder.*

Eve's pudding *1. n.* A British dessert made with apple and sponge cake, which is traditionally eaten with custard. *2. n.* A Biblical term for a lady's *undercarriage*, which is also traditionally eaten with custard.

exam shits *n. medic.* Excessive diarrhoea caused by a student's examinations week diet of Red Bull, Pro-Plus and cups of tea. Examples can be found in varsity *crappers* throughout the land, not least those in the basement of the John Rylands Library at the University of Manchester.

exasturbate *v.* To make an already difficult situation even more fraught through an involuntary deposit in the *wank bank.* *'I already got the massive horn every time she spoke to me, but the other lunchtime she exasturbated things by talking about her tits for a whole hour. Jesus, my nuts were like two tins of Dulux Brilliant White all afternoon. So I just sign here do I, officer?'*

excused shorts *phr.* Of a *well-endowed* school lad or boy scout, who might be embarrassed by his *todger* dangling out there for all to see.

exercise the ferret *1. v.* To pull something thin and hairy from one's trousers and pop it into a muddy hole in the hope of catching something. *2. v.* To pull something thin and hairy from one's trousers and pop it into a muddy hole in the hope of not catching something.

exhaustipated *adj.* So tired that you don't give a *shit.* *'Sorry madam, your three-year-old son may well have swallowed three bottles of headache tablets, been savaged by a pitbull and pulled a pan of hot chip-fat onto himself, but I've been at work since sparrow's fart on Thursday and frankly I'm exhaustipated. Might I suggest that if you are in any way dissatisfied with the prescription for a course of mild antibiotics I have just filled in and handed to you, you might care to take your custom to another hospital.'*

expellianus! *exclam.* Cod-Latinesque conjuration uttered when someone *drops* a magical *gut.*

explosion in the quarry *n.* Following a warning shout of "Fire in the hole!", an uncontrollable eruption of female *love wee*, if you believe in that sort of thing.

extra-Caligula activity *euph.* Any saucy peccadillo of such depravity that it would make even the famously-debauched Roman Emperor blush. *'Fetch me a live goose, a twenty-foot length of washing line, a tub of coleslaw and a small chest of drawers, my dear. I'm going to indulge in a little extra-Caligula activity.'*

eyeball straightener *n.* The *hair of the dog*. An alcoholic tincture that restores the health the morning after a *bad pint*. A *heart starter.* *'On behalf of the crew and myself, I'd like to welcome you aboard this Icarus Airlines flight into the side of Mount Erebus. Captain Plywood has completed his pre-flight checks and had his morning eyeball straightener, so please fasten your seatbelts and secure all baggage underneath your seat or in the overhead compartments and make sure your seats and table trays are stowed in the upright position for take-off.'*

fabric softener *n.* A *low resolution fox* who takes a chap's *giggle stick* on an erotic rollercoaster ride from a state of *diamond cutting* tumescence to marshmallow softness as she comes within range, thus relieving pressure on his trouser frontage.

face fart *n.* A burp or belch. Particularly one that smells of *shit*.

facebonk *v.* To *sleep with*, or indeed *fuck*, someone you met via a social networking site. To *poke*.

facemuck *n. Man mess* produced when idly browsing photos of female friends on social networking sites.

facerucking *n.* Engaging in confrontational behaviour on a social networking site, usually at the conclusion of a smashing night *on the pop*.

facial awareness *n.* Male medical condition closely linked to penile *dementia*; a lowered ability to discern the physiognomical features of a busty woman to whom a fellow has been introduced. *'I'm sorry, Jodie. Have we met before? I'm afraid I don't have very good facial awareness.'*

fadgida *n.* The flabby stomach of a *chubster* that effectively conceals her *fadge*.

faecal expression *n.* The contorted and gurning physiognomical expression of one who is struggling to lay a particularly tricky section of *clay pipe*.

faecal treacle *n.* Viscous *squits, runs,* diarrhoea. *Molarses.*

faeces pieces *n.* Nutty nuggets in a chewy coating.

FAFTAS/faftas *n.* A lady who a sexist pig would happily *empty his cods* up but would be unlikely to pick as his "Phone a Friend" on *Who Wants to be a Millionaire?*. Fit As Fuck, Thick As Shit.

fag burn in a fur coat, he would shag a *phr.* Said of a resourceful chap who displays a willingness to avail himself of whatever recreational facilities might present themselves. *'I wouldn't share a taxi with Toulouse Lautrec, if I was you, Madame Foret. That mucky little fucker would shag a fag burn in a fur coat.'*

FAGUAC *exclam. abbrev.* Of someone attempting to *dine at the Y* but having difficulty locating the *bearded clam* due to an excess of adipose tissue in the vicinity; "Come on, love. Fart and give us a clue."

faint rustle of taffeta *euph.* A vague *whiff of lavender* about a chap whom one suspects may be harbouring a *long-standing interest in fashion*. *'Hmm. He may have won all them medals, but there's still the faint rustle of taffeta about him if you ask me.'*

fairground rifle, she's had more cocks than a *sim.* Said of a lady with a healthy appetite for the old *firing piece*. Also *she's been cocked more times than Davy Crockett's rifle.*

Falklands Islands princess *n.* A lone woman placed in a *cock heavy* environment, such as an oil-rig, a men's prison or an Antarctic research station, thus finding herself suddenly the cynosure of all eyes despite looking like the Elephant Man's less attractive sister. A *Bodleian beauty queen.*

false start *n.* Following a night of heavy refreshment, the happy beginnings of the next day where the subject mistakenly feels that they have escaped miraculously unscathed, only to start getting shaky, sweaty and nauseous as the morning wears on.

fanipulation *n.* The ancient female practice of using the promise of *fanny* to influence the behaviour of men. *'She fanipulated me into putting them shelves up, then she said she had a headache.'*

fannaemia *n. medic.* Debilitating affliction suffered by single men whose diet incorporates insufficient quantities of *mackerel.*

fannished *adj.* Suffering an almost vampiric hunger for a serving of *quim*.

fanny alley *n.* A scenic diversion that takes a gentleman from his office desk to the lavatory cubicles via the secretarial pool.

fanny bag *1. n. US.* What would be called a "bum-bag" on this side of the Atlantic, on account of they call their *arses* "fannies" in America. And a bum is a tramp, apparently. *2. n.* A relatively unattractive woman that a callous man retains as a low-maintenance *bang* during periods of sexual drought. Men are beasts. *'No, your worship. To be fair, she's more of a fanny bag than a girlfriend.'*

fanny banter *n.* Female conversation, such as that enjoyed on programmes like *Lorraine* and *Loose Women*. Also known as *binter*.

fanny clamp *n.* The vice-like grippage of a dirty lady's inner *bacon sarnie* as she has an *organism*.

fanny hole patrol *n.* A chap's eagle-eyed drive home from work, keeping a lookout for any half-decent bits of *tussage* who might be passing. Probably not a phrase, one might suppose, that finds much favour with Suzanne Moore.

fanny out *adj.* Self-explanatory description of a male exotic entertainment venue. *'I like going to Blue Velvet, me. It's not just a titty bar, you see, archbishop. It's fanny out.'*

fannytosis *n. medic.* Bad breath as a result of *cumulonimbus.*

fanny whisperer *n.* A ladies' man. *'Today's birthdays: Aleksay Nikolayevich Tolstoy, Russian author, 129; George Foreman, banjolele-playing boxer and heavyweight grill manufacturer, 63; Rod Stewart, gravel-voiced fanny whisperer, 67.'*

fan of soft furnishings *euph.* A *bad thrower.*

Fanuary *n.* A month during which a woman neglects her neatly-*fanicured ladygarden* and allows it to grow into a magnificent, unkempt *bush.*

farkle *n.* A lady's *queef* from the *front bottom.* A bit like a *fart,* but with extra sparkle. A *muff puff.*

farmer's footprint *n.* A huge *skidmark.* *'That's the last time I let Meat Loaf in to use the Sistine Chapel shitter. The fat bastard's left a right farmer's footprint in the U-bend, your holiness.'*

farmer's omelette *n.* A particularly infirm, runny, yellow motion. *'Apologies, Lady Grantham. I must just pop upstairs for a farmer's omelette.'*

fart & depart *n.* At a social gathering, the act of *dropping a gut* before swiftly moving away to allow someone else to take the credit for your gaseous *largesse.*

fartburn *n. medic.* A stinging blast of curry gas that could set the *fairy hammock* ahad.

farte blanche *n. Fr.* The comfortable stage in a relationship when a chap is able to *step on a duck* in bed without fearing any retribution, or any reaction whatsoever for that matter, from his *significant other.*

fartefact *1. n.* The product of an unexpected *follow-through.* An *objet d'arse. 2. n.* An old *dropped gut* discovered still lingering upon re-entry to a previously vacated room. *'With trembling hands, I inserted the candle and peered in. At first I could see nothing, the ancient fartefacts escaping from the chamber causing the candle to flicker. Presently, details of the room emerged slowly from the mist, strange animals, statues and gold. Everywhere the glint of gold.'* (from *An Account of the Discovery of the Tomb of Jimmy Savile* by Howard Carter).

fartification *n.* The lid of a *Dutch oven,* held down firmly to prevent the egress of noxious *flatus.*

fast and furious *n.* A quick *lamb shank* - the opposite of a *Clapton.*

fatties' loft insulation *n.* Home exercise equipment; gym mats, pink dumbbells, exercise balls *etc.,* which are pressed into service lining the attics of *gustatory athletes* about a week or so after the Argos January Sale.

fattoo *n.* A permanent ink design applied to a *salad dodger.* *'Ooh, Is that your new fattoo, Michelle. What's it of?' 'It's a life-size copy of Raphael's School of Athens.' 'Nice. And what are you going to have on the other buttock?'*

faux pair *n. Fr.* Artificially augmented *jubblies. Beverly hills.* *'I like your faux pair, missus. They're a right tidy sight.'*

faux pie *n.* Not a real pie. One of those bloody microwaved abominations you get in chain pubs, consisting of a misleadingly small amount of gristle casserole the temperature of molten glass hidden under a four-inch thick duvet of puff pastry.

feeding time at the trout farm *euph.* The crowded view that greets one after *dropping off* a three- or four-day collection of *mudbabies at the pool* after *breaking the siege* following an enforced period of *brown drought.*

feejit *n.* An acceptable way of calling someone a "fucking idiot" when in polite company.

fe fi fo fum *acronym. exclam.* A frustrated ululation. Fuck Everything, Fuck It, Fuck Off, Fuck Ur Mum.

Fellaini's flannel *euph.* A decidedly unkempt *ladygarden,* named in honour of Everton's wild-barnetted Belgian midfielder.

fellatio ratio *n.* Out of the total number of people in the room, the proportion whom one might allow to *nosh off* one's *slag hammer.* *'Alan, you can't fire another woman this week. The producer says we've got to keep the fellatio ratio up.'*

fellationship *n.* A loosely-maintained romantic dalliance in which the lady occasionally *gobbles* the bloke *off* in a pub *bog* or behind a skip.

fellow-tio *n.* A chap *sucking the poison out* of

another chap's *giggle stick.*

femme brûlée *n.* A creamy *minge* where you need a spoon to crack your way through the crispy topping.

femme fartale *n. Fr.* A scarlet woman who is prone to expel wind more often than is strictly decorous.

femme fatale *n.* A *clopper* that could prove deleterious to one's health.

Fenton *n. prop.* Named after the famous youtube pooch, a predatory *biddy fiddler.* That is to say, one who chases "old dears" around the park.

fequel *n.* A *crap* sequel or prequel, *eg. The Fly II.*

fer-fetch a cloth, Granville *exclam.* A humorous apophthegm to be uttered in the immediate aftermath of a stentorian *dropped hat.* From the catchphrase of stuttering Yorkshire shopkeeper Arkwright in the 1980s sitcom *Open All Hours.* Also *ease springs; don't tear it, I'll take the whole piece; how much?; keep shouting sir, we'll find you; more tea vicar?; I'm Peppa Pig.*

festive perineum *n.* The famously nondescript bit between Christmas and New Year. *'What are you doing over the festive perineum?'*

fetch hot water and towels! *exclam.* A jocose exclamation to be uttered in the style of James Robertson Justice after someone's *wind has broken,* heralding the imminent delivery of a *bouncing mud child.*

fetch *n. & v.* Spunk. And indeed to *spunk up.* Also *fetch up.* *'Have you seen my other trousers anywhere, Bates? There's fetch down the front of these.'*

FFFA *abbrev.* A reference to the sort of worthless *nonebrities* who rock up on the television these days. Famous For Fuck All.

fiarrhoea *n. medic.* Volcanal eruptions following a night on the vindaloo. *'Hollywood movie stars, world leaders and the crowned* *heads of Europe have all got fiarrhoea after a slap-up feed at the Rupali Restaurant, Bigg Market, Newcastle upon Tyne.'*

fiddle yard *1. n.* A concealed part of a model railway enthusiast's layout where he stores his toy trains and manipulates them away from the gaze of the general public. *2. n.* Another out-of-sight place where a model railway enthusiast manipulates things when he thinks nobody can see him.

fiddler's mittens *n.* Lady's hands. *'You can tell Madonna's older than she looks, though. You've only got to look at her fiddler's mittens.'*

fidge *n. Santorum, sexcrement, shum, toffee yoghurt, poof paste.*

fifty shades of brown *euph.* A phrase used to describe a particularly varied morning of explosive diarrhoea following a hefty drinking session.

fifty shades of gravy *n.* Descriptive of the *fairy hammock* on an unkempt lass's *dunghampers.*

fifty wrist *n.* A frantic, blurred *knob-strangling* session opportunistically enjoyed during the narrow *wank window* which opens when the missus pops out to the corner shop for a paper.

fighting patrol, teeth like a *sim. milit.* Amusingly said of one with substandard dentition, *viz.* "All blacked out with five metre spacing".

file for wankruptcy *v.* To use the last vestiges of your strength to reluctantly put away your stash of *art pamphlets* after emptying *Barclay's vaults.*

Filey fanny *n.* The knees-apart, up-bloomers seated posture adopted by elderly northern ladies at the seaside. Believed to be a means of keeping the flies off their ice creams.

FILF/filf *acronym.* Feminist I'd Like to Fuck. You'd think they'd be flattered.

Filipino palm vinegar *1. n.* A popular recipe

ingredient in western Pacific cuisine. *2. n.* A popular lubricating unguent liberally dispensed wherever *happy endings* are sold.

filofucks *n.* Notches on a young buck's bedpost, by which means he records and tabulates his miscellaneous romantic escapades.

final demand *n.* A "last warning"-style twitch from the *Camillas* which signals that one must drop everything in order to *park the fudge* immediately. A *final demand* usually arrives from the *gasworks* when one has been putting off a *poo* in anticipation of a forthcoming commercial break.

findus, a *n.* Encountering a different type of *meat* than first expected. *'Tits and a findus at every show!'* (promo flyer for the *Ladyboys of Bangkok* tour).

finger discipline *n.* The skilful manual dexterity exhibited by a *heavily-refreshed Glasgow piano* virtuoso. *'You've got to hold the two lemons and nudge that cherry, your holiness. Oi, oi, oi, watch your fucking finger discipline.'*

fingerhut *n.* A small, rude dwelling for the digits, typically found amongst the undergrowth whilst exploring a *ladygarden.* A *moss cottage.*

finishing touches *1. n.* In a *rub-a-tug shop,* the closing manoeuvres of the latter service as opposed to the former, typically costing the client an extra five quid or so. *2. n.* The final few flicks of the *naughty paintbrush* when *painting the ceiling.*

Finnan haddie *1. n.* Gastronomically speaking, a high class fish supper, *viz.* Haddock which has been smoked over peat. *2. euph. Gashtronomically* speaking, a high class *fish supper.* From the lyrics to the Cole Porter song *My Heart Belongs to Daddy,* as saucily performed by Julie London, Marilyn Monroe and Eartha Kitt, and somewhat less suggestively by Herb Alpert, *viz.* "If I invite / A boy some night / To dine on my fine Finnan haddie / I just adore his asking for more / But my heart belongs to daddy."

FIOFI/fiofi *acronym*. A tough-looking, unattractive woman. From (would you rather) Fuck It Or Fight It.

Fiona Bruce *rhym. slang. Blip, milp*. From BBC newsreader Fiona Bruce = fanny juice.

fire alarm *n*. When all hell breaks loose from all your emergency exits as you are settling down for a nice quiet *Betty Boo*. A burning backdraft of *arsepiss, Wallace* and collapsing girders.

firelighter *n*. An exceptionally dry *turd* that has a low flash point.

firewood *n*. The state of penisular arousal whereby nothing and nobody is going to stop it *going off*, not even your gran knocking on the shed door with a cup of tea. *Vinegar string*.

first half shat-trick *n*. A fine achievement by any working man; the *laying* of three *cables* before midday.

fisherman's blues *1. n*. 1988 Waterboys album which reached number thirteen in the UK charts. *2. n*. The deep disappointment and resentment felt by a chap who has successfully *licked out* his missus when she fails to return the favour.

fish fingers *n*. The lingering odour experienced after performing the *cat and the fiddle* on a rude lady's *landing gear*. Hopefully without any ketchup.

fish flakes *n*. The dried scraps of *haddock sauce* left in a gentleman's *rubiks* after a night of passion.

fishing nets *n*. Mesh *undercrackers* infused with the ripe *fent* of seafood.

fishmonger's dustbin *n*. A very flavoursome and aromatic *kipper* that could attract seagulls from miles around. A *blind man's muff, Norwegian's lunchbox*.

fish mouth *n. medic*. The *meatus, Jap's eye* or hog's eye. *'Without warning, the somnolent peace of the dorm was broken by an ear-splitting cry from Jennings's bunk. "Ooyah! Someone call matron!" he screeched. "What on earth...?" yawned Darbishire, clumsily groping in the darkness for his spectacles and knocking his tooth mug onto the linoleum. The light clicked on and there stood Mr Wilkins, purple-faced in his dressing gown and slippers. "What is the meaning of all this noise?" he blustered. "Sorry Sir," said Jennings. "But I've somehow got a biro refill stuck in me fish mouth."'* (from *Jennings Sticks a Ballpoint Pen down his Cock-end* by Anthony Buckeridge).

fish slice *n*. The seam on a pair of tight-fitting jeans which occasions an uncomfortable intrusion down the centre of a lady's *captain's pie*.

fish spa *1. n*. A currently-fashionable treatment whereby women dip their weeping corns into a stagnant fishbowl full of other people's verruca germs. *2. n*. A female version of the *gentleman's wash*, carried out in a pub toilet sink, a *gash splash*.

Fish Street *1. n*. The female vagina. *2. n*. A narrow, damp and cobbled thoroughfare in central Shrewsbury, accessed via Grope Lane and Bear Steps. *'I was in Grope Lane, but I never made it to Fish Street'*.

fistival *n*. A carnivalesque jamboree of *fisting*, for want of a better explanation.

fistorian *n*. A fellow who maintains a keen and active interest in vintage pornography.

fistress *n. Madam Palm*, with whom a man might be tempted to cheat on his missus.

five a day, getting one's *phr*. Euphemistically said of an idle chap sitting at home all day *relaxing in a gentleman's manner. 'Doctor: 'You look quite drained, Mr Jones. Have you been getting your five a day?' Patient: 'I certainly have doctor. Me plums are as flat as a spare tyre.''* (Bamforth's Seaside Chuckles postcard by Donald McGill, 1928).

five card stud with the gangster of love, play
v. To *shuffle one's deck*. *'Can I borrow your Grattan Catalogue, dear? I'm just off down the shed to play five card stud with the gangster of love.'*

five man army, the *1. n.* Title of a 1969 spaghetti western set during the Mexican Revolution, directed by Don Taylor and starring that bloke out of *Mission Impossible*. Not the *short arse* off *Top Gun* who believes in space aliens, him off the telly version who was the pilot in *Airplane*. *2. n.* Title of the fifth track on Massive Attack's 1991 album *Blue Lines*. *3. n.* Those noble soldiers who engage in *hand to gland combat* with one's *purple-helmeted little soldier*. The fingers. *Madam Palm's five sisters.*

five six *exclam.* A gent's means of announcing to his companions that he has espied a buxom young lady in the vicinity. From the erstwhile nursery rhyme "Five six, stick out tits".

five-wheeled snurglar *n.* An office-based *snufty* who eschews bicycle saddles, preferring instead to *quumf* the seat fabric of swivel chairs that have been recently occupied by attractive female co-workers.

flaboteur *n.* An overweight woman, tempting her friends and colleagues with cake in order to spoil their figures.

flaccinating *adj.* Descriptive of a distracting quality or feature in a sexual partner that - once noticed - cannot but lead to a marked loss of turgidity in the *membrum virile*. *'Your voice, Janet. It's ... it's flaccinating.'*

flag hags *n.* Deluded, grinning, toothless old *biddies* who wave Union Jacks at the Queen as she gets whisked past in the back of an hermetically-sealed Rolls-Royce.

flail *n.* The *twitter*. Also *tinter, taint, biffin's bridge, Humber bridge, carse, scran, Barry Gibb, Bosphorus, Botley Interchange, brink, butfer, cleach, clutch, snarse, cosif, crunk, fa-*

noose, or *farse*. "The bit between a lady's flower and her tail".

flally *n.* A flaccid *willy;* a problem in the bedroom but not in the supermarket. From flaccid + willy.

FLAMALAP/flamalap *acronym.* A lady that looks way hotter from behind than she does from the front. Face Like A Man, Arse Like A Peach. Also *golden deceiver, back beauty, backstabber, witch's trick, nolita, kronenberg, boyner* or *ASWAD*.

flap acid *n.* The acrid fluid leaking from a well-used *sump* that is capable of taking the enamel off one's teeth.

flaparazzi *n. pl.* The gutter-dwelling photovultures who wait outside nightclubs in the hope of snapping *upskirt* pictures of knickerless celebrities to sell to the *Daily Telegraph*.

flapmates *n.* A *lesbidicious* couple.

flap oil *n.* Aftershave. The fragranced liquid applied to a male's neck prior to a *cunt hunt* or during a *Scouse dry-clean*. Slagbait, *snogging water, fuck oil.*

flapper *1. n.* A young *piece* of the 1920s, who affected bobbed hair and a short skirt, and who would listen to jazz on a gramophone and do that dance where her legs went out at the sides. *2. n.* A lady with heavy, swagged *Keith Burtons*.

flapsidermy *n.* The art of preparing, mounting and *stuffing* a *bird*.

flap snapper *n.* A photographer who specialises in the depiction of feminine beauty. A *flaparazzo*. *'Today's birthdays: Lucy Davis, TV actress spawn of Jasper Carrott, 37; Jim Bakker, scandal-ridden US televangelist, 70; David Bailey, top drawer flap snapper, 72.'*

flaptop *n.* A portable computer equipped with wireless *binternet* access for the on-the-move bachelor. A *dirty mac*.

flart *v.* To charm a prospective romantic partner with a coquettish burst of flatulence.

flattened some grass in her time, I bet she's *phr.* Said mischievously of a lady who has a "certain look" about her that might lead a casual observer to (possibly erroneously) suppose she might have entertained a *knob* or two over the years, although that may not be the case and we are certainly not suggesting it is. Far from it, *eg. Newsnight's* Emily Maitlis, that Linda out of off of *Casualty*, the Rt. Hon. Harriet Harman QC MP *etc.*

flattery *n.* A slight, unexpected splatter consequent upon a *trouser cough,* which "gets you nowhere", especially during a job interview or whilst modelling *haute couture* silk underpants at a Paris fashion show.

flatue *n.* A comical shape - for example the one-legged, poised stance of the Angel of Christian Charity at Picadilly Circus or Rodin's Thinker - "thrown" by one who is about to noisily *drop a gut.*

flatusfaction *n.* The feeling of blissful, fulfilling contentment experienced whilst dropping a *calling card* as one leaves a crowded lift.

flaunt *v.* Of a young woman, to inadvertently allow herself to be photographed by a *Daily Mail* smudger armed with an enormous telephoto lens. See also *show off, pose. 'After leaving the Ritz Hotel last night, the Princess of Wales flaunted her curves for Parisian photographers whilst being cut out of the wreckage of her crashed limousine.'*

flavour saver *n.* The jazzy tuft of hair betwixt a chap's bottom lip and his chin. The *moip mop, unpleasantness, blip bib* or *batter catcher.*

flick chick *n.* An habitual *invisible banjo player.*

flip chart *n.* Record of one's previous convictions for assault and breach of the peace.

Flipper's burp *n.* A *ladygarden* with a pungent maritime aroma.

flits *n.* Flat *tits.* From flat + tits.

flock of bats or a block of flats *phr.* Said prior to going to the toilet when unsure as to the consistency of *foulage* that may be produced. *'Jesus, my guts are rotten this morning. I don't know whether I'm going to have a flock of bats or a block of flats. Here's Rabbi Lionel Blue with Thought for the Day.'*

Flo job *n.* A toothless *nosh* off a senior citizen.

floodgates *n.* The well-greased *sluices* on a woman who is *dripping like a fucked fridge.*

flumpert *n.* The enlarged *mons pubis* of a mature, salad-averse female, which is reminiscent of the proboscis of a bull elephant seal (*Mirounga angustirostris*).

flushing a dirty buffer *1. n.* In computing, the synchronisation process used when the data on disk and the data in memory are not identical. *2. n.* Some sort of filthy Teutonic carry-on.

flush mob *n.* That group of inconsiderate people who always seem to be occupying the toilet cubicles when you are desperate to *drop off the shopping.*

flying dirty *1.adj.* Description of an aircraft which has its gear and flaps lowered. *2. adj.* Description of a lass who has her *gear* and *flaps* lowered.

Flying Horse, the *euph.* Anal sex. From the name of the alternative hostelry utilised by the residents of *Coronation Street* when their preferred venue of the Rover's Return is rendered unavailable/unusable for whatever reason. *'Fancy a quickie, Dierdre?' 'Sorry Ken, I'm up on blocks. It'll have to be the Flying Horse tonight, I'm afraid.'*

fog on the Tyne *1. n.* Title of a song released firstly as a single in 1974 by erstwhile Geordie boy band Lindisfarne, and later in 1990 with thirsty, poultry-toting, plastic-titted siege negotiator Paul Gascoigne on lead vocals. *2. n.* The dense, noxious fumes produced by habitual imbibers of Newcastle's eponymous Yorkshire-brewed brown ale.

foofbrush *n.* A toothbrush reserved exclusively for use after performing *cumulonimbus*

foo fighter *n.* A female who regularly has to defend herself from the unwanted attentions of amorous *lady golfers.*

food baby *n.* A massive *Eartha* that wakes you up all through the night and leaves you with bags under your eyes.

foogle *n.* A *twat* who thinks they are a world authority on a subject after googling it and scanning halfway through the top paragraph on the first page that comes up. Also *wikiot.*

fool's gold *n.* The false sense of sexual optimism felt by a gentleman upon entering an event where initial appearances suggest a wall-to-wall *birdfest,* but where further inspection reveals the majority of attendees to be *on the bus to Hebden Bridge, eg.* A Tracy Chapman gig or comfortable shoe convention.

footballer's business card *euph.* A tasteful portrait of a premiership star's *cock* and *balls* sent via a camera-phone or webcam. Also known as a *ChatRoulette friendly hello.*

footloose and fanny free *euph.* 'Perennial bachelor boy Cliff simply hasn't found the right girl yet. Now a disarmingly youthful-looking ninety-two, and after more than seventy years in the business, he's as footloose and fanny free as ever.'

footstool *n.* An imperial *feeshee* of impressive length.

forced-air *1. n.* A system of heating, common in N. America, which uses air as its heat transfer medium and a furnace (usually gas-fired) to circulate warm air through a building. *2. n.* The sudden, unexpected, release of *flatus* from the *bomb bay,* which occurs as a result of an over-exertion, *eg.* Moving a piano up a fire escape, stretching in a quiet yoga class or standing up after

being knighted. Usually accompanied by a short, sharp ripping noise and a red face.

forespray *n.* A *frigmarole*-avoiding alternative to foreplay consisting of a quick squirt of *WD over 40.*

forest dump *n.* An *ad hoc* and indeed *al fresco* expulsion of *feeshus* during which you basically always know what you're going to get.

forest gunt *n.* An unkempt *pie hider.*

formula one *n. medic.* Patent medicine that is proven to cure Sunday afternoon insomnia.

ForP?/forp? *phr. abbrev. interrog.* Useful coded word which may be exchanged between gentlemen on a night out, when questioning the circumstances of a lass with a *nice personality, viz.* Fat or Pregnant?

Fosbury flop *n.* An energetic release of the *manhood* from the flies prior to taking a *whizz.*

Fosbury's disease *n. medic.* Condition chiefly characterised by flaccidity in the male reproductive organ. Named in honour of the erstwhile American athlete who won a gold medal in the 1968 Mexico Olympic Games high-jump competition, using the revolutionary "back first" technique that is named after him, Dick Flop. The symptoms of *Fosbury's disease* are usually ameliorated by the administration of a dose of *mycoxafloppin, mydixadrupin* or *bongo Bill's banjo pills,* taken three times a day after meals.

four ball Paul *n.* A *bullshitter* who, if you told him you had three testicles, would have to go one better. Also *racunteur, twat o'nine tales, Bertie big bollocks, two shits.*

FPM/fpm *abbrev.* A measure of the noxiousness of the atmosphere in a crowded lift, taxi cab or Space Shuttle. Farts Per Million.

FQI *abbrev.* A *Hart to Hart* which rises in pitch towards the end, as if posing a query. Fart Question Intonation.

fracking *1. n.* A fashionable means of natural gas extraction. *2. n. Blowing off* whilst on the job.

frass *n.* Caterpillar *shite*, as trod in by centipedes.

fraud fiesta *n.* Mode of vehicular transport favoured by the uninsured young drivers who populate the Dicky Bird (Chesham Fold) estate in Bury. A fraud fiesta is easily identifiable by its out-of-date tax disc, bald tyres and an exhaust pipe the size of a wizard's sleeve.

fraudband *n. Thinternet. 'Eeh, now what was the name of that company that used to do them adverts with Maureen Lipman? You know, the ones where she was on the phone to her grandson talking about "ologies". I simply can't bring the name of the company in question to mind. Why don't you look it up on your fancy new laptop?' 'I would do, Granny, but the fraudband's gone down again. And even when it's on, it only runs at a tiny fraction of the 20Mb download speeds promised in the publicity material.'*

Fred Dibnah *euph.* A woman with a *face like a bag of chisels* who, during intercourse, is capable of "bringing the largest erection crashing down".

Freddie Cougar *n.* A scary, sharp-fingered older woman who interferes with blokes while they sleep.

free beauty treatment *n.* A *Vitamin S*-enriched *facial,* involving the application of copious amounts of *heir gel* and *oil of goolay. 'Congratulations love. You've just won a free beauty treatment.'*

free hit *1. n.* In one-day cricket, an opportunity for a batsman to take a shot without the risk of dismissal. *2. n.* The chance for a man to *bank at Barclay's* without the fear of getting told off by his significant other, for example if she's away on business, staying at her mother's or unconscious.

free range eggs *n.* Muscular *knackers* that can propel a blast of *man gravy* over an impressive distance. *Seven league bollocks.*

freelancer *n.* A short, hairy-palmed man with thick glasses who *works from home.*

Freetown fart *n.* A catastrophic *follow-through.* Named after the capital city of Sierra Leone, a metropolis renowned for its magnificent National Railway Museum, the grandeur of its Cathedral of St George and the unrivalled opportunities it affords to visitors of catching amoebic dysentery. "It's a brave man who drops a gut in West Africa." - Dr Livingstone.

French fringe *n. rhym. slang.* The *foofoo* or *hoo-ha.* From French fringe = minge.

French have been involved, the *phr.* A term from the motor trade when something mechanical is either totally *fucked* or is devoid of any logical method of repair. *'I'm terribly sorry but I had to fail it on the hydropneumatic suspension. The French have been involved, I'm afraid.'*

French hedge *n.* A badly-executed bit of vaginal topiary.

Frenchman's shoe *n.* An item of footwear liberally covered in dog *feeshus. 'Please come in Mr President.' 'I'm afraid I can't, your majesty, as I'm wearing a Frenchman's shoe. Have you got anything I can scrape the shit off with?'*

fresh prince of bell end *n.* A contumelious epithet.

friends with benefits *1. n.* Acquaintances who maintain a sexual realtionship without becoming emotionally involved. *2. euph.* A polite term for the urban underclasses. *'I see there's some more of our friends with benefits on the Jeremy Kyle show, your majesty.'*

frig brig *n.* The bedroom. *'Is your David playing, Mrs Baddiel?' 'I'll just shout him down, Frank. He's up in his frig brig.'*

frigger's freeze *n. medic.* The feminine version of *wanker's cramp.*

friggit Jones *n.* A spinster of the parish who seems to buy an awful lot of batteries.

frogging *n.* Gallic *dogging*. Possibly a mildly racist entry, but it's only the French.

from dashboard to airbag *phr.* The miraculous surgical transformation of a *Miss Lincolnshire* into a *double D tit queen* that may leave one disorientated, seeing stars and suffering from ringing in the ears.

front weights *euph. Lancs.* Breasts. A Lancashire farmers' term, more usually spoken when referring to the counterbalance weights fitted to the front of a tractor. *'By heck, that young piece of tuppence has a champion set of front weights on her.'*

frontal losnotomy *n.* One of them bogies which brings out a substantial part of your brain with it.

frosty biscuit *n.* A variation on the *soggy biscuit* game, as played by mountaineers and Arctic/Antarctic explorers. *'I'm just going outside, I may be some time.' 'Right you are Oates. But don't stay out there too long, we're having another round of frosty biscuit in a minute, just as soon as Bowers can feel his fingers again.'*

frozen mop *n.* A *boner* covered with a frosty layer of dried *mandruff*. *'I fell asleep halfway through the second half, had a dream about a spit roast with Dwight and Jordan and then woke up with a frozen mop. Now, Alan, what did you think of Arsenal's second goal?'*

fruits du nez *Fr.* How a waiter in a posh restaurant would refer to his *greenies*. *'Plat principale: Foie gras de cygne avec saumon fumé, haricots verts, huitres et fruits du nez du Maître d'hôtel; 300 euros.'*

FT *1. abbrev.* Customary contraction for the *Financial Times* or, more entertainingly, the *Fortean Times* newspaper. *2. abbrev. pej.* Family-friendly online shorthand for Fuck Them/Fuck That which can be used with impunity in newspaper comments sections.

fuck a frog if I could stop it hopping, I would *exclam.* An expression of male sexual frustration. A less coarse version of *I would dig up a badger and bum it* for use in refined social situations. *'"Dash it all, Jeeves," I expostulated to the sage retainer. "I've not had any company of the female persuasion for weeks and it's really starting to rag my pip. I tell you, I'd fuck a frog if I could stop it hopping."'* (from *Bend Over and Brace Yourself, Jeeves!* by PG Wodehouse).

fuck à l'orange *n.* A saucy act of penetrative affection performed up one of them *birds* covered in all fake tan, like what you get on *The Only Way is Essex* or *Geordie Shore*.

fuck barrel *n.* An affectionate term for one's *bag for life*.

fucked as a Blackpool donkey *sim.* Expression to confirm that one's physical condition is rather worse than desired, particularly after an evening of heavy *refreshment*. *'A message for the best football supporters in the world. We need a twelfth man here. Where are you? Where are you? Let's be 'avin' you! Come on! Sorry for shouting, only I've got to be honest with you. I'm as fucked as a Blackpool donkey here.'*

fucked fanny, dripping like a *sim.* Descriptive of the condition of a faulty refrigerator.

fucked with his own cock *euph.* Having brought misfortune upon oneself with one's own foolish actions. *'In his summing-up, the coroner said that, in jumping from the flyover whilst drunk and wearing a home made rocket suit, the deceased had been reckless as to his own and others' safety, and recorded a verdict of fucked with his own cock.'*

fuck her while she's still warm *exclam.* Lighthearted cinema/theatre audience heckle to be uttered immediately following the on screen/stage demise of a female character in the hope - at a live performance - of making the actress laugh. *'Juliet, my wife! Death,* *that hath suck'd the honey of thy breath hath had no power yet upon thy beauty.' 'Fuck her while she's still warm, Larry!'*

fuck hutch *n.* A small flat kept as a discreet venue for illicit liaisons.

fuckit list *n.* Personal inventory of all the things you can't be *arsed* to do before you die. *'You going to the away match at the weekend, then?' 'Nah. That one's going on the fuckit list.'*

fucklings *n.* Little treasures, the fruit of one's loins.

fucknuts *exclam.* Multi-purpose oath. *'Oh fucknuts, the humanity!'*

fuck off moment *n.* During a person's morning commute, the point at which they decide enough is enough, mutter a foulmouthed imprecation and switch off the radio. It is estimated that up to 80% of listeners to BBC Radio 4's *Today* programme experience a simultaneous *fuck off moment* at approximately 7.45am each day.

fuck oil *n.* Aftershave. Also known as *snogging water, flap oil* or *slagbait. 'Happy Christmas, granddad. I've got you a bottle of fuck oil off the indoor market.'*

fuckonathon *n.* When an easy task becomes hard work. *'What took you so long? I thought you were just nipping out to change the headlight bulb on your Rover 75.' 'Don't ask. It was a right Fuckonathon.'*

fuck oven *n.* A polite euphemism for a lady's *bower of delight. 'Did you see that strippogram at Terry's leaving do? She was absolute class. She managed to fit a whole coke bottle in her fuck oven.'*

fucksaw *n.* A *dildo* attached to a mainspowered reciprocating saw. Frankly, it's an accident waiting to happen, is that. They should do a Public Information Film.

fucktastic *adj.* Evidently better than fantastic, but neither fucking fantastic nor fanfucking-tastic. From fuck + tastic.

fuckwhiskers *n.* Pubes.

fudge drums *n.* Farts. *'That pasty at the General Synod lunchtime buffet has had me on the fudge drums all afternoon.'*

fudgina *n.* The *arsehole. 'Sorry pet. Genuine mistake. I thought you said fudgina.'*

fu-fu manchu *n.* A sinister, long, straggly *underbeard.*

fulfil your destiny *v.* To ejaculate. After *wanking* so hard it feels like your hand has fallen off.

full A13, the *euph.* An adventurous session of *hanky-panky* that is analogous to a journey from London to the coast along the said thoroughfare, *ie.* A gentleman performs a *Dagenham handshake*, his ladyfriend returns the favour via a *Basildon bagpipe*, and the whole sordid shenanigans culminates in a visit to her "South end".

fun bucket *n.* An unacceptably sexist and offensive way of referring to the *village bike.*

funcle *n.* The same-sex civil partner of a *comfortably-shod* aunt. From female + uncle.

fun dungeon *n.* A lady's *below-stairs* accommodation.

fun sock *n.* A *jubber ray. 'Anything for the weekend, Mr Straw?' 'Aye. I'll have a packet of fun socks, please. Extra small size.'*

fun sponge *n.* The *banana cupboard. 'Up on the table please, Mrs Leadbetter. Let's have a butchers at your fun sponge.'*

fürburgring *n.* An interminable and hazardous circuit around a particularly byzantine *clopper.* The missus's *southern loop.*

furlong *n.* Imperial unit of pubic hair length.

furred game *n.* That which a *cuntry gent* hunts on a Friday night. *Hair pie,* the game meat in a *country supper.*

furry muff *exclam.* A ribald alternative to saying "fair enough" when speaking to an elderly relative, someone in a call centre on the other side of the world or giving evidence in court.

fussell your Russells *euph.* Of an over-excitable young man, to be *up and over like a pan of milk* into his *Russell Grants*. *'Are you trying to seduce me, Mrs Robinson?' 'Yes, but it looks like I'm too late. You appear to have fusselled your Russells.'*

future shit *n.* A space age *dump* that requires no wiping, like everyone will do in the year 2020.

fuzz lite *n.* A Community Support officer. A *potted plant.*

fwank *v.* To desperately stimulate the *ivory tower* whilst trawling through a female friend/colleague's profile pictures on a popular social networking site, in the hope of happening upon some vaguely enticing bikini snaps.

GAK/gak *abbrev.* Grade A Knobhead. *'Jenny Bond, given your extensive specialist knowledge of royal matters and thought processes, how do you think the Prince's family will react to the publication of photographs showing him cavorting naked in a Las Vegas hotel room?' 'To be blunt, Jeremy, it won't come as much of a surprise to them. They've had him down as a bit of a gak for years.'*

game of thrones *1. n.* Title of a fantasy series on the telly that's based on some books. *2. n.* Upon realising too late that there is no *bumwad* in your public convenience trap, the undignified and crab-like shuffle around the other stalls to find some.

garage *euph.* The obliging lady that a chap visits when he needs his *big end* serviced.

gash badger *n.* A voracious *rug muncher* who is not in the slightest put off by thick pile.

gash guzzler *n.* An enthusiastic sipper of the *hairy cup.*

gashion pages *n.* The section of a *haute couture* magazine where the models are actually worth a look, as opposed to the emaciated, freaky-looking miserable skellingtons in all the other pictures.

gash leak *n.* A monthly emergency in one's domicile where the most insignificant spark could result in a huge explosion.

gashmere *n.* The soft, downy strands of *gorilla salad* which form the warp, woof and weft of an upper class *wizard's sleeve* is knitted.

gashtric band *n.* A device designed to drastically reduce a gentleman's consumption of *hairy pie.* A wedding ring.

gashtronaut *n.* An intrepid explorer who boldly goes where no man has gone before.

gashquatch *n.* A particularly hirsute *growler.*

gay and display *1. n. Puddle-jumping* carryings-on in car parks. *2. n.* A gentleman who behaves in an overly camp manner, eg. Him off Channel 4 with the glasses and the teeth who sounds like Dierdre Barlow hyperventilating sulphur hexafluoride.

gay blob *n.* An unexpected case of the *Brad Pitts* which effectively puts the kybosh on the evening's planned *mudlarks. 'Any chance of a bit of backdoor action tonight, love?' 'Sorry Dave, I can't. I'm on the gay blob.'*

gear goggles *n.* When buying six tubs of ice cream at 3am, *Bob Hope*-assisted optical aids which make the woman who works in the petrol station look attractive.

gearstick gargler *n.* A popular and talented young lady who is able to fully accommodate a *meat endoscopy* from a well-made gent without *honking up* her kebab onto his *clockweights.*

generation game *n. Having it off* with one's partner's parent, grandparent, great grandparent or worse; as performed on a daily basis by the delightful guests on daytime telly chat shows. Bring back Peter Ustinov.

genetically modified fruit *euph.* Well-hoofed *plums.* See also *emergency stop button.*

genis *n.* Where the flesh around the base of a *salad dodger's slag hammer* becomes indistinguishable from his general gut area. The male equivalent of the *gunt.* Also *gock.*

genital husbandry *n.* The timeless craft of *winding the clock. Re-setting the crown jewels, nip & twist.*

gentleman's cure-all *n.* Something that brings ease and comfort in any given circumstance. *Coccupational therapy.*

Geordie's passport *n.* A bus ticket. Also *Scouse visa.*

George Herbert *euph. Horatio.* From the poem *Love Bade me Welcome* penned by the eponymous Welsh-born poet, orator and priest (1593-1633), which contains the line "'You must sit down', Says Love, 'and taste my meat', So I did sit and eat." Don't say we never fucking learn you anything.

German pop *n.* Urine.

gesundsheit *n. Ger.* A simultaneous, albeit unintentional, sneeze and *brown trout* in the trousers. A cause for congratulations in Germany, that is.

get engaged *v.* To scratch at your *rusty bullet hole* in public, *ie.* To "pick your ring".

get out and walk *exclam.* Disparaging parting remark, made over the shoulder to a retreating *air biscuit.*

get out of shag free card *n.* An excuse used by a person to avoid taking part in an act of sexual union. *'I'm absolutely gutted. The missus has got multiple compound fractures in each femur, had both her hips dislocated, broken her coccyx in six places and shattered her pelvis after falling into the mechanism of a escalator on the London Underground. No doubt she'll be using that as this week's get out of shag free card.'*

get-you-home spare *n.* A substandard, low performance woman picked up at the end of a frankly deflating night.

get your leather *v.* To have sexual intercourse. *'How did you get on with that pissed-up bird I saw you arresting last night? Did you get your leather in the back of the van?' 'Certainly not, your honour.'*

get your numbers up *v.* Of an individual who is soon to be wed, to work round-the-clock to increase his tally of partners before the prohibition of marriage cramps his style somewhat.

gifted *1. adj.* Of a schoolchild, annoying. *2. adj.* Of a lady, in possession of an impressive set of *qualifications.*

Giggs boson *n.* A vanishingly small, dense point of intelligence which may be present between the eyes of a professional footballer, although such a particle's existence is as yet unproven.

Gillette Fusion girl *n.* A dirty *trollop* who is prepared to go at it like a bull at a gate, thus ensuring that her gentleman friend does not feel the need to *see to his own needs* at all. From the eponymous depilatory product's television advert, which states that use of said razor results in "no pulls or tugs".

Gillian McKeith's Tupperware cupboard, smells like *sim.* Something that is distinctly malodorous, based on the completely untrue rumour that the eminent fully-qualified dietician takes home all the stools she examines on her telly programmes and then secretly eats them.

gincident *n.* Any alcohol-related mishap. *'I'm terribly sorry, officer. There appears to have been a gincident involving my automobile and a bus queue.'*

gingina *n.* A carrot-topped bird's *rusty fusewire gorilla salad.*

Ginster's crust *n.* The unfunny, puckered result of catching the end of one's *windsock* in one's flies whilst doing them up too fast, for example when a policeman appears.

gironaut *n.* A long term benefits claimant.

giroscope *n.* A television set that is rarely switched on before 2pm. *'Switch the giroscope on, Chardonay. Your nan's on Jeremy Kyle.'*

Gi us a squint of yer pooper *exclam.* A poetic romantic injunction which, apparently, rarely fails to oil the wheels of love in the West Country.

give blood *v.* To *release the chocolate hostages* whilst afflicted with galloping *chuckles and smiles.*

give Thumper a reprieve *euph.* To decide to have *one off the wrist* instead of *copping off* with a putative *bunny boiler.*

give yourself a big hand *v.* To celebrate following the achievement of reaching a personal goal. This may include applauding, splashing out on a gift, treating yourself to a slap-up meal, or having a *wank*.

Gladstone *arch. rhym. slang.* Victorian rhyming slang for an act of penetrative congress. From Gladstone bag = shag. *'Her Majesty (at the conclusion of a long perinambulation upon a diminutive horse, accompanied by her faithful ghillie Mr John Brown Esquire): "We have much enjoyed our post-prandial equine constitutional, Mr Brown. Notwithstanding, we observe that your sporran is twitching in a most curious fashion." John Brown: "Och aye the noo, hoots mon and help m'boab, Ma'am. Ye dinnae fancy a quick Gladstone in yon bracken, by any chance, do ye?"* (cartoon by Sir John Tenniel, *Punch*, 1887).

glam-jams *n.* Fashionable "show" pyjamas worn when nipping to the shops or on the school run. Commonly accessorised with *pugg boots* and a high performance outdoor jacket.

glandrail *n.* The raised rim area of the *glans* that stops a gentleman punching himself in the face during *self help*. The *wankstop* or, if you want to get all technical, the *sulcus.*

gland slam *n.* A notable sexual conquest.

gland to mouth existence *n.* A living eked out using acts of *horatio* as currency.

glans end to John O'Scrotes, from *phr.* A reverse *cock lick.*

glans national *n.* An exciting Saturday afternoon spent *jumping* over *bushes,* which could easily end quite badly.

Glasgow piano *n.* A fruit machine.

Glasgow suitcase *n.* A carrier bag. Also *Barnsley briefcase.*

glaze the ham *v.* To *shoot your load* onto a *piece of crackling*'s upturned buttocks, before spreading the *manfat* evenly over both *arse cheeks* in a manner similar to a chef preparing the tasty pig-based dish.

Glitter-ati *n.* A loosely-organised cabal of celebrity *nonces* from the 1970s.

global warming *n.* The generally agreeable testicular sensation experienced by a fellow occupying a public transport seat that has been recently vacated by an attractive female.

glorification of the chosen one *n.* A quintessentially cosmopolitan *J. Arthur* with Stravinsky's *Rite of Spring* playing in the background.

glorious Goodwood *1. n.* Some sort of yearly horse-racing event they seem to get very excited about on Radio 5. *2. n.* An erection of particular noteworthiness that they probably wouldn't get very excited about on Radio 5. In fact, likely as not, if you phoned Victoria Derbyshire up to tell her about it, she'd cut you off.

gloss drop *n.* A salon-quality moisturising serum, enriched with *Vitamin S and* applied to a lady's hair and/or face.

gloyster *n.* A particularly sticky *hockle,* barked into the basin as part of one's morning ablutions, which cannot be loosened even when one resorts to the hot tap on full pelt and the wife's toothbrush.

glue flower *n.* The dried imprint left on clothing/sheets/curtains *etc.* which have been screwed up and used to wipe up *joy gloy* following a romantic interlude.

gnomosexual *n.* A short *puddlejumper.*

gnome's hat, like a *sim.* The appearance of the summit of one's *faceeshus* poking out of the water following a long stint on the lavatory. *'If you think that's impressive you should've been here on Boxing Day, Mr Carson. Her shite was sticking out the pan like a fucking gnome's hat.'*

goat's eye *n.* The "come hither" *tradesman's entrance* on a well-*bummed grumble queen.*

goatshagger's tickle n. A firm handshake. From the strong grip required when doing bestiality.

goblin-cleaver 1. n. A mythical sabre featured in the works of JRR Tolkein. 2. n. The pork sword of a bloke who specializes in the shagging of mingers.

goblin's wattle n. A distended *chicken skin handbag* not unlike the jowly excrescence sported by the character portrayed by Barry Humphries in the film *The Hobbit.*

go Catholic v. To pull out of something at the very last minute. *'Bad news, Lord Coe. G4S have gone Catholic on our arses.'*

goes for the vegetarian option *euph.* Said of a *well-manicured* chap who *knows what's in his wardrobe.*

gokkasock n. Dan. An item of male hosiery pressed into service as a receptacle for *sploff* whilst enjoying a bout of *gentlemans' relaxation. 'Do you want me to fetch you anything from the shops while I'm out, Mr Christian Anderson?' 'Yes, you can bring me some fresh gokkasocks. This lot have gone all crispy. It's like wanking meself off into a cheesegrater.'*

gold medal winner n. One who always *comes* first. A *one push Charlie, minute man, siso* or *speaking clock.* A fellow who always *spends his money before he gets to the shop.*

golden shred n. A marmalade-coloured breakfast *piss* with all chewy bits in it. A *pipecleaner.*

golden syrup n. The viscous amber mixture of *tweedledee* and *jipper* which has to be forced through the plumbing following any form of sexual activity.

Goldilocks 1. *euph.* Trying all three *holes* of a new romantic partner for a "perfect fit". *'Dad, I think this one's a keeper. She's got a breakfast bowl that Goldilocks would be proud of.'* 2. n. prop. A keen *nosher* who doesn't mind swallowing neither. From the fairytale character with a predilection for the taste of porridge.

Goldilocks dump n. A perfect motion - one that is neither too sloppy nor too tough, and which leaves no mark upon the *arse paper.*

go off like a punched icing bag v. Splendid phrase coined by thin-legged, high-haired funnyman Russell Kane on ITV2's *I'm a Celebrity's Little Brother,* during a comedic routine about ejaculation following an enforced period of celibacy.

go offroad v. To leave *Henrietta Street,* cross *Biffin's bridge* and drive oneself up a *dirt track.*

good pull through with a Christmas tree *euph. medic.* Notional treatment regime intended to cure a wide variety of ills. *'Patient: Female. Age: 46. Presented: Headaches, loose teeth, sweating, sore throat, nausea, ringing in the ears, bloodshot eyes, tremors, general lassitude. Treatment: good pull through with a Christmas tree.'*

good time to bury bad news *phr.* An opportune moment which presents itself in a crowded public place when one can offload a particularly noisy *Bakewell* without being detected, eg. At the start of a Formula 1 motor race, whilst Slayer are playing *Disciple,* during a low, high-speed pass at a Red Arrows air display or whilst Janet Street-Porter is speaking.

gooter/goother n. Ir. Dublin slang for a feisty, red-headed colleen's *front bottom.* A *mighty crack.*

gorilla's eye n. A bird's *bodily treasure* that in some way slightly evokes the famous scene in *King Kong* where the *horny* ape looks through Fay Wray's bedroom window.

gory hole n. Like a *glory hole,* but infinitely more terrible, in a scenario possibly involving some *loppers.*

gossip column *n.* A cohort of chatting women moving slowly down a corridor. *'Sorry I'm late, only I got held up by a gossip column.'*

go to work on an egg *v.* To start the day by emitting a series of rancid, brimstone-infused *botty burps.*

Govan go-kart *n.* A shopping trolley, commandeered for joyriding purposes by the high-spirited youths of the eponymous Glaswegian garden suburb.

Grandalf *n.* A *Cumbledore* for the senior citizen.

Grand National *n.* The aftermath of a booze- and meat-fuelled night out, after which it might be the kindest thing to shoot you. An *Eartha Kitt* so sticky that you need to get up into a half-squat and whip at it with a toilet brush, recreating the historic moment when AP McCoy triumphantly rode home his first winner, the appropriately-named "Don't Push It".

granny bollocks *n. Bingo wings* of the legs. *Meat jodhpurs.*

granny's laptop *n.* A cat.

granny's prawn *n.* Distinctly unappetising *seafood* dish which is well past its sell-by date.

grape flicker *n.* A *bumming* enthusiast. A *piledriver.*

grave digging *n.* Resurrecting the deceased dog-ends in an ashtray in an attempt to make a functioning "Frankenstein"-style cigarette which is an abomination against nature.

gravel lorry at the lights *sim.* A bird who is *frothing like bottled Bass. 'I wouldn't say she was gagging for it, Fern. But she was dripping like a gravel lorry at the lights.'*

Gravesend walking stick *n.* Any completely unnecessary perambulatory aid, as used by virtually everyone in the eponymous North Kent locale as a means of backing up their incapacity benefit claims.

gravy leg *n.* The result of *gambling and losing*, possibly - and indeed most probably - after enjoying a dubious, mollusc-based repast.

gravy taster *n.* An individual whose line of work leaves them with a permanently brown tongue. *A shirt fly* or *fart sucker.*

grease me up, I'm going in! *exclam.* The battle cry of a valiant gentleman who is about to go *over the top* into a dancefloor full of fatties.

Great British bake-off *euph.* The act of driving the full length of the A1 whilst absolutely *busting for a shit.*

great escape, the *n.* The act of shaking a loose *German Bight* down your trouser leg, right under the guards' noses.

Greek-style yoghurt *n.* The unpalatable mess found inside a recently *kicked-in back door.*

greggarious *adj.* Popular amongst pies.

greggasaurus *n.* A *pastivorous* monster.

greggbound *adj.* Constipated following over-consumption of savoury pastry comestibles.

greggcited *adj.* Of people who have trouble with their glands, unconscionably thrilled when approaching a branch of the popular high street bakemeat vendors.

gregglets *n.* Rotund children. Also *cub stouts, pork & beanie babies.*

Greggs bosons *n. phys.* The less than mysterious particles that give *plumpers* their mass.

Greggs canapé *n.* A lower-class thing that has ideas above its station. *'I see that comic filled with crap jokes about wanking and shit is in the Tate Gallery, then. There's a real Greggs canapé if ever there was one.'*

Greggs confetti *n.* The pastry flakes that cascade off the savoury sweetmeats offered by the famous high street *bellicatessen.* Also *Greggs dandruff.*

Greggs, go to *v.* To pay a visit to an establishment that is full of *tarts* and *cream pies.*

Greggs hot shelf jackpot *n.* Any trifecta of heated delicacies purchased from the eponymous fooderie by a *bigger-boned* person, *eg.* A sausage roll, a Cornish pasty and a steak bake.

greggspectant *n.* Blooming as a result of pastry consumption rather than pregnancy. *Greggnant, greggspecting.*

greggstra large *adj.* Of a T-shirt or sports top, a size measurement suitable for a person whose glands are full of pastry. *'We've got this shirt in XL, XXL, XXXL or there's this one in XXXXXL, Mr Moyles.' 'Hmm. It's still a bit tight under me bingo wings. Have you got any in greggstra large?'*

Greggs tie *n.* The vertical pastie-flake mess that adorns the front of the shirt, jumper or vest following the swift and careless consumption of a popular high street bakery-sourced comestible.

grenade *n.* A woman with a *lovely personality* in a nightclub, upon whom a selfless fellow throws himself to save his comrades.

grey box *1. n. Eucalyptus microcarpa.* Type of tree with distinctively-coloured bark which is endemic to the Antipodes. *2. n.* The contents of an Australian feminist fircbrand's *undercrackers,* you might imagine. And you'd be right.

Greyfriars jobby *n. Scots.* A faithful, small, brown pal who refuses to leave and keeps on returning even after multiple flushes.

greyhound griller *n.* A particularly miffed *bunny boiler.*

grey matter *n.* A gelatinous organic material intrinsically linked to the thought processes of the male human being. *Spunk.*

grief bacon *n.* Weight gained as a consequence of emotional turmoil. *'I tell you what, after her divorce she's really slammed on the cakes and hit the grief bacon.'*

GRILF/grilf *acronym.* Grandma I'd Like to Fuck, *eg.* Joan Collins, that Purdey out of *The New Avengers* or any woman over the age of 32 from one of our country's less salubrious council estates.

gristle whistle *n.* A "Swannee"-style *blow job,* performed on the *spam kazoo* whilst pulling the *Scotch eggs* up and down.

grit between the pillows *n.* Particularly crusty *men in the rigging* which lead to excessive chafing betwixt the *mudflaps. 'Captain Peacock: Mr Humphries. Do you have to walk across the shop floor in such an affected fashion? Mr Humphries: I'm sorry, Captain Peacock, only I spent the weekend camping with a digger driver in a quarry near Golders Green and ever since I got back under me own duvet I've had terrible grit between the pillows.'* (Extract from script of *Are You Being Served?,* BBC TV 1978).

grolly *v.* To do that thing professional footballers do where they cover up one nostril and blow *snot* out the other one. *'Can you believe that, Richard? Female linesman. Never mind the fucking offside rule – she probably don't even know how to fucking grolly.' 'Course she don't, Andy. Daft cow probably thinks you do it down both fucking nostrils at once. Do me a favour, love. Still smash it, though.'*

Grolsch washer *n.* An anal sphincter resembling the trademark orange rubber seal used on the bottle-tops of the popular Dutch beverage. *'That vindaloo I had at the Rupali Restaurant, Bigg Market, Newcastle upon Tyne last night has left my Grolsch washer in tatters, doctor.'*

gromble *n.* A chap who makes good use of the *bongo mags* that the everyday folks leave behind under bushes. A *grumble womble.*

grond *1. n.* In the *Lord of the Rings,* the battering ram that shattered the gates of Minas Tirith, for any viewers who managed to stay awake that long. *2. n.* A *log* of terrifying proportions that could smash its way through even the most tightly-clenched *nipsy.*

groovement *n.* A cool *dung* taken whilst listening to your favourite funky jams.

grope-atunity *n.* An unexpected and fortuitous, albeit morally dubious, chance for a bit of a *feel*, which comes knocking out of the blue. *'The missus turned over in bed last night so I took the grope-atunity to get me tops. And now over to Rob Bonnet with the sport.'*

grotweiler *n.* An unacceptably sexist and offensive term for an aggressive-looking, mangy old *dog* in a readers' wives-type publication.

groundsman's hut *n.* The *back door*, where one lodges a stiff complaint when the *turf* round the front is unplayable.

group-on *n. coll.* A gathering of erections.

group stages *euph.* A degree of erectile tumescence so unimpressive that it fails to warrant classification as a *semi* or even a *quarter.*

gruffalo's hand *n.* Harsh and hairy *parts of shame*.

grumble strip *n.* A well-pruned *minge* of the sort that would provide an attractive landing site for an experienced *bush pilot.*

grumbs *n.* The flakes of pastry-based confetti that accumulate throughout the day around the entrance to famous high-street bakeries. From Greggs + crumbs.

grunting bunting *n.* Lavatory tissue. Also *shit scrape, arsewipe, bumwad. 'Throw us up another roll of grunting bunting, will you love?'*

Guantanamo Bay *rhym. slang.* Said of one who prefers the company of "a few good men". Also *Colwyn, Whitley, Cardigan, Jessie J.*

guard fog *n.* A vicious *arse barker* unleashed in the hall immediately prior to going out, which hangs around waiting to catch an unsuspecting burglar and bite him on the nose.

guard's whistle *n.* A series of shrill blasts warning that the *brown train* will shortly be leaving *arse station. 'I've got to dash, your holiness. That's the guard's whistle. I'll give you a bell in the week, yeah?'*

guilt chip *n.* The single, token French fry left by a *salad dodger* after they have just troughed their way through three Big Mac Meals.

guilty pleasure *1. n.* In disc jockey *hyperbole*, a cheesy record that outwardly-cool people can't help liking in spite of their better judgement. A floor-filler. *2. n.* An autoerotic act of sordid *personal delight.* A *sock-filler.*

gumgam style *n. Horatio* performed following the considerate removal of the false teeth, possibly accompanied by up-tempo music.

gun front *1. phr. milit.* Term used by tank commanders when moving their vehicles' weapons into the forward elevated position prior to firing. *2. phr. milit.* Term used by squaddies when they *pitch a tent.*

gunning *n.* In a prison or similar secure facility, the light-hearted act of *cuffing the suspect* through the bars of one's cell at a passer-by. As seen in *Louis Theroux's Miami Mega Jail, The Silence of the Lambs* and *Porridge.*

gun slinger *n.* In a public lavatory environment, a *sharp-shooter* who manages to enter a neighbouring cubicle, empty his *chamber* and leave the saloon before you've managed to pull anything out of your *back holster*, let alone take aim or fire.

gusher *n.* A dirty lady's orgasmatromical *parts of shame* that would daunt Red Adair himself.

gut beret *n. Fat hat,* as worn by a chap performing *cumulonimbus* on a *roll model.*

gutbutt *n.* Affectionate epithet for an extremely obese person, the folds of stomach hanging down out of their t-shirt, resembling nothing so much as a pair of extra, frontal *mudflaps.* Also *fruttocks.*

gut soup *n.* A bowl filled with particularly runny, steaming *foulage.*

gutter butter *n.* The off-white stain of *blip* found in the *gusset* of a *tart's applecatchers.*

gut the turkey *v.* To tickle the missus's giblets. To *firkyfoodle, feed the pony.*

haberdashers' handshake *n.* A *banjo string* duet.

had more sausage than a fat German butcher, she's *exclam.* Said of a *bird* who's had *more cocks than Davy Crockett's rifle, seen more Japs' eyes than a Toyota wing mirror etc.*

hag reflex *n.* Involuntary early morning retching caused by looking across at the lady occupying your bed and realising that what looked like Dannii Minogue last night now, in the cold light of day, looks more like Danny La Rue. And not in a good way.

hagover *n.* Saturday morning penile headache caused by an excess of sex on Friday night. *'I knew I shouldn't of fucked that last slapper in the Red Lion. I've woke up with terrible hagover. Anyway, today's recipe is braised leg of mutton with caper sauce.'*

Hagrid or Hermione? *exclam. interrog.* An inquiry as to whether a particular young lady possesses an unkempt, hirsute vagina, or a tidy, neatly-clipped one. Named after the contrastingly-haired characters out of *Harry Potter. 'I say, mister Roy. Mate of mine reckons he's seen a photo of Germaine Greer's cunt on the internet.' 'Really Basil? Was it a Hagrid or a Hermione?' 'Hagrid. Very much so, he said. Like a fucking collie's chest, it was apparently. Ha-ha! Boom! Boom!'*

hail damage *n.* Cellulite on the legs of a bird who has *relaxed her fitness regime.*

hair grip *n.* The distinctly uncomfortable sensation of getting a bit of *fusewire* tightly entangled under one's *fiveskin* and around the brim of the *farmer's hat.*

hairline crack *1. n.* A minor structural defect found in, for example, a motorway flyover or aircraft wing. *2. n.* A *minge* that has been shaved within an inch of its life.

hairy bath *n.* A *shag. 'Did you get a noshing off that bird behind Lidl, then?' 'No, she'd* got her braces in so she just gave me cock a hairy bath.'

hairy cod mother *n.* A heavily-*battered fish supper.*

hairy heroes *n.* The testicles. *John Wayne's hairy saddlebags*, the *clockweights, knackers;* the *gonk-faced Mother Teresa sisters* or *McSquirter twins.*

hairy tree *1. n.* A legendary, hirsute sapling in Girvan, Scotland, supposedly planted by erstwhile troglodyte cannibal Sawney Bean's daughter. Now the subject of an epic Holy Grail-style quest by former Ipswich Town, Coventry and Scotland forward Alan Brazil. See also *stumpy tower. 2. n.* A chap's moss-covered *twig and berries. 'Fancy a wee climb up the hairy tree, love? Thought not.'*

hairy wink *n.* A friendly twinkle of encouragement vouchsafed by a lady's *nether eye* to a novitiate *cumulonimbalist. 'A nun gave me the hairy wink / I got meself some close-up pink / What would the Holy Father think? / When I'm cleaning windows.'* (lyrics to *The Windowcleaner* by George Formby).

half a wank *euph.* Something that's not worth doing, *eg.* Going for "a couple of pints".

halibut handshake *n.* A *fistful of mackerel.*

halibutosis *n. medic.* A condition often affecting those who *quaff at the furry cup.*

Hallowe'en cake, face like a *sim.* Said of an aesthetically unconventional person. *'He's won seven Tony awards, three Grammy awards, one Oscar, fourteen Ivor Novello awards, seven Olivier awards and a Golden Globe. He's a giant of British musical theatre and he's got a face like a Hallowe'en cake. Put your hands together and give a rousing Over the Rainbow welcome to Andrew Lloyd Webber.'*

hamazon, like going up the *sim.* A reference to paddling one's *skin boat* on a voyage of discovery up a particularly overgrown and swampy *meat delta*, which is possibly infested with leeches, fire ants and them really long millipedes.

ham clam *n.* A sturdily-constructed yet juicy *snapper*. More compact than a *ham bucket*.

ham salad *n.* An unlikely-sounding, yet ingenious, home-made masturbatory aid, consisting of a hollowed-out cucumber lined with ham and placed in the microwave prior to use. Even better, it counts as one of your five-a-day.

hammerfat *1. n.* The typeface familiar to pasty-faced, bedroom-bound players of old-fashioned Atari video games. *2. n. Wanked*-up *joff, jaff, spiff, spaff.spoff, spangle, spungle* or *spingle*. Something else that will be familiar to pasty-faced, bedroom-bound players of old-fashioned Atari video games.

Hampstead grief *n.* The plight of a chap who *knows what's in his flowerbeds* who gets mugged by a scoundrel masquerading as a fellow *bottery barn* habitué.

hand cuddle *n.* A *wank*. *'I'm feeling a bit lonely, mum. I'm just nipping upstairs for a hand cuddle.'*

hand grenade *n.* A palm-sized incendiary *squib* which detonates messily when *tossed*.

hand luggage *n.* The penis. *'Will your hand luggage fit in the overhead locker, sir?' 'I've not had any complaints yet, pet.'*

hand practice *n.* Solitary monomanual labour for the housebound bachelor who wishes to keep his wrist in.

handsome *n.* Neither a threesome nor a twosome. A *one-in-a-bed romp* or ménage à un.

handular fever *n.* Condition suffered by those who *work from home*. *'Have you finished those reports yet, Russell? The board needs them for the big presentation this afternoon.' 'Sorry, I've had handular fever all week so I never got them done.'*

happy clappy *1. adj.* Annoyingly full of the love of God. *2. n.* Not really bothered about having *cock rot*.

happy medium *n. Lucky Pierre*. The filling in a *spud fumble*r sandwich.

happy sealion, do the *v.* To enjoy vigorous coitus, the whole performance accompanied by a wet clapping sound, damp whiskers and a strong smell of fish. *'And there goes the Royal couple, leaving the Cathedral in the golden State Coach. And no doubt Prince William be looking forward now to a lavish reception and banquet at Buckingham Palace, followed by a night of doing the happy sealion whilst thinking about his sister-in-law's shitlocker.'*

happytwat *n.* Any modern, upmarket sex shop, *ie.* One that doesn't smell of sweat, despair and *spunk*.

hard as the knobs of Hell *sim.* Traditional Cheshire phrase for something that is very hard indeed. Also *hard as a Chinese wordsearch, hard as a policeman's knock, hard as Stephen Hawking's homework*.

haroldite *n.* A super-gluey adhesive in a cylindrical tube which is invaluable for sticking the pages of *art pamphlets* together. Also *population paste, joy gloy, Aphrodite's evostick, jazz glue, prick stick, man mastic, pyjama glue* and *cockidex*.

harp strings *n.* Residual strands of *man mess* left hanging 'twixt the upper and lower jaws following a bout of oral tomfoolery.

Harry Ramsden's fingers *1. euph.* Descriptive of the state of the digits after fiddling with an excitable woman's *haddock pastie*, *ie.* Covered in batter and smelling of fish. *2. n.* Title of Kim Carnes's less successful follow-up to *Bette Davis Eyes*.

Harry Ramsden's skip *n.* A mingsome *snatch*. *'Kleptomania was powerless to resist. His eyes burned into hers like Swarovski crystals. His strong arms enfolded her body as she felt herself being swept away on a pontoon of passion. Gently, Tarpaulio's roughly-hewn lumberjack's fingers teased down her bloomers as he got down on his knees to lick her out. 'Christ on a bike, love,' he cried. 'It smells like Harry Ramsden's skip down here.'* (from *The Countess and the Tree Surgeon* by Barbara Cartland).

Harry Styles *n.* An annoying pain in the *arse*.

Harvey Keitel *n.* An urgent clean-up operation after *cacking* yourself or having a *wank* that gets out of control. Named after the infamous scene in *Pulp Fiction* when the eponymous actor is called upon to clean up a terrible mess.

have a wank on it *phr.* A procedure that any gentleman should undertake when there is a big decision to be made in order to afford himself the opportunity to make his judgement with a clear mind. And *knackers*. *'I just don't know. I'd really like a Porsche Panamera, but on the other hand the missus needs that eye operation in Switzerland to stop her going blind.' 'Tell you what, sir. You go home and have a wank on it.'*

Hawley's gift *n.* The selfless and munificent dispensation to perform an act of *horatio* upon his turgid person which is granted to his ladyfriend by a gentleman on the occasion of her birthday. From the line in the eponymous Sheffield-based crooner's song *For Your Lover Give Some Time, viz.* "It was your birthday yesterday. I gave a gift that almost took your breath away."

head start *euph.* Oral foreplay. *'I gave her a head start but I still came first.'*

heart starter *n.* A bracing breakfast-time snifter, for example a few cans of Special Brew, a couple of pints of cooking sherry or a bottle of Tesco Value gin, taken to invigorate one's semi-comatose body following the previous evening's merriment. An *eyeball straightener*.

hedgehog through a cheesegrater, like a *sim.* The polar opposite of *an otter off the bank, viz.* An extremely painful *shite* that seems takes ages to shift.

hedge quimmers *n.* A *fannicurist*'s lady shaver.

heirdo *n.* A funeral.

helicopter, the *n.* Post-rugby match entertainment: Whipping out one's *chopper* and whirling it around a bit at a high angular velocity.

helium heels *n.* Affectionate nickname for a woman who tends to end the evening with her legs in the air.

help around the house *v.* To attempt to wash *shit* stains off the inside of the *bum sink* by half-heartedly aiming one's *piss* stream at them during the ad break in *Dickinson's Real Deal*.

Henry *n. rhym. slang.* An act of *monomanual self pleasure*. From the name of the well known Yorkshire-based gun shop Henry Krank = Sherman tank.

Henry the eighth *n.* A temporary, but nevertheless full-bodied, Tudor-style red beard formed on a man's chops after *dining at the Y* when *Arsenal are playing at home*.

herbal essence *n.* The pulchritudinous likes of Helen Mirren, Lorraine Kelly and possibly, but probably not, Gillian Taylforth, who are "still giving you pleasure after 40 years". Actually, *definitely* not Gillian Taylforth.

here come the warm jets *exclam.* What Brian Eno says to his missus when he wakes up in the night with bad guts.

Hergest ridge *n.* An exceptionally unkempt and overgrown *biffin's bridge*, as immortalised by him who done the music for *The Exorcist* and *Blue Peter.*

Hermione's handbag *n.* An endlessly capacious *kitten purse,* named after Hermione Granger out of Harry Potter, who cast a magical spell on her reticule in the latest film so she could squeeze limitless quantities of stuff in it. *Mary Poppins's bag.*

heteroflexible *adj.* Said of a gent who is basically straight but occasionally hops onto *the other bus* for a couple of stops.

hi-ho *1. exclam.* Half of the customary collective salutation employed by the vertically challenged when embarking on an ante-matitudinal journey to their subterranean place of employment. *2. exclam.* A friendly greeting to a good time girl. *'Hi-ho.' 'Hi Mr Rooney.'*

hidden track *1. n.* An annoying, unwanted bit of music that suddenly comes on after a couple of minutes of silence at the end of an album. *2. n.* An extra bit of *turd* that unexpectedly makes its presence felt when you've already wiped your *dot* and pulled your *trolleys* up. *3. n.* A supplementary drip of *jitler* that drops out the end of the *giggle stick* about ten minutes after you've *crashed the yoghurt truck.* The *missing fish, Japanese teardrop.*

hiding denim *euph.* Exhibiting a *camel's toe. 'Blimey, your nan's hiding a lot of denim today.'*

hillbilly toothpick *n.* The bacula. A small, rod-like penis bone common to many mammals, such as skunks, raccoons and gophers. Typically used by inbred rural Americans to pluck corn dogs, chitterlings and hominy grits from what's left of their dentition prior to appearing on the *Jerry Springer Show.*

himulsion *n.* The white gloss which a keen *do-it-yourselfer* applies in a carefree manner to the ceiling, the walls, his wife's hair *etc.*, whilst flicking his *naughty paintbrush* about.

Hindenburg, hatch a *v.* To work up an incendiary abundance of highly inflammable *poopane gas* in the *rear hangar*, usually after eating broccoli. To release seven million cubic feet of explosive gas, causing onlookers to cry "Oh, the humanity".

ho *n.* What a sexist rapper calls his *bitch.*

hockler's draught *n.* A slimy, green *prairie oyster* produced the morning after a night of brown beer and *Harry Wraggs.* A *docker's omelette, gold watch, greb, gilbo, sheckle, gonga, Old Leigh oyster, phlegm brûlée, tramp's breakfast, greeny* or *Dutch pikelet.*

Hockley Heath beef eater *n.* A sexual position much favoured in the West Midlands. Named in honour of a well known clandestine *shagging* hotel near the M42.

hog roast *n.* An act of sexual congress involving two short-sighted centre forwards and an aesthetically challenged female.

hogwarts *n.* Fleshy excrescences around the *privates* that herald an urgent trip to the *pox doc.*

hoist the vein sail *v.* To obtain a *stiffy.* To *round Cape Horn,* in the expectation of a faceful of salty spume.

hokey cokey *n.* A *grumble*-inspired *money shot*; one that goes "in, out, in, out, shake it all about", if you will.

hole milk *n. Vitamin S.*

hole of the moon *1. n.* Title of a single taken from The Waterboys' 1985 album *This is the Sea. 2. n.* The art of manually parting the buttock cheeks in order to give passers by a better view of one's *chocolate starfish* when *mooning. Hanging your hole, playing Brigadoon.*

Holland Street hopscotch *n.* Light-hearted game played by residents of the eponymous East Hull boulevard, as they avoid the vast amounts of *hound rope* on the pavement whilst making their way to Fulton's Foods and Greggs.

Hollywood halo *n.* A considerably waxed and bleached *ringpiece*, affording a glorious view replete with undoubted star quality to anyone approaching from the *gasworks end.*

Hollywood loaf *1. n.* A high-quality, lovingly-crafted and crusty cake of brown bread made to the exacting standards of Paul Hollywood, top pastry chef star of *The Great British Bake Off*. *2. n.* A similarly high-quality and aesthetically pleasing *U-bend blocker* which also results from several hours of being lovingly baked.

hombrero *n.* A *titfer* that is worn for style reasons as opposed to practicality. A *twhat.*

home brew *n.* The offspring of an ill-judged value vodka-fuelled liaison between two members of the same family, usually - but not exclusively - to be seen having a shirtless punch-up on the *Jerry Springer Show*. *'Yeah, there's definitely a touch of the home brew about that one. Have you seen the size of his fucking ears?'*

home entertainment system *n.* A bachelor's pride and joy; his frequently-polished genitals.

homegrown *n.* Hallucinogenic gases produced from one's own *anus*, courtesy of which it is reputedly possible to "get high on your own supply".

Honey Monster's eyelids *euph.* The visible top half of a buxom lady's *funbags* when she is sporting a strapless frock.

hoo-ha *1. onomat.* Noise made by a person doing an impression of Al Pacino. *2. n.* The female *parts of shame*. *'Britney, for the last time will you put your fucking underkecks back on. No-one wants to see your hoo-ha.'*

hook, line and sphincter *phr.* A measure of the ardour with which an *arse man* falls for the crinkly object of his affections.

hookie nookie *n.* A day spent indulging in penetrative *how's your father* with one's new girlfriend, whilst officially stricken down with "that one day tummy bug that's been doing the rounds lately". A *duvet lay.*

hop o'my thumb *1. n.* Fairy tale written by Charles Perrault, about a tiny child who overcomes adversity and steals some boots off a giant. *2. n.* An unenthusiastic *third leg jump*, the issue of which which fails to clear one's opposable digit, thus temporarily precluding the possibility of one living happily ever after.

horse blowing after the Grand National, blowing like a *sim.* Suffering from stentorian flatulence; a reference to the similar sound produced by one of the few nags who survive to the end of the popular steeplechase/glue manufacturers' productivity drive.

horse curtains *n. Beef curtains* that are definitely not as advertised.

horse that has been machine-gunned in a tunnel, fanny like a *sim.* A charmingly poetic figure of speech for an aesthetically displeasing *lady garden* apparently coined by cheeky family entertainer Frankie Boyle.

hosepipe ban *n.* A seasonal veto on *the other,* imposed by the missus.

hoss piss *n.* A Cumbrian term for an extremely protracted act of micturition following a night of heavy drinking.

hostilery *n.* Public house which extends a less-than-wholehearted welcome to its patrons, *eg.* The exact opposite of the Northumberland Hussar on Sackville Road, Heaton, Newcastle upon Tyne. See also *chapel of rest.*

hot cross bun *n.* Pattern often seen on the face of certain lady actresses performing in artistic filmed dramas.

hot desking *1. n.* In business, the practice of several employees sharing the same workspace. *2. n.* In the lavatory, the uncomfortable sensation of sitting down on a toilet seat that is still warm from the previous patron. Also called a *Shoeburyness* in the *Meaning of Liff.*

hot fog *n.* A *guff* with the unmistakeable, cloying aroma of oxtail soup.

hot plate *n.* When a *lady of the night drops a log* on a customer's chest. Also something to cook your tea on, though you may well be off your food, all things considered. See also *Boston pancake.* Or rather, don't.

hot stones *n.* The buckshot-like, high temperature slurry passed the morning after a spicy *cuzza.* The lumps that articulate the consonant sounds in a *Calcutta splutter.* Also *solar stones.*

hovercraft, the *n.* A *queef* causing a substantial set of *Keith Burtons* to billow outwards, the overall effect somewhat reminiscent of the bulging skirts on one of the popular air-cushioned comedy boats of the 1970s.

HP Lovecraft *euph.* A monstrous *beast of chodbin.* From the eponymous author's habit of giving his books such stirring titles as *The Thing on the Doorstep, Lurker at the Threshhold, The Dunwich Horror etc.*

HSBC *1. abbrev.* The old Midland Bank as was, now Hongkong and Shanghai Banking Corporation Holdings plc. *2. n.* A special fellowship of those afflicted with *Chalfonts.* The Half Shit & Blood Club. *3. abbrev.* A discreet session of under-duvet *banking with Barclays.* Hand Shandy Below Covers.

HTC *1. abbrev.* Popular manufacturer of mobile telephones. *2. abbrev.* A *two-push Charlie* who always *spends his money before he gets to the shop.* One who is *up and over like a pan of milk.* Hair Trigger Cock.

hubsidised *adj.* Of a married woman's ludicrous, loss-making business venture that is only kept afloat thanks to regular cash injections from her husband.

Huddersfield quidditch *n.* The traditional sport of running away from taxis without paying in the Cash Converter-riddled Yorkshire Shangri-La.

Hughie Green face *euph.* The surprised, monocular expression of a lady whose consort has, "just for fun", elected to withdraw just prior to the conclusion of an act of *horatio,* thereby depositing his base spendings in one of her eyes. Also, variously, a *Gabrielle, Velma, King Harold, spoff monocle, German eyebath* or *St Valentine's Day mascara.*

humous kebab *n.* See *bulldog chewing porridge.*

humousexual *adj.* Of or pertaining to a fellow who prefers to partake of light, effeminate dishes such as tofu, cous-cous, quiche, meringue, salad, fruit *etc.*

hundred and thousands *n.* The left-over bits of toilet paper often to be found sprinkled about a drunken lady's genitalia. *Spandrels, men overboard, croutons, tiger nuts.*

hung like a mousetrap *adj.* Prone to sudden, premature ejaculation. *'Is that it, Lord Archer? Half a push?' 'Yes. I'm hung like a mousetrap, but please don't tell anyone. Here's two thousand pounds in an envelope.'*

Hungarian hopscotch *n.* A distinctly unlikely-sounding *gentleman's relaxation* technique, whereby the subject squats down, places his turgid *membrum virile* between his ankles and then hops up and down until he either *brings himself off* or has a heart attack, whichever happens sooner.

Hungarian, fluent *euph.* The utterly incomprehensible language which is evidently being spoken by one's drinking companions when one arrives late and stone-cold sober at a social engagement after being unavoidably detained *en route*.

hungry hippo *euph.* From the popular children's game of the 1970s, a woman who has "had a lot of balls in her mouth".

hunt for red October *1. n.* Film starring Sean Connery as a Scottish/Russian submarine captain, if memory serves. Or that might be *Gorky Park*, come to think of it. *2. n.* A saucy bedroom game whereby a lady who is *up on blocks* invites a lucky chap to seek out and remove her *blobstopper* using only his teeth. No, it was William Hurt in *Gorky Park*.

hurr *v.* To breathe forcefully, theatrically and at close quarters onto an item of food or drink before temporarily leaving the room for whatever reason, in order to put off anyone who might otherwise be tempted to *scouse* it in your absence. *'And don't touch that lemon meringue pie while I'm on the shitter, Cora. I've hurred on it.'*

hurt locker *1. n.* 2008 movie starring Jeremy Renner, Anthony Mackie and Brian Geraghty. No, us neither. *2. n.* The *nipsy, dot* or *freckle* after any one of the following (or combination thereof); a portion of the late Abdul Latif's Curry Hell - the world's hottest curry, excessive/incorrect/overly-vigorous wiping with cheap *arse paper, anal fisting* or the passing of a gargantuan *Thora*.

I 'ate that duck *exclam.* Said in the style of ventriloquist Keith Harris's comedy monkey Cuddles after someone emits a *botty quack.*

ibeerprofen *n.* A popular alcoholic painkiller, an overdose of which can lead to vomiting, memory loss and liver failure. *Canaesthetic, canadin.*

iced by a blind baker *euph.* Said of a *tart* who has been the subject of a saucy *bukkake* attack from several ill-aimed *egg white cannons.*

icing the cake *n.* After *fouling* oneself, squeezing the *crap* down the trouser legs and out of the turn-ups in order to deposit discreet chocolate rosettes on the floor, in the style of a baker decorating a gateau. With *shite* out of his *kegs.*

idiot lantern *n.* A television set. The *shit pump.* *'What do you think of me new idiot lantern? Now I can watch Cash in the Attic in high definition 3-D widescreen with Dolby Pro-Logic 5.1 surround sound.'*

Iggle Piggle's potty *n.* Rhetorical description of an area redolent of the stench of freshly-deposited human excrement, named in honour of the popular baby out of off of *In the Night Garden.* *'I'd avoid the end trap if I were thee, mate. It kefs like Iggle Piggle's potty.'*

illigiterate *n.* An ignorant *bastard.*

I'm a grow-er not a show-er *exclam.* A thoroughly convincing explanation of why a man's flaccid member may, at first glance, appear misleadingly tiny.

I'm Peppa Pig *exclam.* A humorous aphorism that can defuse the hostile atmosphere that sometimes obtains following a *lusty snort* from the *nether snout.* Also *ferfetch a cloth, Granville; someone let him in; someone's tinkered with Herbie; speak on, sweet lips that never told a lie; I'm ready for the question, Noel.*

I'm ready for the question Noel *exclam.* Humorous interjection after someone *steps on* a fortissimo frog. Also *I'm Peppa Pig; speak up caller, you're through; taxi for Brown; what's that, Sweep?; sew a button on that; mighty fine words, preacher.*

I'm with a client *exclam.* Said when someone knocks on the *bog* door when one is ensconced on the *shit hopper.*

inchilada *n.* A spicy morsel which smells of hot cheese.

independent thinker A *fucking mental.* *'Today's birthdays: Bob Holness, dead quiz show host and saxophonist, 82; Errol Brown, seventies slap-head, 62; Charles Manson, independent thinker, 76.'*

indoor league *1. n.* Show which was cheaply produced by Yorkshire Television between 1972 and 1977, in which pipe-smoking, cardigan-toting ex-cricketer Fred Trueman introduced coverage of such pub sports as shove ha'penny, skittles and arm wrestling. *2. n.* Code word for *cottaging* used in working class boozers throughout the north. *'I'll see thee in the toilets for a spot of indoor league.'*

inebriati, the *n.* Shadowy, secretive brotherhood united by a shared fondness for Communion wine, Communion white cider and Communion extra-strength lager.

injured in the warm-up *euph.* Said of a footballer who *shits* himself and is forced to retire disconsolately from the field of play for an early bath.

instant diet *n.* A huge *pony* that allows you to do up your belt a couple of notches.

instoolments *n.* The successive episodes of a *trilogy* or *mini-series.* *'I'm paying for that slap-up feed at the Rupali Restaurant, Bigg Market, Newcastle upon Tyne, in instoolments, you know.'*

intercourse work *n.* Modular weekend and evening tasks typically researched online.

interior decorator *n.* In a *bukkake* session, the chap who actually gets to *do it* with the *plasterer's radio.*

interview at Butlins *euph.* A *knock-up* during *cricket week,* whereby one "comes out with a red coat".

in the soft drinks aisle *euph.* Completely mental, as in "past crackers and nuts". *Mad as a Maltese roundabout.*

in the wet *adj.* Well and truly *cunt-struck.*

investment wanker *n.* One who forks out for a subscription *bongo* service from Sky television in the expectation of getting a substantial return on his holding.

invincibility cloak *n.* That drink-fuelled shield that gives a man the ability to fight like Tyson, escape from the police in a single bound and fall off scaffolding without harm.

iPhear *n.* The sensations of dry-mouthed panic, horror and trepidation experienced by a chap when his missus picks up his iPhone and opens Safari.

Irish appendectomy *n.* A dramatic *buoy from the black stuff* which appears to contain an internal organ, or at the very least some sort of vestigial gland.

Irish tumble drier *n.* Unacceptably racist and offensive term for a cement mixer, which we can categorically assure our readers would never find its way into a publication with such high editorial standards as what this one do. Has.

irons his socks, I bet he *euph.* Said of a fellow who *knows what's in his flowerbeds.*

I say, the tail-gunner's trigger happy today *exclam.* To be said in clipped RAF tones when subjected to unexpected *arse flak.*

iScar *n.* A 9" long red welt on the upper abdomen, caused by the one-handed balancing of a tablet-style media device thereupon whilst *surfing the web for antiquarian books.*

Italian enema *n.* The first strong coffee of the day, ensuring a smooth morning *dump. Ex-laxpresso, Laxwell House.*

it fits like a cock up a puppy's arse *phr.* '*I told you this garage was big enough for a Range Rover, and I was right. It fits like a cock up a puppy's arse, look. Careful you don't scratch the paintwork while you're climbing out of the boot, nan.'*

I think I ate a clown *exclam.* Apologetic phrase issued from one's water closet cubicle after *dropping a particularly large pair of shoes out of the loft.*

it's a good answer, but it's not right *exclam.* Said in a soft Ulster brogue in the style of Roy Walker following a polite, after-dinner *clearance of the nether throat.*

i-zooming *n.* The action of two fingers trying to pry open a lady's *hangar doors*, reminiscent of the pincer-like movement required to enlarge a picture on the screen of a mobile telephone.

JAC/jac *acronym.* Useful nickname for the sort of "celebrity" you've never ever heard of who rocks up on programmes like *Dancing on Ice, Celebrity Coach Trip, Celebrity Come Dine With Me, Celebrity Love Island* or *Celebrity Embarrassing Bodies*, who usually turns out to be off *Hollyoaks*. Just Another Cunt. See also *FFFA*.

Jackanory *n.* A slow and gentle attempt at anal sex, involving a tub of marge, patience and repeated enquiries of "are you sitting comfortably".

jack cheese *1. n.* The stringy stuff they put on hamburgers in Britain to make them sound more authentically American. *2. n.* The stringy stuff chefs spread onto the food of unpopular customers. *'The chef's just wanking some jack cheese out of his knob onto your main course, Mr Winner.'*

jack of all trades *n.* One who can manage a *fish supper* and a *sausage dinner* in one sitting. A *happy shopper.*

jack rustle *n.* The tell-tale sound of a fellow who is surreptitiously *wagging his tail.*

Jackson Bollocked *adj.* Of a lady's face, decorated in an Abstract Expressionist manner using a *naughty paintbrush.*

Jacob's ladder *n. medic.* The tearing of the stitches holding a recent mother's *joybox* together.

Jacqui Smith *n.* Getting *bummed* in prison. Named after the erstwhile Member of Parliament for Redditch, who famously got her "back room touched up" for free by a few hardened convicts while she was the Home Secretary.

Jagger's lips *euph.* Used to describe the distressing anatomical repercussions of a high-pressured *trouser cough. 'That last fart left my arse feeling like Jagger's lips, your majesty.'*

Jamaican chocolate volcano *n.* The exotic Caribbean cousin of the *Cleveland steamer,* fuelled by enthusiastic consumption of spicy jerk chicken and Red Stripe beer.

James Bond pants/007 pants *n. Undercrackers* of a certain vintage that a bachelor sniffs in order to check if they'll "do another day".

jam salvage *n.* Retrieving a *fanny mouse* that has accidentally got pushed two or three inches up a lady's *clopper* during an *ad-hoc cricket week scuttle.*

jam tart *1. n. rhym. slang.* A *Bakewell.* From jam tart = Exchange & Mart. *2. n.* A rough *piece* who has *got the painters in.*

jap off *v.* To remove stubborn excrement smears from the *chod pan* using a stream of fluid directed from *Jap's island.* To make use of the *yellow toilet brush* or *piss chisel. 'Sorry about the pebbledashing in the shitter, darling. If you give me half an hour or so, I'll have a few cups of tea and get it japped off for you.'*

Japanese dismount *n.* Falling off something. From that far eastern gymnast who fell off the pommel horse and later claimed it was actually his dismount, thus costing the British team their Olympic silver medal. *'After landing well clear of the ramp, the front forks of the bike collapsed, and Knievel performed a Japanese dismount which left him with two broken legs, a shattered shoulder, four cracked vertebrae and compound fractures in both wrists, as well as a ruptured spleen, concussion and life-threatening internal injuries.'*

JAT sandwich, dry as a *sim.* Moistureless. A reference to the desiccated in-flight provender served on Serbia's national airline. *'Shall I just give up, love? Only I've been giving you the halibut handshake for half an hour now and you're still as dry as a JAT sandwich.'*

jaw warmer *n. Scots.* A threatened spot of *chin music* from a *doorknob. 'Get oot o' here noo, Jimmy, before I give ye a jaw warmer.'*

jaxidermist *n.* A gentleman who has a penchant for stuffing bottoms.

jazz hands *1. n.* The action of displaying and agitating one's palms in time to a syncopated musical accompaniment. *2. n.* The action of shaking the *jitler* off one's *wanking spanners* following a vigorous rifle through the *rhythm section* of one's favourite *bongo book*.

jazzholes *n. Arseholes* who affect to like the sort of free-form music which is so clever that it sounds like a piano, double bass and drum-kit being kicked down a fire escape.

jazzma *n. medic.* Male condition which is characterised by shortness of breath; a symptom which typically presents when the patient's *bag for life* gets back from the shops unexpectedly early.

jazz scavenger *n.* A fellow in the midst of *working from home* whose wireless broadband router goes down so he is forced to frantically search for a neighbour's signal to piggy-back onto. A *jazz passenger.*

jeaneology *n.* The scientific study of young women's *arses* viewed through tight denim. A learned discipline which is principally practised by male motorists in neck-braces.

Jennifer Canestan *n. prop.* An attractive woman who is riddled with *gash rash. Lady Chalk of Billingsgate.*

jerk sauce *1. n.* The special secret ingredient that is apparently added to the KFC Reggae Reggae Box Meal. *2. n.* The special secret ingredient added to every meal that the late Michael Winner ever consumed.

Jessie J *adj. rhym. slang. Colwyn Bay.* 'Fancy a quickie behind a skip?' 'No thanks, madam. I'm a bit Jessie J.'

jessticles *n. Knackers* that have been *wanked flat* whilst watching two consecutive days of women's Track and Field.

jet slag *1. n.* A woman who is always *up for a bit* in the *crappers* on a plane. *2. n.* A woman whose morals are somewhat looser than usual due to extreme tiredness brought on by travelling from a different time zone.

jibbles *n.* The involuntary vibration of the *jester's shoes* just before the *custard pie gets thrown.*

jim-jam wigwam *n.* A conical teepee pitched in one's nightwear, using a fleshy tentpole for support.

Jim Kardashian *n.* A convincingly *bootylicious tranny.*

Jimmy Savile Row *Scrote couture* style of shell-suit tailoring sported by scratters on inner city estates. See also *Savile Row.*

Jimmy Savile's running shoes, colder than *sim.* A turn of phrase evidently coined in honour of the late Leeds-based charity marathon-runner and cigar-chomping *sexcase.* 'Fuck me, shut those tent-flaps will you, Tensing. It's colder than Jimmy Savile's running shoes in here.'

jinker *n.* That up which one may be rhetorically invited to stick something. 'Can I interest you in today's special lunchtime menu at all, madam?' 'Stick it up your jinker, sonny.'

jipper *n.* Cod yoghurt.

jit lag *n. NZ.* State of exhaustion experienced by men who are suffering from a zinc deficiency. 'Can't make it to the pub tonight, lads. Only I've just got me broadband working and I'm suffering from severe jitlag.'

jizzappointment *n.* The underwhelming experience suffered when a keenly-anticipated *popshot* fails to live up to expectations.

jizzazzle *v.* To *vajizzle.* To give the missus a sparkly, sticky decoration around the *downstairs area.*

jizzdens *n.* Masculine reference material that a man consults studiously during *cricket week.*

jizzery *n.* The sorrowful form of *monomanual delight* practised by a newly single man.

jizz hands *euph.* Shaking sticky *Thelonious* from one's *wanking spanners* at the conclusion of a productive *five knuckle shuffle.*

'So, Mr Winner's soup was on the way out of the kitchen when I suddenly realised that not a single employee had wanked into it.' 'Christ on a fucking bike, what did you do?' 'Only one thing I could do, Kirsty. I rubbed out a quick one and gave it the jizz hands over the bowl as the waiter went by.' 'And what is your fourth record?'

jizz lamp *n.* A special torch favoured by fictional crime scene investigators looking for feloniously-deposited *man spackle* on mattresses.

jizzle *n.* In *dogging* circles, a mixture of *jipper* and light rain on a car windscreen. Thankfully, the intermittent wipe is usually all that is required to deal with a minor fall of *jizzle.*

jizz ships *n.* The flotilla of small *egg drop soup* tankers and *friggits* which float about on the surface of the bath after a chap has played *up periscope.*

job application forms *n.* Sheets of *bumwad* filled in whilst visiting the *job centre. Shit tickets. 'Mam! Can you lob up another roll of job application forms onto the landing?'*

jobby well done *n.* The sense of pride one feels after serving up a *gorilla's breakfast.*

jobby clock *n.* The internal precision chronometer that keeps one's *Camillas* running on schedule, and which can easily become confused by a holiday, a surfeit of hard-boiled eggs or a visit to a hard water area.

job centre *n.* The *crapper, chod bin, jobbie engine.*

jockey's bollocks, neck like a *sim.* Dysphemistic description of one whose *noggin* is somewhat unimpressively attached to their shoulders, *eg.* Multi-phobic, semi-conscious *turd*-sniffer Dr Gillian McKeith PhD.

John McCririck's wanking pants, dirtier than *1. sim.* Used by a mother to describe the unkempt state of a room. *2. sim.* Said of a woman who has a refreshingly open-minded attitude to sexual matters. *'Fuck me, that blonde piece doing the weather looks dirtier than John McCririck's wanking pants.'*

John Zorn *1. n. prop.* Way-out, hardcore, experimental jazz musician. *2. n. prop. rhym. slang.* Way-out, hardcore, experimental jazz. *'Got any John Zorn, mate?' 'Yeah, I keep it in the back room, Mr Brown.'*

Johnny Cradock's collar *n.* A foulsome, unwashed *brim*, named in honour of the eponymous, monocled seventies lush, whose missus famously had to clean his filthy shirt neck by rubbing it with a bar of Fairy soap.

join the soil association *v.* To befoul one's *grundies. 'I do beg your pardon. I just bent over to tie my shoelace and accidentally joined the soil association. Where was I? Oh yes, Dogger, Fisher German Byte, rain, one thousand and six, good, rising slowly.'*

jolly green giant *n.* A virescent *dreadnought* that appears as a result of the over-consumption of fresh liquorice. Unlikely to provoke much laughter.

Jossy's giants *1. n.* Title of a popular 1980s children's television series about a Geordie football team, the Glipton Giants, written by late, over-educated TV darts commentator Sid "that was like throwing three pickled onions into a thimble" Waddell. *2. n.* Big *tits* on a Newcastle lass.

judge the fudge *v.* To assess the state of one's health by examining the contents of the *pan* for evidence of disease.

juggosaurus rex *n.* A monstrously large-breasted woman, as mentioned in *The Inbetweeners.*

Jugsy Malone *n.* A well-built lady who could cause lots of cream to fly about.

jump start *v.* To allow a mate to step in and do the hard work involved in getting your *ride's knicker engine* fired up for you.

junction x *euph.* A versatile, geographically-specific insult to a *fugly* woman, depending on where she lives in relation to the nearest motorway interchange. *'Have you met my wife? I call her Junction 11 because she's the Banbury turnoff.'*

jungle jitters *n.* Term coined by *TOWIE* alumnus Mark Wright whilst a contestant on *I'm a Celebrity* to describe the sensation of being trapped in the dark heart of the Australian rainforest with nothing but platypus *fannies,* crocodile *bollocks* and kangaroo *nipsies* for sustenance. *2. rhym. slang.* Loose stools, diarrhoea. *'Ooh, I tell you what. I'm bad with the jungle jitters today, and no mistake. Not guilty, your honour.'*

jungle junction *1. n.* Popular children's television programme featuring an entertaining selection of zany woodland characters. *2. n.* An unkempt *growler* found in a lady's *fork.*

junior hacksaw *n.* The act of *finger banging* a lady's *blurtch* in the rapid style of an impatient metalwork teacher cutting lengths of 10mm mild steel stock for a forthcoming lesson.

junkie's carpet, rough as a *sim.* Descriptive of one who looks, smells and feels awful. And would probably be sticky if you stepped on them. *'And how are you this morning, Lady Bellamy?' 'I'm as rough as a junkie's carpet, Hudson.'*

just take it for a walk, will you? *exclam.* A jocose rejoinder to one who has a *brown dog scratching at the back door.*

kakophany *n.* The noise of *a load of old shoes falling out of the loft.* A *flock of pigeons, musique concrète.*

kale force winds *n.* Brassica-assisted *trouser breezes.*

Kalihari bushman *n.* An expert at foraging through the undergrowth. A *deep sea muff diver, gashtronaut.*

kami khazi *n.* A *depth charge* travelling at such speed, and with such little regard for its own safety and wellbeing, that hits the water and is immediately carried round the U-bend and out of sight by its own momentum.

kanji *1. n.* An ancient form of Japanese writing. *2. n.* The *shit* that encrusts itself around the bowl of a student lavatory bowl, and would presumably provide something interesting to read for any ancient Japanese person who happened to pop in *to turn his bike around.*

Karen carpenter's biscuit tin *n.* Something which is rarely used or in pristine condition. *'Winsome and Welshman are delighted to be able to offer this 1926 Rolls-Royce 20 HP landaulette with gleaming, original maroon coachwork by HP Mulliner. Formerly the property of the Maharajah of Kalahandi, this exceptional automobile has covered just 26 miles since new, and has been maintained in its original condition regardless of cost. Take our word for it, this truly stunning time-warp classic is a real Karen Carpenter's biscuit tin and is offered with new MOT and 6 months tax. £350 ono. No tyre kickers.'*

Kate Humble's jumper, like *sim.* Said of the soft and downy nether regions of a lady.

Kate Moss's chip pan, as much use as *sim.* Said of something that is utterly useless and redundant, probably a footballer. Also *Anne Frank's drumkit, tits on a fish.*

kebabbledash *n.* The semi-durable rendering compound produced by the careful mixture of real ale and late-night *stomach fillers. 'Oh* no, I'm never going to make it up the stairs in time. I'll just have to stop here and kebabbledash the neighbour's front wall.'

kebabby *n.* See *beerby.*

kebab compass *1. n.* Drunken navigation system which allows a chap to retrace his steps by following the trail of dropped salad along his "walk of shame". *2. n.* The hand-held device which late night revellers can be observed waving around on street corners in an attempt to get a bearing on their front door.

kebab TV *euph.* The "adult" channels to be found on Channel 950 upwards on Sky that are typically viewed whilst *pissed as a Bishop* in the early hours, when the prospect of ogling a muted ex-Page 3 girl with a floppy *boner* in your right hand and a floppy doner in your left seems perfectly proper.

keep the cap on the sauce bottle clean *euph.* Said of a fellow who's a tad *left hand down a bit. 'Keep it under your hat, but I have it on very good authority that that Alan Carr off the telly is known to keep the top of his sauce bottle clean.'*

keepy-puppies *n. Tits* so droopy they could be used for football practice.

Keighley lullaby *n.* A soothing small hours *berceuse* enjoyed by the somnolent residents of the salubrious West Yorkshire Shangri-La, consisting of drunken shouting, breaking glass, sirens, and rights being read by arresting officers.

Keighley picnic *n.* A box of Stella Artois, for *al fresco* consumption.

Keighley wedding *n.* A fight.

Kenny Lunt *n. rhym. slang.* A woman's *Jeremy Hunt.* Named after the spooneristically inopportune Hereford United football player, *viz.* Kenny "Lenny" Lunt = Chris Brunt.

Kentucky battleship *n.* A not particularly seaworthy *tugboat.*

Kentucky breakfast *n.* A *heart starter* or *eye-*

ball straightener. A bracing, ante-meridian tincture, which might be followed by a short power-nap on a park bench or a refreshing *piss* in one's trousers.

kerb-ab *n.* A park-dweller's late night snack from the gutter buffet. *'Do you know what'd just round the night off smashing after all them metal polishes? A nice kerb-ab.'*

kettle wank *n.* A gent's weekend morning five-minute *act of self delight*, typically prefaced with a request that his wife "just nip downstairs and make us a cup of tea, love."

KFC *abbrev.* A Kiss, a Fuck and a Cuddle. *'I'm bored with this ambassador's reception, Phil. Fancy a KFC?'*

kicked over trifle, fanny like a *sim.* A term much used in Stoke-on-Trent to describe a lady's *bodily treasure* that is not particularly pleasing to the eye. A *butcher's dustbin.*

kick fart *v.* To initiate an act of *internal bumbustion* by raising one leg.

kidney disturber *n.* A bloke with an impressive endowment in the *trouser department*, such as might inadvertently interfere with the nephritic arrangements of a ladyfriend. *'Today's birthdays: Ken Russell, formerly-purple dead film director, 85; Fontella Bass, pipe-smoking dead female soul singer, 72; Stephen Pound MP, kidney disturber, 64.'*

killing a bear *n.* Passing a notably monstrous, grizzly, brown *arse brute*. *'Romeo, Romeo, wherefore art thou, Romeo?' 'Be down in a second, love. I'm just killing a bear.'*

kinder surprise *n.* The gift of a smelly egg in the pants of a pre-school infant, found by a teaching assistant even while the father is sprinting up the path after depositing his child at the nursery.

King Diamond with his bollocks caught in a mangle *phr.* Description of an unusually high-pitched voice. Named after the screeching lead vocalist of heavy metal band Merciful Fate, whose unusually high-pitched singing would no doubt be even more unusually high-pitched if his *bollocks* got caught in a mangle.

King Lear *n.* A stentorian, dramatic *flapper rattler* that will wow them in the back row of the Upper Circle. From, as everyone knows, Lear's line which opens Act III Scene 2 of the famous Shakespeare play, *viz.* "Blow, winds, and crack your cheeks!"

King's Cross - St Pancras *euph.* An elegant, sophisticated lady and her squat, mundane-looking constant companion. A *cruiser and tug.*

kipper dinghy *n.* A lady's *secret bower of pleasure*. *'Olympia is reminiscent in its subject matter of Ingres's Odalisque with a Slave. However, that is where the similarity ends, for in this case the artist does not present us with a depiction of an idealised nude. Instead, with his harshly direct lighting and his deliberate use of a limited colour palette and crude brush-strokes, Monsieur Manet has painted a naked courtesan, reclining on a chaise longue with her hand on her kipper dinghy.'*

kipper hamper for gentlemen *n.* An item in the Botham's of Whitby catalogue, consisting of Fortune's kippers, Landlord beer, fruitcake and some ginger & double chocolate biscuits.

kipper's twat, fishy as a *sim.* Said of something distinctly questionable, *eg.* Channel 4 funny man Jimmy Carr's tax arrangements.

Kleenex, own shares in *euph.* A polite way to suggest that you think someone is a bit of a *wanker. 'If you ask me, that Sting looks like he owns more than a few shares in Kleenex.'*

knacker elastic *n.* The rubbery bands that hold the male *clockweights* in place within *John Wayne's hairy saddlebags*. The high tension suspension cords in *Dierdre's neck.*

knee knocker *n.* An abnormally large *tallywhacker. 'I'm terribly sorry, Archbishop Welby, only the cat seems to have taken a liking to your* *knee knocker. Do let me know if he's bothering you at all and I'll put him out. More tea?'*

kneeling cushions *n*. Long, padded *tits*.

knickerbocker glory *n*. A *back scuttle* effected whilst pulling the female's *anal floss* to one side.

knicker giblets *n*. *Bacon strips* which can be boiled up to make a rich stock.

knobtard *n*. One whose performance has failed to impress. Derivation unknown.

knock the table *v*. To suffer from constipation. From the conventional behaviour used by domino players to signify when they "can't go". *'I had a three goose-egg and black pudding omelette for my tea the Friday before last and I'm still knocking the table.'*

knocking in the bat *1. n*. In cricket, the mysterious tradition of "seasoning" a new bat by beating it for six hours with a cricket ball or special magic mallet. *2. n. Self abuse.*

knows her way around an engine *euph*. Said of a lady who eschews uncomfortable footwear. Also *good at reverse parking*.

knows his way around Brighton *euph. Light on his feet.*

knuckle down *euph*. To lock oneself in a dark study on the pretext of getting to grips with a pressing work engagement/novel deadline/political speech, belying one's true intention of indulging in an *ADW. 'How's it going working from home, then?' 'Well, you've just got to knuckle down and get on with it, haven't you?'*

korv med mos *n. Swed*. A term used by patrons of the Tantogardens Park mini golf course in Stockholm to describe the state of the bogs next to the championship course. Literally *bangers and mash.*

kraptonite *n*. A *shite* that gives off such an *ignoble gas* that it would bring Superman to his knees in his Fortress of Solitude.

krautside lane *n*. Outer division of the motorway which seems to be exclusively reserved for drivers of expensive German motor cars.

Kung Fu tits *n*. Anomalously-proportioned *lady lumps* that require a fellow to adopt a braced, martial arts-style stance in order to tackle them front on.

Kurts *1. rhym. slang. medic*. Diarrhoea. From German artist and typographer Kurt Schwitters = skitters. *2. rhym. slang. medic*. Haemorrhoids. From German composer of the Threepenny Opera Kurt Weills = piles. *'Ooh, doctor. These fucking Kurts aren't half playing havoc with me Kurts.'*

Kyle-ie *n*. A female guest on the *Jeremy Kyle Show* who is semi-attractive, if only by that programme's usual low standards, *eg*. One with some teeth.

Kyleys *n*. Literally, those who appear on ITV *scratter* parade the *Jeremy Kyle Show*. The underclasses. *'I wouldn't leave my car there if I was you. The local Kyleys'll have the wheels off it the moment you turn your back.'*

labia-rador *n.* An extremely hairy *growler* that smells of tripe.

ladder legs *n. medic* Debility, tightness and cramping in a male's lower limbs caused by having to repeatedly stand on tip-toes whilst pleasuring a taller lady, or one wearing high heels. *'What's up, Bernie? Why have you stopped?' 'I've got ladder legs, Fabiana. You couldn't pop down to the kitchen and fetch me a chair to stand on, could you?'*

lady ga-garden *n.* A *front bottom* that has all big pieces of raw meat hanging off it. A *minge* blessed with pendulous *steak drapes.*

lady graeme-garden *n.* A *front bottom* with big, hairy sideburns and leather elbow patches.

Lady Sa Ga *euph.* An old *hound* dressed up in outrageous and inappropriate clothing.

lager of la mott *1. n.* 1980s lager-style beverage, famed for its somewhat overblown Sword & Sorcery-themed television advertisements. *2. n.* Any bitter liquid quaffed with relish from a *furry cup.*

lambrini surprise *n.* The mischievous act of drinking a surfeit of fizzy wine, *pissing* in the empty bottle and leaving it in the park for a thirsty *professional outdoorsman* to happen upon. A *tramp trap.*

lambs are screaming, the *1. exclam.* In James Herriot film *The Silence of the Lambs*, the repressed childhood memories of agent Clarice Starling that result in emotional trauma in later life. *2. exclam.* Expression of an urgent need to evacuate one's *Simon Cowells* if emotional trauma in later life is to be avoided.

Lampwick *n.* Of a person who has received a gent's *spendings* in their mouth, the Proustian recreation of the regurgitatory noises made by the late Dick Emery's old man character James Maynard Kitchener Lampwick, who sounded like he was juggling a mouthful of false teeth and *hockle*

at the start of every utterance.

landing a shark *n.* Whist spending a day *working from home*, the arduous and spirit-sapping task of attempting one's fifth act of *procrasturbation*; a largely pointless exercise for even the most dedicated *onanist.*

landlord's supper *n.* An item in the Botham's of Whitby catalogue, consisting of a delicious Botham's fruitcake, served with real Wensleydale cheese and a bottle of Timothy Taylor's Landlord beer.

lap of honour *n. Going down* on the missus when you really don't feel like it. See also *cuntractual obligation.*

lardcore *adj.* Type of explicit erotica principally concerned with the carryings-on of *chipwrecked* females.

lardette *n.* A generously-proportioned, pint-swilling, *salad-dodging bird* who engages in raucous behaviour when suitably *refreshed.*

lard on *1.n.* A pornographic journeyman's perfunctory *hard on* which does the job, but only just. A *satiscraptory* erection. *2. n.* The state of non-sexual excitement felt by a *bigger-boned* gentleman when approaching a Ginster's display. *3. n.* The sort of small erection experienced when looking at a *filfy plumper. 4. n.* Term used to describe the sort of high-cholesterol *boners* enjoyed by fat slobs like that twat who used to do the Radio 1 breakfast show.

last metrosexual *n.* A *sophistipated* person who, after failing to cop off with a member of the opposite sex in Newcastle's Bigg Market on a Friday or Saturday night, resorts to chatting up any old *floor sweepings* available on the "last Metro" train out of Monument Station in the hope of getting a bit *fiddle.*

last minute platform alteration *n.* During a *brief encounter*, an unexpected announcement from the man that he is about to attempt a *tight brown* rather than an *easy* *pink. Changing at Baker Street, playing the B-side.*

last piece of the jigsaw, looking for the *euph.* To be unavoidably detained whilst wiping one's *Marmite pot*. *'Your tawdry jubilee barge awaits, your majesty.' 'With you in a minute, pal. I'm just looking for the last piece of the jigsaw.'*

last supper *n.* The final lard-filled blowout which *piabetics* invariably enjoy prior to going into hospital for their gastric band or stomach stapling surgery, after being told by their doctors to have a light meal on the evening before their operations to avoid dying whilst under the anaesthetic.

last turkey in Tesco *n.* An amusing gents' changing rooms cabaret impression, in which the *scrotal skin* is pulled up and over the *bollocks* to create a vivid simulacrum of a lonely, unloved fowl sat shivering in a fridge at the eponymous supermarket. Also *the last turkey in the shop, Bob Cratchitt's pantry.*

launch a fragrance *v.* To roll out your *signature scent. 'Jesus, Kylie. What's that smell? Has a platypus died under the floor?' 'Ah, that's me, Jason. I was bad on the Supershine last night and I've just launched a fragrance.'*

lava lamp *euph.* A female who is "very hot but not terribly bright".

law of beverages *n.* The system of precisely-defined scientific axioms that govern the effect of booze upon the human body. *'Look dear, I'd had a skinful. It's hardly surprising in the circumstances that I woke up in your sister again. It's the law of beverages.'*

Lawrence of a labia *euph.* One who enjoys the occasional munch on a *magic carpet.*

Lawrence Olivier *n.* The *ne plus ultra* of excrement; the definitive *Richard the Third.*

Laws on *n.* An erection which springs into life whilst watching Nigella on the telly, but rarely whilst watching her dad or brother for some inexplicable reason.

laxident *n.* A *slip of the bum* whilst dosed up on the sennapods.

lazy Susan *n.* Lackadaisical *Boris Johnson* position whereby the woman reclines on her back with her head dangling over the end of the bed.

le cock spurtif *n. Fr.* An iconic, non-trade-marked logo adopted by novice and expert graffiti artists alike. Frequently essayed in public toilets and textbooks, and drawn in the dirt on the backs of vans, it consists of a stylised ejaculating *membrum virile* set atop a cursory *chicken skin handbag*. Also known as a *three-line pud.*

leave everything on the water *1. phr.* Cliché much used by Olympic commentators when referring to Olympic rowers expending maximum effort in order to win a race. *2. phr.* Doing an immense, personal best *shit.*

leave the brown barge in the lock *v.* To fail to flush properly. To leave a *night watchman* floating in the *chod pan.*

lech-tacles *n.* Sunglasses. Also *perv windows.*

Lecter's lunchbag *n.* A young lady's *farmyard area* that takes on the appearance of a bloody bag of nibbled lips and lobes once a month, when the *tomato boat is docked in tuna town.*

Leeds Christmas tree *n.* Roundhay Park shrubbery bedecked with tightly-knotted bags of *lawn sausages.* Also *brown baubles, Warrington baubles.*

Lee Evans's suit, as wet as *sim.* Said of a sexually aroused lady at her moistest. *Dripping like a fucked fridge, frothing like bottled Bass, wet as Dermot O'Leary's shirt.*

leg byes *n.* Diarrhoea dribbling out of the *popping crease* and down the *leg gully* after one has failed to avoid the *follow through.*

Lego garage, like I've shat out a *sim.* Turn of phrase spoken by one who has recently been delivered of an uncomfortably hard arse baby. 'Christ. I knew I should of chewed them fucking crisps up a bit more last night. I feel like I've shat out a Lego garage. Anyway, welcome to In Our Time. This week I'll be discussing the teachings of St Thomas Aquinas with Dr Patrick Pending of Cambridge University, Sir Basil Herb, emeritus professor of Theology at Imperial College, London and the philosopher Alain de Bottom.'

Lego pineapple n. An extremely knobbly and uncomfortable *Thora*. *'Now there's some sad things known to man / But ain't too much sadder than the tears of a clown / When he just crapped out a Lego pineapple.'* (from *The Tears of a Clown* by Smokey Robinson and the Bandits).

lemon enders n. A variety of female nipple that may be squeezed onto pancakes.

lemon meringue n. The deeply unedifying sight of a bowl of bright yellow *piss* topped off with a frothy morning *flob* that the previous bastard has failed to flush. *'Fuck's sake, Posh. You've left a lemon meringue in the shit pot again.'*

Lenovo lunch euph. A veritable feast of crumbs and dead skin obtained by turning your laptop upside down.

lepers' finger buffet, like a sim. Said when something is a mess. *'Don't you think it's about time you tidied the house up a bit, dear? The boss is coming round for dinner tonight and the place is like a lepers' finger buffet.'*

les beau n. A dandy fellow who enjoys the company of *three-wheelers*. A *dykey likey*.

lesbeen n. A *lesbidaceous* has-been. A *hasbian, wasbian*.

Les Dawson Creek n. Any area populated by women who resemble the aesthetically-challenged eponymous late comedian in drag. *'Wish me luck. I'm off on the pull at the disco in the downstairs bar at Brough Park dog track.' 'I wouldn't bother, mate. It's like Les Dawson Creek in there.'*

let's have a record exclam. A conversation-restarting phrase, to be deployed after a sudden *dropped gut* has silenced the room. To be delivered in the manner of Kirsty Young on Radio 4's *Desert island Discs*, introducing the next tune after her guest has reminisced themselves to a standstill whilst re-living some childhood trauma or other.

let the dog out v. To release a ferocious *arse barker* immediately upon waking. *'Sorry about that, love. I had to let the dog out, only it's been scratching at the back door all night.'*

let the wife down euph. Of peripatetic musicians, *banging* groupies whilst on tour. *'Hello? Claridges Room service?' 'Yeah, could you send up a cine camera, a length of rope and a live mudshark to room 308 please? I'm about to let my wife down.' 'Certainly Mr Bonham.'*

Libyan uprising euph. A morning of violence in the *Benghazi area*. A stinging dose of the *Dickie dirts* after a plethora of dark beer and piquant provender.

life and arsehole of the party euph. At a convivial social gathering, one who is about as popular as a *bellend* infection. A *pisswizard*.

lift and separate n. Named in honour of the erstwhile *titpants* advertising slogan; a sophisticated, eco-friendly and modern *buttocks*-spread *shitting* technique that saves a fortune in *arse paper*.

lift the latch n. To shift one's bodyweight onto a single cheek in order to facilitate a release of *carbon dibaxide*.

light bender n. A person of such large proportions that their enormous bulk distorts space-time, causing light to distort around it, as explained in Einstein's *Theory of General Relativity*. *'Today's birthdays: Lil Wayne (real name Dwayne Michael Carter), rap singer, 29; Alvin Stardust (real name Shane Fenton & the Fentones), pop star, 69; Meat Loaf (real name Alvin & the Chipmunks), light bender, 64.'*

light the brown touchpaper v. To initiate the *shitting* process. Usually achieved via the first smoke and coffee of the day, after which one should stand well back with one's fingers in one's ears.

like starting an outboard motor *sim*. Descriptive of the action required to lovingly remove a string of anal beads from one's inamorata's *rusty sheriff's badge*. A *Suffolk punch*.

lion's breakfast *n*. A particularly unkempt *gorilla's wallet*.

lion walk *n*. Sticking your *balls* out backwards between your legs and - not surprisingly in the circumstances - roaring in the style of a big cat.

lip service *1. n*. Hollow compliments that a gentleman gives to a piece of *blart* upon whom he has designs. *2. n*. The act of dining at the Y. *3. n*. The missus's visit to the *snatch dentist* for her annual *mot test*.

lirthy *adj*. Both lengthy and girthy.

little fluffy clouds *exclam*. A suitable phrase which can be used to great effect in the immediate aftermath of a rousing *rumpet voluntary*. *S*poken in a girlish, nasally-congested voice similar to that of Rickie Lee Jones with a heavy cold as heard on the eponymous record by The Orb.

little pink bag of shit *n*. An alternative to the more clichéd "little bundle of joy" used to describe a *fanny apple*. *'Births: Locksbottom. At the Portland Hospital, London. To Lady Fellatia (née Smegmeaux) and Sir Turdfrith, a boy, Stradivarius, brother to Bendibus and Clitorice. Mother and little pink bag of shit doing well. Deo Gracias.'* (*The Times* Jan 30th 2012).

llama's top lip *n*. A *camel's toe*.

Llandudno handbag *n*. A colostomy bag.

LNS *abbrev*. Quality time spent peacefully communing with the world. A Late Night Shite.

loaf that dare not speak its name *euph*. A freshly-baked, crusty *log* that could easily ruin a man-about-town's reputation.

lock on, achieve *v*. When mentally thumbing through ones *mammary banks* whilst *knocking oneself about*, one *achieves lock on* when a particularly debasing erotic episode is recollected, leading to a satisfactory conclusion to proceedings. *'I tried my best to take advantage of a rarely issued pink ticket but sadly didn't manage to achieve lock on before the missus returned from the shops or seeing her poor old mum or feeding the birds or whatever the fuck it was. To be honest I wasn't listening, your honour.'*

log book *n*. Suitable material for reading whilst *laying a cable*.

log burner *n*. A ferocious *Ruby* that provides a handy source of blistering heat around which the family can gather on cold evenings.

log cabin *n*. The *khazi*.

logging material *n*. Reading matter perused whilst *chopping butt wood*. Also *shiterature, loo reads*.

log in the woodburner, got a *euph*. A genteel expression of one's urgent need for a *sit down lavatory adventure*. *'And God said unto Noah, I will bring a great flood upon the earth to destroy the corruption and evil that I hath created. Make thee an ark of gopher wood; rooms shalt thou make in the ark, and the length of the ark shall be three hundred cubits, the breadth of it fifty cubits, and the height of it thirty cubits. And you shall fill it with all the animals of the earth; the fowls after their kind, the cattle after their kind and every creeping thing of the ground by his kind, two of every sort shall come unto you, to keep them alive. And Noah said unto the Lord, I'll get it started in a minute once I've had a shite, only I've got a log in the woodburner at the moment.'* (from *Genesis* 6:13-15).

logzilla *n*. A monstrous *duty* that causes onlookers to run away screaming.

sews his own buttons on *euph.* Said of a *sensitive* man who is *good with colours, knows what's in his flowerbeds, bakes a light cake, doesn't play poker* and is *first on the dancefloor.* A chap with *nice nails.*

sex drive *n.* A jolly motorised sojourn to a *dogging* site in one's shooting brake. *'I'm off for a sex drive, dear. Do you want anything bringing back while I'm out?' 'Ooh, can you get me Steve McFadden and Stan Collymore's autographs please, love?'*

sex meringue *n.* The sticky, white, albuminious foam that's created after an over-aggressive bout of *stabbing the cat.*

sex pat *n.* A chap of a certain age whose only reason for leaving the shores of blighty to live abroad is his propensity for encounters with local ladies and/or ladyboys who are young enough to be his daughters and/or daughtersons.

sexual outercourse *1. n.* Masturbation. *2. n.* Dogging.

Shackleton's shaft *n.* A dire state of genital hygiene resulting from failing to clean one's *bellend* or change one's *undercrackers* every month as one is supposed to.

shady milkman *n.* A seedy character who flogs his *man jam* down at the local *wham bank* on a daily basis.

shag pile *n.* A subsidiary residence maintained principally as a venue for penetrative, extra-marital liaisons. A *fur trapper's cabin* or *stabbin' cabin.* *'Mr Plywood has been MP for Fulchester Sunnybrook since 1987, and was recently appointed Minister for Family Values in the coalition government. He lives in the constituency with his wife and three children, and has a small shag pile near the Palace of Westminster.'*

shake a seven *v.* To *gamble and lose.*

shake 'n' bake *1. n.* Some sort of proprietary breadcrumb-based coating for pork or chicken. *2. n.* The peculiar physiological phenomenon whereby a person who is on a jog or run feels the sudden, inexplicable need to *lay a cable.* *'Today's birthdays: Bob Guccione, US bongo magnate, 82; Bernard Hill, Yosser Hughes actor and Baxter's Beetroot Chutneys and Sauces ad voiceover man, 68; Paula Radcliffe, Olympic Marathon-running shake 'n' bake champion, 39.'*

shakes on a plane *n.* Joining the *mile I club. Making like a Chinese helicopter pilot* in an aeroplane toilet.

shame glaze *n.* The shimmering crystalline sheen of ignominious varnish left upon one's person following an act of *self harm. Dutch polish.*

shammy batter *n.* KY jelly. Also *phoney batter, I can't believe it's not batter, granny batter, fuck butter, pork pie jelly.* *'TERRY: Eurgh! June, this margerine tastes horrible. JUNE: That's not margerine, Terry. It's Great Aunt Lucy's tub of shammy batter.'* (script of *Terry & June*, BBC TV, February 1832).

Shane *n.* A once grubby, rowdy mate who has formed a new relationship and simultaneously undergone a complete makeover of both appearance and behaviour. From Australian cricketer Shane Warne, who seems to of went all metrosexual now he's *banging* that Liz Hurley.

Shane McGowan's toothbrush, it looked like *sim.* Descriptive of a particularly heavily-soiled *bogbrush* of the sort typically found in a bookies' toilet.

shank *n.* A multi-tasking lavatory adventure. From shit + wank.

share a tent *euph.* To be *on safari. 'Didn't you hear? (name removed on legal advice) off (programme removed on legal advice) used to share a tent with Princess (name removed on legal advice).'*

shaternity leave *n.* A statutory period of rest and recuperation after the birth of a *mudchild,* during which one is not required to do any work. *'I'm afraid the doctor can't see you now. She's on shaternity leave.'*

shatoll *n*. The highest part of a mound of *dumpage* which breaks the surface of the toilet water, thus forming a small, brown island which is unsuitable for human habitation. A *misty mountain top.*

she can give it back to me as small as she likes *exclam*. Said by a sexist fellow in appreciation of a lady that he would ideally like to *slip a length to.*

Sheila feeler *n*. An Antipodean *lady golfer.*

shelf restraint *n*. The admirable willpower which must be summoned by a fellow in order to resist the temptation to treat himself to a nice new *niff mag* at the newsagent. *'For God's sake Mr Larkin, show some shelf restraint. That ceiling's going to come through if you try to put any more cunt-books in the attic.'*

shelter belter *n*. A young lady who specialises in *having it off* at bus stops.

shepherd's pie *n*. A main course in the *pan;* a layer of hot brown *bum-mince*, topped with a fluffy white "mash" of *arsewipe* and finished off with a yellow "crust" of *Tweedledee.*

Shergar, do a *v*. To mysteriously disappear during a night out, only to turn up later in a kebab shop.

shick *v*. To defecate and vomit at the same time, following a cracking night on the ale. From shit + sick.

shift a round bale *1. v.* On a farm, to transport one of them big bundles of hay, usually tightly wrapped in black or white polythene, usually at 4mph during rush hour so as to cause the maximum annoyance to other road users. *2. v.* To *forklift* a lass *with a lovely personality*, especially if she is wearing an ill-advisedly skintight black or white outfit.

shifting cement *n*. A fatiguing act of *one-handed filthy concrete* mixing. *'Anyone seen Dave with my copy of Nuts?' 'Yeah, he's shifting cement with it in the crapper.'*

shirt snifter *n*. Of a normally red-blooded male, a brief, temporary foray into a previously unknown world of interior design, male grooming products or cookery.

shit an angry squid *euph*. To pass a less-than-solid motion.

shit bumpers *n*. Polite euphemism for the b*ttocks. *'Phwooar! That Serena Williams has got some rare old shit bumpers on her, eh Cliff?'*

shit chisel *n*. A stout tool used when *mining for gold* in *kak canyon.*

shitecap *n*. A well-deserved *poo* just before bedtime.

shit in a doorway, stand out like a *sim*. *'"What do you think of my new trousers, Jeeves?' I expostulated. 'These knee-length houndstooth twill bags are all the go at the Drones Club this season, you know. I thought I'd wear them for Tuppy Glossop's wake tomorrow, but I'm wondering if they might not be a little ostentatious for such a sombre bash.' 'Ostentatious isn't, if you'll excuse me for saying so, sir, the word,' opined the perspicacious manservant. 'If you wear them kecks for a funeral, I can guarantee that you'll stand out like a shit in a doorway.'* (from *I Was Only Following Orders, Jeeves* by PG Wodehouse).

shit in the Queen's handbag, it would be easier to *sim*. A measure of the difficulty of a task. *'Removing yourself from Facebook is theoretically possible, but to be frank, it would be easier to shit in the Queen's handbag.'*

shit knot *n*. A knot made by re-tying lots and lots of little knots in the vain hope that it will hold. Like a slip knot but *shit. 'I simply can't imagine why that wardrobe came loose from the roof of my car in the fast lane, officer. It was fastened securely with a length of stout garden twine which I tied to the radio aerial with a large shit knot.'*

shit lips *n*. Affectionate term for a sycophantic person. *'Situations vacant: A national pop music radio station is looking to recruit an experienced shit lips to sit in the studio and agree with an overweight, sweating fuckwit on its breakfast show.'* (advert in *Broadcast* magazine, 2003).

shit shoveller's crack *n*. A less than fragrant *bottom burp*. *'Jesus, your majesty. No offence, but hat one smells like a shit shoveller's crack.'*

shit shy *adj*. Constipated. *'Strewth, doc. Can you squirt something up there, only I ate fifteen Scotch eggs for a bet and I've been shit shy for a fortnight.'*

shit the bed *1. euph*. To make a big mistake. *'Addressing the Parliamentary Committee on Culture, Media and Sport, BBC Director General George Entwistle admitted that he had really shit the bed over his handling of the Newsnight investigation into Jimmy Savile.'* 2. *exclam*. A sudden shout of alarm or frustration when one realises one has made a big mistake. *'Shit the bed! I've agreed to go and address the Parliamentary Committee on Culture, Media and Sport this afternoon.'*

shit thickener *n*. Any foodstuff taken on board in an attempt to stem the flow of rusty water from one's *arse* following a night *on the pop*. *'Ooh, I feel terrible, your holiness. I must have had a bad pint or something.' 'Bless you my son. Here, have some of me scratchings as a shit thickener. Oi, not that many, you theiving cunt.'*

shitelight *n*. The big light that goes on in the bathroom when having a *sit down toilet adventure*, even on the sunniest days, due to its being wired to the same switch as the extractor fan.

shitoris *n. medic*. The sensitive bundle of nerves up a fellow's *jacksie* that get stimulated during *bottery*. The prostrate gland, *tremble trigger* or *walnut*.

shitpickers *n*. Dog owners. *'Cruft's is the world's greatest dog show, and once again dishevelled shitpickers from all over the country have descended on the NEC here in Birmingham, all hoping to win the trophy for Best in Show.'*

shitter's smirk *n*. The stoical rictus grin that accompanies the experience of squirting *dirty water* through a tattered *Wigan rosette*.

shittoon *n*. The *thundermug* or *porcelain god*, especially when in receipt of something less-than-usually solid. From the other side of the room.

shitzkreig *n*. An unstoppable, hostile force which overwhelms one on the toilet.

shiver shit *v*. Of a constipated dog, to labour particularly hard whilst laying an *egg*. 2. *n*. A disparaging monicker bestowed upon one who wimps out of a soft task, *eg*. Taking his 5-year-old on the 'Ben 10 - Ultimate Mission' family rollercoaster at Drayton Manor.

shoe horn *n*. The glottal contortions apparent in the tongue of a *grot* actress when she is preparing to swallow a broad-fitting foot.

shoot oneself in the cock *v*. To perform a self-destructive act that unintentionally scuppers one's chances of scoring with a member of the opposite sex. *'With the benefit of hindsight, it was a definite error of judgement to tell my mother-in-law about the Rugby Club World Brothel Tour of 1986-2007 that took in Soho, Hamburg, Thailand, Amsterdam and Leeds, on our first date. I definitely shot myself in the cock there.'*

shopkeeper *n*. Someone who is not in the vicinity of the bar when it is their round, but who miraculously appears when it is someone else's shout. Named after the proprietor of the fancy dress shop frequented by single man Mr Benn in the 1970s children's television series of the same name, who would materialise "as if by magic" when his sole customer entered his seemingly-empty establishment.

short back and sympathy *euph*. A cod haircut performed by an indulgent barber upon the pate of a balding gent, which involves making clipping noises near the customer's ears whilst throwing a bit of hair about to add realism.

shovel recce *euph. milit.* Used by members of HM Forces on manoeuvres when they wander off in search of somewhere quiet to *drop the shopping.*

shower babies *n.* The clingy offspring of a spot of *self delight* in the shower.

shower cock *n.* The ideal penis size when using a communal shower facility; neither too small nor too erect. A *quarter-on, Goldicock.*

shredded wheat *n.* A large, wholesome, vigorous and surprisingly well-groomed blonde *landing strip* of the sort which is found on most German ladies of a certain vintage, apparently.

shreddies 1. *n. Underchunders.* 2. *n.* The tiny little threadbare *Hitler 'taches* typically seen on videographic models.

shwiss *n.* Portmanteau term for a comprehensive trifecta of toilet functions performed by a person with a busy schedule. From shit + wank + piss. *'Baggs the Brand, you're fired. I'm off for a shwiss.'*

sick off *n.* A competitive event where contestants attempt to vomit the furthest, normally from a raised platform, balcony or dais. *'It's a good job finally Ed won it on the unions vote. The rest of the results were so close we thought at one point we were going to have to decide it with a sick off.'*

signalman's rag, stiff as a *sim.* A colourful turn of phrase dating from the days when a railway signalman would spend all day alone in his box with little to do except while away the hours *relaxing in a gentleman's way* - a tradition still kept alive by volunteers at heritage railways throughout the country.

silent roar 1. *n.* Trade name of the small pellets containing lion excrement, the smell of which scares cats from flower beds for up to six months. 2. *n.* A *feeshus* dropped in the toilet, the smell of which keeps everyone out of the bathroom for up to six months.

silly cones *n.* Implausible fake breasts.

silver blurtch *n.* The withered fleece to be found 'twixt the legs of a *coffin dodger. Gash in the attic.*

Simba *n.* Holding one's mobile phone skywards like out of that bit in *the Lion King* in a vain attempt to to acquire a signal whilst in a rural area. Or, if you're on Vodafone, whilst anywhere at all, including standing on a ladder next to a Vodafone aerial mast.

simpleston *n.* A dim-witted fellow who finds nothing more amusing than them fucking GoCompare meerkat adverts.

sinky *n.* The *gentleman's wash* taken by a married man in preparation for his annual *Boris Johnson.*

Sir Alan's lieutenants *n.* The sour-faced duo who hang around underneath one's *Lord Sugar. The gonk-faced Mother Teresa sisters, McSquirter twins.*

sitting, standing, leaning 1. *n.* One of the hilarious, totally improvised rounds in the hilarious, totally improvised gameshow *Whose Line is it Anyway?,* throughout which each of the three contestants was required to adopt one of the specified postures at all times. 2. *n.* In any *troilistic* pornographic scenario, a common arrangement of the participating artistes, adopted in order to facilitate the filming of *DPs, spitroasts, anal titwanks, sticky belly flapcocks etc.*

situation room, the *n.* The *water closet.*

six knuckle shuffle *n.* An act of *personal pollution* enjoyed by one who lives in a rural community on the Norfolk, Lincolnshire and Cambridgeshire borders.

skagamuffin *n.* A colourful street urchin with the impressive ability to transmute shoplifted goods, his landlord's furniture and friends' giros into narcotics.

skate wings *n.* Very large, fishy, pink *piss flaps.* Often served with a white, creamy sauce.

sket vet *n.* The clinic where a fellow must take his *cocker* when it picks up a *Doonican* such as *happyrash,* the *pox* or *galloping knob rot.*

ski-ba bop-ba-dop bop *exclam.* Said as one is just about to *go down* on a partner's anal cavity. Aptly taken from the lyrics of the one-hit-wonder *I'm a Scatman* by Scatman John.

skidney stones *n.* The solid consequences of *netting a serve*, found rolling around in the *sump* of the *underchunders.*

skidoo *n.* A Glühwein-fuelled *wind sketch* in the salopettes that is accompanied by a high-pitched buzz reminiscent of an over-revved two-stroke engine.

skiff *v.* To rub one's sweaty *arse vinegar* onto an item to be used by another person. *'Room service was good, although I noticed that my toothbrush, face flannel and shaving brush had been thoroughly skiffed by the maid whilst I was enjoying my splendid full English breakfast in the elegant Tudor dining room.'*

skimming *n.* A discreet act performed by a gentleman who secretly wants to avoid getting his broody missus up the stick; regularly *beating his meat* in order to "skim off" the healthiest *tadpoles* from his *man milk.*

skinstick *n.* A tumescent *bum beater.*

skin the rabbit *v.* To forcefully pull the pelt off an *old friend.*

skunking *n.* The rejection of one's partner's amorous advances by employing a defence mechanism similar to that of the American stink badger, namely the release of a noisome scent from the anal region. Usually an even more effective deterrent than claiming to have a headache.

skunt *n.* A person what skis. From ski + cunt.

skwype *v.* To clean the screen of one's computer following an adult-oriented video conferencing session.

skydiver's mouth *n.* A post-coital *flange* that resembles nothing so much as the *gob* of a thrill-seeking dangerous sports enthusiast as he plunges vertically and inevitably towards a shattered pelvis.

Sky News sofa slot *n.* Before they have to leave the house on their morning commute, the window of opportunity afforded to satellite television subscribers from 7.45am Monday to Friday to squeeze out their morning *fruit juice* whilst savouring the visual delights of a selection of inappropriately-dressed Sky News anchorwomen. Female viewers have to make do with a *bean flick* to the appropriately-surnamed James Whale.

skyrim *1. n. Dungeons and Dragons*-style Space Invaders game played by translucent adolescents. *2. n.* Contactless form of *anilingus* as depicted in cheaper foreign *art pamphlets* with names like *Asshole Fucker - In Action!* (3.99 from most kiosks in Jerez, Spain).

slag-a-pult *n.* An aircraft belonging to a budget airline. So called due to the fact that its primary function is to fire drunken young ladies across Europe.

slaggle *v.* To barter with a *lady of the night* for a better value *knock up*.

slashback *n. A wet penny in the pocket.* Visual evidence of leakage in the *honeymoon area* following a trip to *turn one's bike around.*

sleepover *n.* The sort of miraculous hangover enjoyed by students, jobseekers and bar personnel the world over whereby, following a surfeit of booze, they simply remain comatose throughout all the unpleasantness and wake up on the other side with a slightly dry mouth and feeling a bit hungry.

slip on *1. n.* A type of shoe worn by someone who doesn't know how to tie his laces. *2. n.* A petite lady whom a gent can lift easily and "slip on" his *knob. A fisherman's sock.*

slob *n.* A *slight lob*, not even a quarter of a teacake. Certainly nothing to write home about.

slow puncture *n.* The soul-destroying act of attempting to keep *shagging* after you have *chucked your muck*. From the fact that "you can keep it hard as long as you keep pumping, but as soon as you stop it's all over." *'Pass the tissues, Kate. I seem to have a slow puncture.'*

sluice noose *n.* The string that hangs off the end of a *jam rag* which is *in situ* when *Arsenal are playing at home*. The *white mouse's tail, Fishwick.*

Sly TV *n.* Illegally-accessed satellite television. *'Right love, I'm off to the boozer to watch the footie on the Sly TV. It's beamed in from Uzbekistan on the Eurobird, so the commentary will be all tits and thumbs.'*

smack fairy *n.* A cheeky imp that gives you a right leathering. *'Fucking hell, Shane. What happened to you?' 'I don't know, I was like this when I woke up. I must've got a visit from the smack fairy in the night.'*

smash *1. n.* Brand of instant mashed potato popularised by tin Kermits with Dalek voices in the 1970s. *2. v. Grumble* channel-specific euphemism for "fuck" popularised by lycanthropic, unemancipated ex-Sky Sports presenter and offside rule expert Richard Keys.

smashed tarantula *n.* An hirsute *butcher's dustbin.* Also *stamped bat.*

smash it like a cheap glass, I'd *phr.* Humorous exclamation that signals a lecherous, overweight, impotent, sweating, purple-faced television football pundit's intention to engage in momentary coitus with an attractive young lady.

smash or dash? *exclam. interrog.* Humorously rhyming question of the sort typically posed to one another by TalkSport presenters when they spot a female in the street.

smashturbate *v.* To *wank* so violently that you damage your *plums.*

smeg pegs *n.* Buck teeth which are particularly useful for grating the cheese off a chap's *herman gelmet. 'Don't forget to brush your smeg pegs before you go to bed, Janet.'*

smellody *n. Chamber music* played on a *wind instrument.*

smoke a fag *v.* To perform a *Boris Johnson* upon a gent who *sews his own buttons on.*

smoke out the mole *v.* To avail oneself of the laxative effects of the first *Harry Wragg* of the day.

smoker's cough *n.* The phlegmy substance that the *bag for life* leaves in the *Rick Witter* after you have been *boffing* her up the *whispering Bob* all night.

smooth as snake shit *sim.* A phrase used to describe a bloke who has unrivalled success chatting up the ladies, such as Callum Best, and can also be used to describe the miraculous effect of Gillette's new 10-blade razor on one's chin. Also *smoother than silkworm shit.*

smunt *1. n.* A freshening mint surreptitiously inserted into the folds of a particularly malodorous *furry hoop* prior to performing an act of *cumulonimbus* thereupon. May range in size and strength from a Tic-Tac to a Trebor Extra-Strong, depending on the relative aroma level and the space available. Also *bint imperial, crack bullet* and *sminge. 2. n.* A smug *cunt.* From smug + cunt. *'Sebastian! Sebastian! Big smile over here for the Standard, you smunt.'*

smut butter *n. Man paste, jazz funk, baby gravy, Winner's sauce.*

smurf's hat *n.* A freshly-filled *dunky. 'Please dispose of sanitary napkins and smurf's hats in the receptacle provided.'*

snack whore *n.* A lady who *does it* for a Greggs vanilla slice, a steak bake or a bag of pickled onion Monster Munch rather than freebase cocaine.

snake eater *n.* A *nosh artist* whose skills rival with that of a mongoose. A *sword swallower.*

snap ET's neck *v.* To *crimp off a length of dirty back.*

snarting *n.* Simultaneously snoring and *farting.* *'I couldn't get to sleep last night. The missus wouldn't stop snarting.'*

snatch fit *adj.* Back on active service after a week on the *blob bench.*

snatchoo *n. onomat.* A sudden sneeze from a lady's *quimpiece* either during, or just after, intercourse. *'Snatchoo!' 'Bless you, Sue.'*

snatchos *n.* Dried flakes drizzled with sour cream and festooned with cheese, sometimes served with a spicy meat filling in the back row of the cinema.

snedds *n. Lincs.* Flatlander argot for *winnits.*

snicker stool *n.* A vegetarian's nut-enriched *arse bar.*

snish *n.* The result of a person with poor bladder control sneezing. From sneeze + pish. Also *a-pissue.*

snoaking *n.* The time-honoured pastime of putting a lady's used *dunghampers* up to one's face, covering the nostrils and mouth and inhaling the *fent* from her *smush piece.* *'I'm sorry Lord Archer. You'll have to leave the premises. This is a no snoaking brothel.'*

snood *n.* A *fiveskin* that bunches loosely around the neck of the *tallywhacker*, due to historic *banjo string* trauma.

snowcapping *n. milit.* Whilst on manoucvrcs, to lose one's *officer's mess* onto the summit of a mountain of ordure, Kilimanjaro-style. A bit like *icing the log*, but with a larger pile of *feculant.*

SOC/soc *acronym.* A.N. Other. Some Other Cunt. *'That wasn't me who put dog shit in the collection box, vicar. It was SOC.'*

SOCK/sock *acronym.* Some Other Cunt's Kid.

sock monkey *n.* A single man who is well-versed in the art of *self pollution.*

sockrifice *v.* To forfeit an item of male hosiery on the altar of *gentlemanly relaxation.*

soda scream *n.* The unintelligible *pop shot* outburst of a chap who is *getting busy with the jizzy.*

soda stream *n.* An underwater bath-time trump. An *Edward Woodward, tottle, blooper* or *bottle of olives.*

sodcasting *n.* The act of a *scratter* relaying the ringtones, clownstep remixes and new monkey mash-ups off his mobile telephone for the benefit of the other passengers on the bus, train *etc.* A term coined by Radio 4 presenter Evan Davis on that station's flagship *Today* programme.

soggy mag *n.* An *al fresco art pamphlet* found in a lay-by or under a hedge. *Grummer.*

soggy pocket *n.* A lady's *minge* which is deep enough to stash your car keys and loose change in. Not as capacious as *Mary Poppin's bag.*

solitaire *1. n.* A procrastinatory single-player card game featured in a 1973 song by disproportionately large-*noggined* US crooner Andy Williams. *2. n.* A *procrasturbatory* game played by lonely gentlemen whereby they repeatedly *deal themselves a losing hand.*

solitary joy, the *euph.* The monomanual vice of monks and teenage boys.

someone's moving in next door *exclam.* A witty rejoinder when someone *steps on a duck.* A reference to the sound of heavy furniture being dragged across barc wooden floorboards in an adjoining room. Also *ooh, get her!; language Timothy; that tuba needs tuning; that's all I have to say on the matter; thank-you for the music.*

sonic & knuckles *1. n.* A mid-nineties Sega Mega Drive game starring a colourful hedgehog. *2. n. One off the wrist* performed at the speed of sound.

SONPA/sonpa *acronym.* A *bit on the side* who knows her place. Sex Only No Public Appearances.

sook the pish oot her knickers *exclam. Scots.* A colloquial phrase emphasising the attractiveness of a member of the opposite sex. *'Och, Granpaw. Did ye see yon tits on thae Sophie Raworth readin' the news last nicht?' 'Aye, Wullie a did. She's got a braw pair, thae lassie. Y'ken, ah'd sook the pish oot her knickers.'*

SOS *abbrev.* A Shirt Off Shit. A proper blue collar act of defecation that makes you feel all manly like the bloke hitting the gong at the start of a Rank film or a galley slave in *Ben Hur.*

sound of trumpets, going in to the *euph.* Undertaking a desperate, last-ditch cavalry charge to the *khazi to the accompaniment of* a stirring *brass eye* fanfare.

sovereign's entrance *1. n.* The gate of Victoria Tower at the Palace of Westminster, which is only accessed on very special occasions such as the State Opening of Parliament. *2. n.* The *bumhole.*

spacehopper caught in a snare *n.* The upsetting *backside* of a larger *bird* who has unwisely decided to effect a thong. And has an orange *arse* with a big tattoo of Parsley the Lion on it.

spaffa cake *n.* A middle class version of the classic *soggy biscuit* game.

spaghetti girl *euph.* She who can be persuaded into *lesbism* when sufficiently aroused. One who is "straight until she is wet".

spaghetti bollocknaise *n.* The multiple thin white strands draped over an actress's face in the final scenes of a *Frankie flick.*

spaghetti spunk *n.* The impossible-to-remove residue which remains after straining the popular cylindrical Italian foodstuff. *'Have you done the washing-up, Charles?' 'Yeah, but I couldn't get the spaghetti spunk out the sieve I'm afraid, Nigella.'*

spam chow mein *n. Silly string* that you want another portion of after ten minutes. *Popshot noodles, chopper suey.*

spank plankton *n.* Bath-borne *tadpoles.*

Spar jellyfish *n.* Soft-bodied marine wildlife often seen floating in the waters off Britain's east coast. Discarded carrier bags. Also *Londis jellyfish, Iceland man o' war.*

sparf *n.* What comes up when a *bird's* gag reflex fails while she is chowing down on a *love dagger.* From spunk + barf.

special resin *1. n.* The viscid fluid used by Gavin from the Autoglass adverts to fill chipped windscreens. *2. n.* A viscid fluid used to fill ladies' *twats.*

speed bumps *n.* An impressive set of *top bollards* on a new conquest which means that one approaches the *vinegar strokes* somewhat more quickly than usual.

speedballing *n.* Bizarre sexual practice whereby the female lies on her back and repeatedly punches a straddling fella's *knackersack*, bouncing it off his arse and shaft and building up a rhythm in the style of a boxer at the gym.

spegg *n.* An incredibly unappealing person who makes one ponder the 300 million-to-one miracle of human reproduction. From sperm + egg. *'Today's birthdays: Celine Dion, long-faced Canadian screecher, 43; MC Hammer, low-gussetted US rapper, 49; Piers Morgan, cuntish spegg, 46.'*

spermaid *n.* In the absence of a proper *fluff mag*, any depiction of a female which is pressed into service as inspiration during a bout of *monomanual self pleasure, eg.* Any half-decent bird found on a holiday brochure, knitting pattern or Quality Street tin.

spewnami *n.* A tidal wave of *puke.* From spew + nami.

sphincter gnats *n. medic.* What feels like an army-sized infestation of belligerent, stinging *arse wasps.* *'Sort out your sphincter gnats with these wet wipes, now half price until April. Every little helps.'*

spider man *n.* A chap who has white, sticky hands after spending all day "on the web".

spinnickers *n. Underchunders* as worn by

more amply-*arsed* women. Named after the large, baggy sails hoisted by yachtsmen on still days. Though a lack of wind's probably not so much of a problem round the stern of a fat *bird*.

spinster's Ginster's, drier than a *sim*. A *slice* that is notably lacking in moisture. The *pie* of a woman who is long past her best before date on the motorway services fridge shelf of life.

spin the jam/spread the jam *euph*. To *finger* a lady who's *on the blob*.

splash one's clogs *v*. To have a *wee*.

splash the mash *v*. To ejaculate onto your *bird's tits,* leaving a residue which looks like a bit of your grandad's dinner.

split from the peloton *euph*. After a prolonged period of severe constipation, to finally put some distance between oneself and one's *foulage*.

spoilt paper *n*. A saucy photogravure that has been fouled with *jipper.*

spray egg *v*. Of an excitable female, to *ejillulate.*

spring roll *euph*. When one has more skin than meat on a cold day, due to *shrinkage.*

sprogs or logs *phr*. Mankind's eternal dilemma, *viz*. Whether to go for the *easy pink* or the *difficult brown.*

SPSM *n*. *Ad hoc* unit of measurement used by local councils and police forces to categorise certain *economically challenged* locales. Staffies Per Square Mile.

spuff leach *n*. A small slug of congealed *jipper* clinging tenaciously to the leg of a chap who has just *gripped the lather.*

spunch *n*. A forceful *facial* that causes the stunned recipient to recoil. A *white hook.*

spunk cousin *n*. A member of a fellow's extended *spam-ily tree* who has slept with the same woman that he has. Also *custard cousin.*

spunk dado rail *n*. A crusty frieze-like excrescence at about waist-height on the bedroom wall of a single young man.

spunktastic *adj*. Erotically enervating. *'Have you seen Kylie's lingerie video? It's absolutely spunktastic.'*

spunktrough *n*. The conveniently-located elliptical depression found atop a lady's sternum at the base of her throat, which forms a convenient receptacle for any overflowing semi-viscid liquid which may dribble from her mouth for any reason.

spunk trunk *n*. A prehensile *cock* that could easily spray *jipper* all over Johnny Morris. Let's just stop and savour that mental image for a moment, shall we.

spurt curses *n*. Involuntary profanities shouted out by a bloke as he arrives at the *Billy Mill roundabout*. *'Sorry, Mrs Harris. That was just some spurt curses.' 'That's okay, Cliff. Now quick, get in the wardrobe. I just heard Jet's key in the front door.'*

squeezy beef oxo *n*. Rich *bum gravy* that requires intense abdominal clenching to expunge from the *Simon Cowells.*

squirrel's nostril *n*. An exceptionally tight, tufty *ringpiece.*

squit thrusts *n*. Involuntary spasms in the *nipsy* during a bout of diarrhoea, that precipitate a rapid and bountiful ejection of *fizzy gravy* and a sore *arse* for afters. *Spurting superstars.*

SSSWSO *abbrev. Pol*. She Said She Was Sixteen, Officer.

stab wound in a gorilla's back *sim*. A charmingly poetic evocation of an ungroomed *blurtch.*

staggered start *n*. A marathon *dump* session in which the release of *runners* is punctuated by distinct periods of frustrating inactivity. A *handicrapped race to the beach.*

stamp licker *n*. A *bird's quimpiece* which is so wet that it could be usefully employed in the despatch department of a busy mail order business.

starching your socks *euph. Relaxing in a*

gentleman's way into a convenient item of hosiery. *'MARGO: Jerry! Jerry! Open this door immediately! What are you doing in there? JERRY: (pokes head round door) Just starching my socks, dear. It's just that Barbara's bending over to plant some spuds next door. And if I crouch on top of the wardrobe and angle the dressing table mirror just right, I can get a great view of her arse.'* (Extract from script of *The Good Life Easter Special*, BBC TV 1978).

starfish enterprise *n.* Guile and native cunning used when attempting "to boldly go where no man has gone before".

start up Guinevere *euph.* To pull the handle after dropping six brown balls and a bonus.

start up Hearts *v.* To produce an extremely loose *flock of pigeons*, from the similarity of the sound to that produced at the beginning of the eponymous card game which is bundled with Windows. To *drop a load of old shoes out of the loft.*

staying up to watch Family Guy *euph.* White lie told by a gent to his better half at bedtime, allowing him the opportunity for a spot of uninterrupted *self pollution* over the ten-minute *fanny*-free free-view on the *fanny channel.*

stealing petrol, sucks cock like she's *sim.* Said of a fellatrix who goes at it enthusiastically like a *scratter* syphoning unleaded from a car in a lay-by.

steel steamer *n.* A foaming, rearing, thoroughbred *horse's handbrake* that appears to be giving off vapour like a Grand National winner.

steam off ma lash *phr. Scot.* An infinitessimal estimation of the value of someone or something. *'Och, ye paid how much to see yon Michael MacIntyre in concert? I wouldnae gie him the steam off ma lash.'*

steeped in theatrical tradition *euph.* Pissed as an astronaut. *'My next guest is steeped in theatrical tradition. Ladies and gentlemen, a big hand for Mr Oliver Reed.'*

Steinbecks *n. Chalfonts, Tate & Lyles* or *farmers.* Named after the Pullitzer Prize-winning author of T*he Grapes of Wrath,* not to mention *Of Mice and Haemorrhoids. 'Ooh, Jesus wept. These fucking Steinbecks are giving me some gyp today, I can tell you. And now over to Daniel Corbett for the weather.'*

stella stairlift *n.* Ascending to one's bedroom on one's hands and knees at the conclusion of a heavy night on the *Nelson.*

St Elmo's fire *1. n.* 1985 hit by Worksop-born American hairdresser John Parr. *2. n.* Luminous plasma due to a coronal discharge from a grounded object in an electric field, for example around the rigging of a ship, caused by the influence of Catholic martyr St Erasmus of Formiae. *3. n.* The dramatic rectal side effects of a particularly devastating Indian meal, such as one prepared in the kitchens of the Rupali Restaurant, Bigg Market, Newcastle upon Tyne.

stench manicure *n.* The result of a badly-timed structural failure of one's lavatory tissue, leaving one with miasmatically abhorrent cuticles.

Stephen Hawking's homework, hard as *sim.* Said of something particularly unyielding. *'Effluvia was powerless to resist. Imbroglio's eyes burnt into hers like hydrogrossular garnets. His muscular business magnet's arms enfolded her softly yielding body as she felt herself being swept away in a tropical cyclone of passion. Holding her close, he put his lips close to her ear and whispered the words she had longed to hear off him for so long. 'Come and have a suck on me cock, love. It's as hard as Stephen Hawking's homework.'* (from *The Lady and the Man* by Barbara Cartland).

stew-pé *n. Fr.* A *faux* pie, typically bought as part of a pub meal. A dish of stew that sports a pastry wig, but doesn't have any fucking pastry on the bottom or round the sides like a proper pie.

stick a long one in the slot *phr.* Humorous instruction to play a lengthy record given by an afternoon radio presenter to his "posse" (short for suppository) when taking leave from his studio to *park his breakfast* in the Radio 2 *shitters. 'Here's a factoid for you. That lamb phaal I had last night is playing havoc with me Simons. I might be gone for some time, so best stick a long one in the slot just in case. And that's copyright.'*

stick your hand up my arse, I've got piles *phr.* A wittily epigrammatic rejoinder that can be employed whenever one is asked for change by carol singers, *Harold ramps* or *chuggers*.

stiffy graph *n.* Scientific scale for the quantification of erectile function in males watching lady tennis players. The parameters of the *stiffy graph* range between zero (Betty Stove lumbering about with her bandaged leg) to ten (Anna Kournikova in a short skirt, bending over to receive a good hard service. Or even playing tennis).

stillborn stoat *n.* A *dead otter* that slips silently under the water's surface.

stinger *1. n.* A device used by the police to impale the tyres of cars driven by criminals and thus instantly slow down the pusuit. *2. n.* A mental image conjured up by a gentleman to instantly slow things down during a *scuttle, eg. One Show* gardening expert Christine Walkden.

stinky toffee pudding *n.* A distinctly unappetising, post-Sunday-dinner *Douglas* with remarkable adhesive properties, meaning that it requires great perseverance to successfully polish it off.

stir the gravy *v.* To agitate the *marmite pot* with the *naughty whisk*. Or something.

St John's wood *n. medic.* A bout of unwanted tumescence which manifests during a christening or funeral.

Stobart *v.* To deposit one's *load* having carefully driven one's *semi* up a particularly tight *loading bay.*

Stoke on Trent *adj. rhym. slang. Whitley Bay. 'Have you met Oscar, Bosie? I'm sure you'll get on like a house on fire. He's well Stoke on Trent too.'*

stomach statue *n.* Easter Island-quality *morning wood.*

stoolmate *n.* The situation that obtains when two persons are seated in adjacent public *crapper* cubicles, each desperate to *drop off their shopping* but waiting for the other to make the first "plop" noise. In a *stoolmate,* neither player is able to move their *Camillas,* and so, after about an hour and a half, a draw is declared.

stool stool *n.* An item of bathroom furniture that doubles up as a makeshift stirrup, enabling one to raise one's ankles while sat on the *bum sink* to ease the delivery of difficult *arse babies.*

straight from the whore's mouth *phr.* A clever figure of speech which can be effectively employed as a rhetorical device during heated debates with members of the opposite sex. *'There you have it, ladies and gentlemen of the jury. Straight from the whore's mouth.'*

strain a Penny Lane *v.* To perform an impressive *rumpet voluntary* that resembles nothing so much as the high-pitched brass solo from the eponymous Beatles song.

straw pole/poll *1. n.* Something carried out for *Newsnight* when there isn't any proper news. *2. n.* A masculine *membrum virile* which, whilst of adequate length, is of such thin and reedy girth that it flops about and could be easily bent, snapped or tied in a reef knot.

stream of unconsciousness *n.* Mystical body of fluid in which one's lower torso is dipped whilst asleep following a surfeit of *happy juice.*

strike a burnt match *v.* To fruitlessly attempt to re-ignite one's *wood* immediately after *blowing one's load*. *'Sorry love, you'll have to give me another twenty minutes. It's like striking a burnt match at the moment.'*

strike gold *v.* Whilst *pan-handling* up another's *creek*, to get a lucky nugget of sweetcorn lodged in one's *Jap's eye*. To have a *kernel blink*.

strike it lucky *phr.* Offer made by a lady whereby a lucky gent can choose which of her sundry orifices in which to *tip his filthy concrete, viz.* Mouth, *minge* or *arse*. Named after the erstwhile *spud-fumbler* and failed swimming pool lifeguard Michael Barrymore's catchphphrase in the erstwhile eponymous gameshow: "Top, middle or bottom. Where do you want to go?"

stringback *1. adj.* Of a pair of gloves, suitable for use whilst driving a Sunbeam Alpine. *2. n.* Whils*t talking to God on the great white telephone*, a thick strand of viscid saliva/vomit that makes contact with the contents of the bowl, thus allowing the *spew* germs to travel back to their progenitor.

stringvestite *n.* Word coined in an episode of *Are You Being Served?*, describing a fellow that *electric-lawnmower-owning* menswear salesman Mr Humphries has met over the weekend at a party in Newcastle upon Tyne.

strumboli *n.* Any fast-fingered solo that builds to a crescendo involving a dramatic eruption.

student's elbow *n. medic.* Undergraduate-specific repetitive strain injury resulting from a combination of excessive masturbation and attempting to knock out a 10,000 word dissertation in three hours using a biro nicked from Argos.

stump grinding *1. n.* Arboricultural practice whereby the remnants of a felled tree's base and roots are removed from the ground using some sort of power tool. *2. n.* Giving one's *wood* a thorough pasting.

stumpy tower *1. n.* The former gaol in the town of Girvan, Scotland. See also *hairy tree. 2. n. 'Fancy a wee climb up the stumpy tower, love? Thought not.'*

stupor glue *n.* Powerful adhesive which keeps a student stuck to his mattress until the morning's lectures have finished. *Booze, degreevostik.*

submarine *n.* A lady whose available holes are all being simultaneously bunged up by a variety of gentleman callers, resulting in her being, a-hem, "air tight and full of semen".

subsidise the arts *v.* To pay a professional dancer to take her clothes off; to visit the *peelers. 'Oi, what have you done with the children's lunch money, you dirty bastard?' 'Sorry love, I've been subsiding the arts with it.'*

suck her shit through a tramp's sock, I'd *exclam.* A romantic declaration of undying love. *'Then plainly know my heart's dear love is set, On the fair daughter of rich Capulet. Though lovers ever run before the clock, I'd suck Juliet's shit through a tramp's sock.'* (from *Romeo and Juliet* by William Shakespeare, Act 2 scene iii).

suetcide *n.* Self-inflicted death by cake.

sugars *n.* The *clockweights*. A reference to UK-based entrepreneur and *Apprentice* host Lord Sir Alan of Amstrad, whose gnarled, wrinkled face covered in wiry whiskers looks not unlike half a scrotum.

suicycle *n.* Any massively-overpowered sports motorbike purchased by a balding, paunchy middle-aged bloke in order to bring his mid-life crisis to a swift conclusion. See also *midlife cricycle.*

suitable advice *euph.* In police terminology, a *fucking* good kicking. *'Constable Penrose, the gentleman in cell three has been banging on the door all night. Go down and give him some suitable advice, will you?'*

Sundance *n.* The slightly more feminine half of a pair of *carpet munchers, ie.* "The one who isn't Butch". A *mug runcher*.

Sunday stopper *n*. A *mystery meat* kebab purchased and consumed on your way home from the pub on a Saturday night that effectively ruins all your plans for the Sabbath by keeping you ensconced on the *crapper* till well after *Antiques Roadshow* has finished.

Sunderland hotdog *n*. A popular pastime in the north eastern holiday resort; a refined *Barclays* performed with the *giggling pin* wrapped in raw bacon. A *pig in a blanket, pork scratching*.

Susie Dent *n. prop. rhym. slang. Colwyn Bay*. From Susie Dent = Stoke on Trent.

suspect remains at large, the *exclam*. Euphemistic police speak for a post-coital *lob-on*. *'I took down her particulars and banged her in the back of the black maria, sarge, but the suspect remains at large.'*

Suthen *1. n. prop.* An eleventh century Queen of Scotland who, according to Shakespeare, was "oftener on her knees than on her feet" and hence *2. n.* Any lady who frequently provides oral pleasure. Don't say we never learn you any fucking culture.

Swedish roulette *n*. An act of onanistic gambling in which the *wanksmith* plies his trade whilst watching an Abba video, hoping that - at the moment of truth - the screen will be displaying the blonde *piece*, or at the very least the brunette.

Swilly salad *n*. A pasty and a blob of tomato sauce, as enjoyed by the health-conscious residents of Plymouth's swish North Prospect estate.

swizzjizz *n*. A synthetic, vegetarian alternative to genuine *baby gravy*. A mixture of icing sugar and warm water, *swizzjizz* is most often used as a cinematic aid or enhancement during the dénouement of lower budget *scud vids*. Also *fake man, spray-onnaise*.

swoo *n*. The viscid emulsion of perspiration and excrement found in the *arse-crack* of one who has been exercising vigorously, for example an overweight bachelor attempting to manhandle a filing cabinet up a fire escape on a particularly clammy day. From sweat + poo.

synipsis *n*. A brief précis or pithy resumé of one's anal health, issued irrespective of whether anyone wants to hear it. Which they don't.

SYNT/synt *acronym*. Polite and lexicographically accurate pronunciation of "See You Next Tuesday". *'Lovely mass, father. See you next Tuesday, you synt.'*

syruptitious *adj*. Of a balding gentleman, furtively and undetectably be-wigged.

tabs *n.* The external labia. *'Phwooar! I tell you what, I wouldn't mind getting my hands on her tabs. And it's a new Olympic Women's High Jump record! Now back to John Inverdale in the studio.'*

taint week *n.* The pointless period that falls between December 25th and January 1st. Because "it taint Christmas, it taint New Year and it taint worth going back to work". See also *the perineum, the festive perineum.* *'Hello. Is that the police? There's a masked man with an axe trying to smash the front door down.' 'Sorry love. I can't send anybody out till a week Tuesday at the latest, only it's taint week and there's nobody here.'*

take matters into your own hands *v.* To *finish yourself off* after your partner fails to successfully bring you to *organism. 'I'm sorry Trudie, but this has gone on long enough. It's reached the stage where I'm going to have to take matters into my own hands. Pass me that copy of Readers' Wives Bums Special. It's on the bedside table under my lute.'*

takes his time shopping *euph.* Said of he whom *bakes a light cake.*

take the A train *1. n.* Title of a jazz classic penned by Duke Ellington and Billy Strayhorn, also famously played by Dave Brubeck. *2. v.* To travel in the missus's *caboose, buffers* permitting.

take the ball into the corner *v.* To go for a *shit* in the works *bogs* at about half past four on a Friday afternoon in order to kill time and wind down the clock until home time. *'Where's Lord Sugar, Nick?' 'He's taken the ball into the corner, Karren.'*

take yourself to town *v.* To have a *five knuckle shuffle.* On the bus.

taking in washing *euph.* Having the *gorilla's knuckles. 'I see Kylie's taking in washing in her new video, then.'*

tampax dancing *n.* A cool new disco craze, as seen in countless *jam rag* adverts, that requires the carefree participant to be "Up tight, out of sight" and, indeed, "into the groove".

tandoor clay oven *n.* A post-curry, smoke-infused, under-duvet miasmatic *blanket banquet* which one's better half is forcibly encouraged to enjoy. Like a *Dutch oven,* but rich with the spicy aromas of the mystic east.

tappit clearance *1. n.* Something on a motor car engine that a real man would understand, and possibly be able to adjust using a hammer. *2. n.* Measurement of the *Toblerone tunnel* between a lass's legs where her *beetle bonnet* resides.

tar baby *1. n.* Something that perennially challenged the powers of imagination of the various artists hired to illustrate *Brer Rabbit. 2. n.* A loose *tom tit* that could certainly not be picked up and held.

tart-an *n.* The traditional pattern worn by young ladies who are generous with their affections.

tartoo *n.* Any permanently-inked design located in a lady's lower lumbar region or *splashdeck.* A *tramp stamp, slag tag* or *whoremark.* Also *arse antlers.*

Tarzan's feet, as hard as *sim.* Said of someone who is good with his fists. *'I wouldn't fuck about with that big bouncer on the door, Professor Hawking. He's as hard as Tarzan's feet, him.'*

taste of your own medicine *n.* An unwanted dose of *Vitamin S;* when kissing goodbye to someone who has just *noshed you off,* inadvertently receiving a savoury soupçon of your own *special sauce.*

tattoo tipp-ex *n.* Whilst *back-scuttling* a young lady, the act of whipping out one's *chopper* at the onset of the *vinegar strokes* in order to *white out* the *tramp stamp* just above her *arse crack* with *erection fluid.*

tavern tumour *n. medic.* Benign male abdominal growth believed to be linked to chronic, repetitive stress on the right elbow joint. A *beer gut.*

TCP *abbrev. medic.* Temporary Cock Paralysis. A morning after symptom of *Post Traumatic Sex Disorder. 'What about a quickie before you go to work, Chief Constable?' 'Sorry love, I've got TCP.'*

TDS *abbrev.* Turd Dumping Session. *'Pull over whenever it is prudent to do so please, Miss Berryman, using the gears, brakes and making appropriate signals to other traffic. I'm off behind the fence for a TDS.'*

teabag left in the pot *1. euph.* A *white mouse* still at home. *'Not again, Gladys. There's a teabag left in the pot.' 2. euph.* An *unexpected item in the bagging area. 'Not again, Gladys. There's a teabag left in the pot.' 3. euph.* The discovery of a *night watchman* on the *starting line at Brand's Hatch. 'Not again, Gladys. There's a teabag left in the pot.'*

teams are in the tunnel, the *1. exclam.* The sort of banal expression uttered by potato-faced football presenter Adrian Chiles before handing over to Clive Tyldesley and Andy Townsend in the commentary box. *2. exclam.* The awkward, alarming feeling that often comes between *touching cloth* and *touching socks.*

tear jerker *1. n.* A particularly painful masturbation session. *2. n.* A particularly joyful masturbation session. *3. n.* A particularly poignant masturbation session.

teazle *n.* The alluring glimpse of luxuriant *faff* observable from the rear of a *bird* via her *Toblerone tunnel. Reverse peach, coconut husk, coffee bean.*

Ted Bundies *n. rhym. slang. US.* Blood-soaked *undies,* named after the infamous American murderer. *'I do wish you'd occasionally pick your Ted Bundies up off the goldarn bathroom floor, Sue-Ellen.'*

Ted Rogers *n. prop.* A special sort of *gusset typing* utilising the lightning fast, dextrous finger

technique made famous by the eponymous, late, fast-talking host of erstwhile purgatorial Yorkshire TV dustbin-based gameshow *3-2-1.*

teddy bear smile *n.* Condition affecting the *front bottoms* of ladies in leggings. Also *camel's foot, camel's lip, knicker sausages, Twix lips, cloven hoof, Cyclops' hoof, gorilla's knuckles, moose knuckles, the pig's trotter.*

telling bone *1. phr.* An expression used by 1970s children's TV character *Catweazle. 2. n.* A twitching bulge in the front of a pair of speedos that indicates that a fellow likes what he sees at the beach/swimming pool/ Olympic Beach Volleyball event.

temperature, take her *n.* To insert one's finger into the missus's *Gary Glitter.*

tenis *n.* A tiny *manhood,* such as that belonging to Jack Straw or Bobby Davro.

ten metre board *n.* The toilet seat; the place from where a *Tom Daley* is launched.

Tennent's elbow *n. medic. Scots.* Chronic muscular/skeletal ailment caused by repetitive flexing of the humeroulnar ginglymus. Particularly prevalent amongst Glaswegian *professional outdoorsmen* the Monday after an Old Firm game. Also known as *tramp's cramp. 'I'm sorry Mr Floyd. I'm afraid you've got an advanced case of Tennent's elbow.'*

ten o'clock to nine o'clock, move my *euph.* Humorous way to inform one's secretary that you'll be taking your morning *tom tit* an hour earlier than usual. *'Hilary, that double espresso you gave me means I'll need to move my ten o'clock to nine o'clock. Has the Washington Post arrived yet?'*

ten of clubs *n.* The polar opposite of *drawing an ace,* from the busy appearance of one's used *bumwad.* That is to say, the aftermath of a messy *chod* that leaves a person's *nipsy* like an open jar of Nutella, thus leading to a wiping job that is akin to the mythical Fifth Labour of Heracles.

ten of diamonds *n.* A cheeky trick played by

one's *council gritter* when one is attempting to *draw an ace* at the end of a game of *craps* with *Famer Giles.*

tension in the Balkans *1. euph.* Period of uncomfortable apprehension experienced by the residents of the eponymous geopolitical region in the period between the assassination of Archduke Franz Ferdinand and when it all kicked off. *2. euph.* A build-up of *spoffological* pressure in a chap's *bulgars* following a period of sexual inactivity. *'There's tension in the Balkans, Sue. I'm going to have to put on a larger pair of tennis shorts.'*

tentertainment *n.* Any recreational diversion that entails a small, cloth-covered erection being pitched.

terminal two *n.* The *shitter. 'This won't hurt a bit, Mr Trubshaw. I'm just going to pop a rubber glove on and stick my finger up terminal two.' 'Is that strictly necessary? After all, I'm only applying for a Nectar card.'*

terrapin *n.* A firm *tod* that busts one's *Jeremy Kyles,* thus leaving livid red streaks along its neck in the style of one of the popular pond-dwelling tortoises.

Tescos barcode fault *euph.* Named after the recent highly-publicised fiasco whereby the supermarket chain inadvertently mispriced Terry's Chocolate Oranges at 29p instead of the usual £2.75, causing canny customers with an eye for a bargain to go into a frenzy of panic buying; thus, to "fill your trolleys with chocolate". *'Can you stick these in the boil wash please, pet? I've had a bit of a Tescos barcode fault on me way back from the pub.'*

Tessa Munt *n. rhym. slang.* A *Kenny Lunt.* Named in honour of the Liberal Democrat MP for Wells in Somerset who, amusingly enough, is apparently a governor of the Hugh Sexey Middle School.

Tetley trot *n.* Conveniently short bout of s*xual intercourse that happily finishes before your cup of tea has a chance to go cold.

Tex Ritter *n. rhym. slang.* The *cludgie,* named after the famous country music singer and film star. From Tex Ritter = Rick Witter. *'Kindly excuse me, your majesty. I'm just off to the Tex Ritter to rub one out over these topless pictures of your granddaughter in law.'*

Thaiarrhoea *n. medic.* A temporary loosening of the *foulage* as a result of eating spicy delicacies from the faraway south-east Asian kingdom.

Thai lottery jackpot *n.* On an exotic holiday, the thrill and excitement felt when *picking up* a couple of far eastern *hotties* which quickly turns to horror when you get them back to your hotel and discover that, between you, you have "six matching balls".

thank *v.* From think + wank. *'What's the matter, Wills? You've gone limp again. Is it Pippa?' 'Yes darling. I was just thanking about her before I came to bed. Especially her arse.'*

thank-you for the music *exclam.* The opening lines from Abba's melodious hit single of 1977, which can be pressed gnomically into service (to include as much of the rest of the song as may be deemed appropriate in the circumstances) as a tuneful expression of gratitude and enthusiasm following the release of a particularly harmonious *dropped hat.* Also *someone's moving in next door; that's how I attract the bitches, that's right Doodles* and *that's the chairs arranged then; back to bed Peppa!*

Thatcher's funeral *n.* Any ludicrously expensive event, trip or occasion desired by a few but which, nevertheless, everyone has to pay for.

the Chancellor of the Exchequer will now read a short statement *exclam.* Declared as a jocular means of announcing imminent flatulence. Also *please welcome to the stage Nickleback/Peter Kay/Skrillex etc.*

the plop thickens *phr. medic.* Medical saying

when administering foodstuffs with the intention of restoring a patient's loose *foulage* to a more healthy consistency.

the power of Christ compels thee *exclam.* Incantation to exorcise the foul demons of the *chod bin* when the room becomes possessed by a particularly evil *out of botty experience.* Most effectively delivered whilst emptying a can of Airwick in a North-South-West-East orientation, in a style reminiscent of a Papal blessing.

there go the Maldives! *exclam.* A humorous rejoinder following a voluble release of *brownhouse gases.* The potent, climate-chaanging nature of *carbon dibaxide* is widely believed to contribute to rising sea levels, which currently threaten the eponymous low-lying, Indian Ocean-based chain of atolls.

there is unrest in the south, colonel *exclam.* Phrase used when suffering from untrustworthy *Simon Cowells,* and one dare not venture far from the *throne room* in case *the rebels should charge the gates.*

there's Bully - you're out of time *exclam.* Humorous utterance to be employed when someone emits a low frequency, bovine *Exchange & Mart.* From Jim Bowen's gentle chastisement of slow-witted contestants on erstwhile darts-themed eighties Sunday teatime gloomfest *Bullseye.*

thesbian *n.* A talented heterosexual actress who convincingly portrays a *tuppence licker* in a film or *jazz mag.*

thightanic *n.* A lady whose upper legs have enormously *lovely personalities.*

thinge, the *n.* A lady's *undersmile* so monstrous that it resembles an animatronic special effect from a 1980s horror film directed by John Carpenter.

thinternet *n.* The diaphanously gossamer worldwide web which intermittently manages to squeeze asthmatically out of your router after you pay a major national telecommunications company for 20MB broadband. *Fraudband.*

third and bird *1. n.* Title, apparently, of a charming CBeebies programme. *2. n. rhym. slang.* A *feeshee.* *'Hold my calls please, Moneypenny. I'm off for a third and bird.'*

thirsty alsatian, lap it like a *sim.* To commit the filthy act of *cumulonimbus* with all the gusto of a parched *shit machine* with its nose in a puddle.

thirsty binman, faster than a *sim.* A classist description of someone doing something very hastily, in the manner of a sprinting refuse collector who is keen to finish his shift and tuck into a few jars and a farmhouse breakfast. *'Here's my column for the Sunday paper, Lloyd.' 'Fucking hell, Tony. You've written that faster than a thirsty binman.'*

thoracic park *n.* Any venue heaving with ladies who possess well-developed *chest-bumps.*

Thornton *n.* One who practises "the art of the chocolatier".

thought for the day *euph.* Switching off the bedside wireless at about 7.50am and embarking on one's last bout of *how's your father* before getting up for work.

three bogs full *n.* An impressive volume of *feeshus* that requires multiple flushes of the *jobby engine* before the water in the pan returns to its usual consistency. A *long haul shite.*

three-in-one oil *n.* Any expensive *tart fuel* that is pretty much guaranteed to ease access to all the important areas of a *slapper.*

three S's, the *euph.* A chap's morning ablutions, *viz.* "A shower, a Shit and a Shave". Not really sure about the apostrophe in there, but what can you do? And you'd probably want to have the shower *after* the shit, all things considered. The *shushes.*

three wank hangover *n.* Semi-terminal *brewer's flu;* a bout of *beer cancer* so brutal that the sufferer cannot even consider getting out of bed before he has committed a trio of *monomanual self-debasements*.

Thresher's shark *n*. An inebriate who circles around outside the town off-licence offering to buy drink for under-18s in return for a small commission.

throat singing *1. n.* Popular form of vocal entertainment in the Inuit community. Like Lee Marvin doing *I Was Born Under a Wonderin' Star* but by an Eskimo. *2. n.* Vomiting loudly after downing twelve pints of watered-down lager at a rock festival.

throne call *n*. A mobile phone conversation during which the recipient is unaware that you are simultaneously *dropping the kids off at the pool.*

throw air *v*. To play a tune on one's *brass eye.*

throw the clay *n*. To commence the construction of a *coil pot* on the *potter's wheel.*

thrushian roulette *n*. The risky practice of *slipping* the missus *a length* while she's cooking a small loaf of *cunt bread.*

thrush's chest *n*. The appearance of the *Ark Royal landing deck* following a visit from any bird of the genus *Turdus. The starting line at Brands Hatch.*

thunderdoming *n*. A *spitroast* which is prematurely curtailed due to one of the male participants pulling out after remembering he has left the gas on or similar. Named after the cage-fighting venue superintended by Tina Turner in the third *Mad Max* film where "two men enter - one man leaves".

tiger's face *n*. The startling *wind sketch* left in your *Bill Grundies* after a soggy *air biscuit.*

tight as a bullfighter's pants *sim*. Particularly parsimonious. *'Don't expect my brother to get a round in. He's tight as a bullfighter's pants.'*

Tilbury triathlon *n*. A race to evade arrest when caught thieving at the picturesque Essex port, which alternately involves running, swimming and cycling. And rucking and climbing fences.

time off in loo *n*. Industrial productivity lost due to lavatory breaks during working hours.

Tim Henman's trophy cabinet, as empty as *sim*. Wittily descriptive of something that has little or no contents. *'I'm going to have to go shopping soon. The fridge is as empty as Tim Henman's trophy cabinet.'*

Tinkerbell *n*. A delightfully delicate *dropped gut* of the sort that would follow a charming young lady round like a spangly cloud of irridescent glitter.

tippexing *n*. The act of *whiting out* a tattoo on the small of an Essex lady's back. *'I had not intended to love Mr Rochester; the reader knows I had wrought hard to extirpate from my soul the germs of love there detected; and yet now, as he stood up and wiped his bell end on the curtains after tippexing my tramp stamp, they spontaneously revived, great and strong!'* (from *Jane Eyre* by Charlotte Bronte).

tired dog's mouth, loose as a *sim. Aus*. A charmingly lyrical figure of speech which may be applied to the more accommodating young lady. *'Have you met my sister, Archbishop? I wouldn't say she's easy, but she's as loose as tired dog's mouth.'*

Titmuss paper *n*. The *spooged*-on tissues which are the residue of a solitary pleasure session involving images of the eponymous celebrity. That's Abi Titmuss, by the way. Not the Middlesex, Surrey and England cricketer who was the unwitting subject of the Half Man Half Biscuit song *Fuckin' 'Ell It's Fred Titmus.* His name wasn't even spelled the same.

tit on your own doorstep *v*. To buy *rhythmic literature* at one's own local newsagents, thus running the risk of being spotted by neighbours or loved ones.

tits on a stick *n*. An affectionate, informal epithet for a bony *tart* with big *churns.*

tit tap *n*. A nipple which, when tweaked, opens a lady's *floodgates.*

tittage *n.* The average weight *avoirdupois* of the *knockers* on a group of women at a bus stop, for instance.

titterati *n.* The top quality, large-breasted *blart* such as Keeley Hazell, Lucy Pinder, Rhian Sugden, who inhabit the pages of didactic journals such as *Nuts, Zoo, Loaded etc.*

tit winch *n.* A powerful bra. Also *tit pants.*

titzkreig *n.* A group of buxom young *frauleins* on the pavement, dazzling oncoming chaps with their *searchlights.*

TK man *n.* A gent with a *membrum virile* so long that it can comfortably accommodate "ten knuckles" gripping it at once.

toasticles *n.* Very hot, buttered testicles.

TOFU/tofu *acronym.* Tastes Of Fucking Underpants.

toilet truffles *n.* The pungent nuggets found ensconced in the *earth closet* after *gurning out* a hot, dry curry.

Tomatina, la *1. n. Sp.* Yearly festival held on the last Wednesday of August in the Spanish town of Buñol, during which locals and tourists spend a morning pelting each other with tomatoes, rendering the entire town centre a deep red colour. *2. n.* The missus's *rag week.*

tomato varnish *n.* The Mozambican term for the clear, colourless solution secreted by the *plums,* which provides the *tadpoles* with something to swim in. Also *ball glaze, guardsman's gloss, perseverance soup, dew on the lily, clear smear.*

Tom Daley's forehead *n.* A buoyant *floater* that bobs back up at the water's edge shortly after flushing.

tool of the trade *n.* The *twat* who everyone hates at a place of work.

tooth dryer *n.* Any repair required on your car, house, or a domestic appliance that requires the recruitment of a qualified tradesman and will thus, once the surly *twat* has finished sucking air through his in-

cisors, end up costing you a *sodding* packet.

top gun *n.* In the works *bogs,* the honour awarded to the *porcelain pilot* whose *afterburner,* upon inhalation, literally "takes my breath away".

top shelf quick *adj.* Lightning fast. From the Zorro-like rapid reflexes of a man in a newsagents staring steadfastly at the *Radio Times* until the moment the shop empties, then reaching for a *Fiesta,* slapping it on the counter and in one smooth movement simultaneously proffering the exact change and slipping it into an opaque carrier bag before exiting. 'I tell you what, Seb. Usain was top shelf quick out of the blocks there.'

top up a half-pint *euph.* Having *drawn an ace* in the *thunderbox,* to take the opportunity to have a *piss* before standing up. *'Have you finished in there, Jonny? Ravi's just gone out to bat.' 'I'm nearly done. I'm just topping up a half-pint, then I'll get me pads on.'*

torpedo cupcake *n.* A guided, deadly bubble of *sulphur dibaxide* released under the jacuzzi water to pop up under an unsuspecting fellow bather's nose.

tortoise *n.* A *kiddy fiddler.* From the fact that he "gets there before the hair".

total wifeout *n.* A one-man, against-the-clock *sexual assault course,* enjoyed whilst the missus is at the supermarket on a Saturday evening, which involves large red balls, squirting liquids and the risk of serious back injury.

Tottenham millionaire *n.* Anyone who has a job of any sort in the picturesquely strife-torn North London locale.

touching a snail's face, like *sim.* The effect of cold *wanking spanners* on the *old chap* when popping behind a tree to *drain the lizard* in mid-winter.

tough mudder *1. n. milit.* An arduous assault course. A test of a combatant's grit, spunk and determination to succeed. *2. n.* A difficult *rear entry.*

TOWIE *abbrev.* A reference to the preferred style of congress enjoyed by the tangerine-faced denizens of the uncouth southern county. The Only Way Is Essex, *viz.* a *back scuttle* up the *wrong 'un*.

toxic socks syndrome *n. medic.* An allergic reaction to a room-mate's feet, principally symptomised by a tightening of the throat, involuntary gagging and watering eyes.

tracer bullets *n.* Hard, difficult-to-digest items, such as corn, peanuts or Lego, that show up in *Thoras* and provide a good estimate of the time it has taken for a meal to negotiate the digestive tract.

Tracey Island *n.* A *Camilla* movement of such volume and consistency that it forms a compelling simulacrum of the erstwhile International Rescue base as it rises majestically above the waves of the *chod pan*.

track and field *euph.* To stimulate a lady's *clematis* in a vigorous, two-fingered manner reminiscent of playing the eponymous classic 1980s "button-basher" arcade game.

tradesman's nudge *n.* A firm blow which is delivered with the intention of making a broken object operational again. *'Mission Control can now confirm that the crew of Space Shuttle Atlantis today visited the Hubble Space Telescope in order to give the malfunctioning Cosmic Origins Spectrograph and Wide Field Camera a tradesman's nudge with a big fuck-off hammer.'*

training lager *n. Piss weak* beer. *'As God is my witness, I'm as sober as a judge. I've been on the training lager all afternoon, officer.'*

trampadol *n.* Powerful prescription sedative used as a recreational drug by the financially-challenged. *'We're out of vodka and fauxcaine, so it's time to break out the trampadol left over from your car crash, mam.'*

trampari *n.* A turpentine substitute aperitif taken as an appetiser before a bin-rifling buffet.

trampede *n.* A stampede of tramps. From tramp + stampede.

tramp in her bin cupboard, she's got a *euph.* Said of a lady who has a *personal daintiness* problem.

tramp l'oeil *n.* Refers to a cheap *dollymop* who looks *good from far, but far from good* at closer range. A *low resolution fox*.

tramp on a kipper, like a *sim. Con gusto.* *'Will you lot fucking shut up, I'm trying to ironically watch Pan's People on BBC4 here. Phwooar! I tell you what, though, I'd be on that like a tramp on a kipper. Thirty-five years ago, obviously.* Pass me the tissues, nan.'

tramp on a sandwich, like a *sim.* Enthusiastic - if not very hygienic - *noshing*. *'Granted she's not much to look at, but get your charlie out and she's like a tramp on a sandwich, your Honour. And I would hope that the court would take this mitigating factor into account when deciding upon its sentence. The defence rests its case.'*

tramp's alarm clock *n.* A loud, early morning *Bakewell* that would rouse its progenitor from the deepest slumber, and may even cause him to leap out of the bed and change the sheets.

tramp's baby *n.* A large bottle of white cider nursed tenderly in the crook of his arm by a *gentleman of the road*.

tramp's lips *n.* A poorly-maintained *glovebox*.

tramps' office *n.* A conveniently located hub where *Balham ballerinas* hold meetings to decide on their future business strategies, core business criteria, mission statements *etc.* For example, the salubrious branch of Burger King on the other side of Euston Road from Kings Cross and St Pancras stations. The bit round the corner from where the staff behind the counter can't see them.

tramp's trilby *n.* A plastic bag pressed into service as an impromptu rain protector.

trancock's half hour *n.* An errant thirty minutes spent surfing *flipper* pornography on the internet, before returning to normality.

tranny cranny *n. medic.* A bubble&squeak-style *minge* knocked up from leftover bits of *meat and two veg* as part of gender reassignment surgery. *'Bloody hell, love. Do we have to watch these Channel 4 documentaries about sex change operations while we're having our tea?' 'Yes we do, it's educational. That doctor's just made Pete Burns a nice new tranny cranny, look.'*

transit of Venus *1. n.* Something astronomical that only happens twice in the average lifetime, and is typically obscured by clouds. *2. n.* A *passion wagon, spambulance* or *fuck truck*. Effectively, a van with a dirty old mattress lobbed in the back.

transporter bridge *1. n.* Petrochemical wonderland Middlesbrough's most famous landmark. *2. n.* The no-man's-land between the *freckle* and the *Mary Hinge*. Also, variously, the *Humber bridge, taint, tinter, notcher, carse, biffon, scran, twernt, Berlin Wall, Botley Interchange, Barry Gibb, Bosphorus, brink, crontis, clutch, joy division, Potsdamer Platz, butfer, snarse, biffin bridge, Checkpoint Charlie, varse* or *Wirral peninsula*.

trap three trepidation *n.* Understandable feeling of anxiety about what one is about to encounter upon venturing into the last operational cubicle in the *Rick Witters. Crapidation.*

trap *v. naval.* To *pull*. *'I went down to Pompey docks last night and trapped the Commander's missus.'*

travelled through shit *phr.* Said of a particularly smelly *dropped gut*. *'Christ on a fucking bike, that one had travelled through shit alright, Mr President.'*

trawler trash *n.* Lower class fisher-folk.

trifle *n.* The multi-layered mess residing in the bottom of the *shit pot* after a bhuna too far.

trim the wax *v.* To clean the build-up of *hedam* from under the brim of the *farmer's hat*.

trip to Trumpton *n.* A visit to the *cludgie* where one sits on the *Barney McGrew* and farts several times.

Trojan flick *n.* The act of removing the last globules of *love porridge* from one's *tackle* by firmly holding the penile shaft and applying a single firm shake in the style of a fly fisherman.

trolley dash *n.* An urgent sprint towards the supermarket *crappers* in order to avoid an *unexpected item in the bagging area*.

troot's mooth *n. Scots.* The *meatus, Jap's eye, hog's eye. 'Och maw, come quick! Gran'paw's stuck a wee pencil doon his troot's mooth!'*

trotter's knot *n.* The anal twitching of one afflicted with *the runs* who is trying not to dramatically *drop the shopping* whilst availing themselves of a lavatory which is not theirs.

trout gout *n. medic.* An inflammation of the female genitals, causing a fishy-smelling discharge. Particularly prevalent amongst *good time girls* who ply their trade near ports and dockyards.

trout pocket *1. n.* A large, secret, slimy, fishy pouch concealed inside a poacher's waxed cotton coat, and hence *2. n.* A lady's minge with a coshed salmon hidden in it.

trucker's cushions *n. Ker-nockers. Manchester Cities.*

trucker's mudflap, face like a *sim.* A reference to a lady who has evidently fallen out of the ugly tree and hit every branch on the way down. And then landed face-first in a pile of ugly gravel. And then been *twatted* with an ugly frying pan.

truffle hunter *n.* An unnecessarily contumelious epithet for a *right fugly salad dodger.*

truffle pigs *n. Big-boned* folk with their snouts pressed up against the counter in Greggs.

trumpaphone *1. n.* One of the less classy instruments of the orchestra; a brass/woodwind hybrid which is basically a trumpet fitted with the mouthpiece from a saxophone.

2. n. A windsome *freckle* put to musical use, making a sound not unlike *1.*

trunking *n.* An amusing gentleman's party trick whereby he pushes his *dobber* up his own *nipsy*, in a style that is charmingly reminiscent of the way an elephant pushes a bun into its mouth.

trunkles *n.* Ankles that are so big they look like tree trunks.

trycoxagain *n. medic.* Treatment which may be efficacious when attempting to alleviate symptoms in short-tempered, overly-emotional *splitarses.* *'What's up with her, doctor?' 'Oh, nothing a dose of trycoxagain couldn't cure.'*

tub thumper *n.* One who is not averse to the odd game of *up periscope* on bath night.

tugboat *1. n.* A chunky *skiff* who is no oil painting but nevertheless provides an efficient *pulling* service. *2. n.* The small *frigspawn* vessels which navigate the bath after a chap has *gripped the lather.*

tugbutt *n.* A saggy *caboose* that has lost its fight with the force of gravity and begun accelerating towards the centre of the earth at a rate of thirty-two feet per second squared.

tugger's remorse *n. psych.* The more-or-less instant feeling of self-reproach experienced by a *merchant* who has just *banked with Barclays. Wangst, wanguish, Crying over spilt milk.* *'There once was a man with a horse / Who found a jazz mag in some gorse / He went in his stable / Wanked all he was able / Then suffered the tugger's remorse.'* (from *Nonsense Rhymes I Tossed Off in Five Minutes* by Edward Lear).

Tulisa's hanky, as wet as *sim.* A reference to a degree of moistness on a par with an *otter's pocket*, named in honour of the NDubz singer's penchant for bursting into floods of tears on *The X Factor,* when a contestant says their granny's got piles.

turbo shandy *n.* A male who is completely

shitfaced after a couple of pints. A *two pot screamer* or *halfpint Harry.*

turd bath *n.* The *bum sink.* *'Hello, this is Prince William in the Honeymoon Suite. Can you send someone up to unblock the turd bath please? It's all clogged up with Kate's bangers and mash.'*

turd girdle *n.* The feeling of uncomfortable abdominal tightness and cramping in the *Roddies* which is experienced when one's unborn *mudchild* is approaching full term. *Concraptions, turdle.*

turd in the hole *n.* Unpleasant, albeit compulsory, game played in rustic French campsite toilets, whereby the participant is required to *crimp off a length of dirty spine* whilst squatting over a hole the size of a coffee mug without *dropping his shopping* into his trousers.

turdish delight *n.* The feeling of pride and well-being which results from an enjoyable and productive session on the *jobby engine.*

turdo-prop *n.* A once-in-a-lifetime *Eartha* that presses down on the bottom of the U-bend whilst still firmly attached at the *nipsy*, thus providing its proud parent with much-needed support. A junior *neckbreaker.*

Turkish breakfast *1.n.* Coffee, a cigarette and a bit of *anal. 2. n.* The foul gases emitted as a *bottom burp* first thing in the morning after a large *catbab with all the shit,* which sets one up nicely for a busy day of sitting in a darkened water closet, sweating and sobbing.

turtle beach *n.* The lavatory, where you drag yourself late at night to *lay your eggs,* hopefully without David Attenborough crouching next to you with a torch.

turtle mat *1. n.* Revolutionary mud-trapping doormat as endorsed by digitally-challenged beardy ice-plodder Sir Ranulph Fiennes. *2. n.* The *autographed jelly hammock* of the *dunghampers* when one is *clutching Bungle.*

turtle nudger *n.* A *fruit fumbler.*

turtle's head revisited *n.* A fond, nostalgic look back at an old pair of *autographed grundies.*

turtle stew *n.* A well-stocked *can* of *bum soup.*

turtle wipeout *n.* The careful removal of a small brown deposit from the *dot* of a chap who has *gambled and lost.*

twangling *n.* The jaunty action of a lady's *independent front suspension* under a T-shirt, especially in the summer months.

twangs my banjo string *phr.* Said of a woman who *floats your boat. 'Did you see that fascinating programme about medieval illuminations on BBC 4? It was an absorbing insight into the way that elaborately illustrated manuscripts bestowed power on a sixteenth century monarch and united his kingdom in an age of plague, warfare and rebellion. And that hottie who presents it really twangs my banjo string and all, I can tell you.'*

twataclysm *n.* An horrific event involving *twats,* such as the celebrity-studded opening of a "fashionable London bakery".

twatapult *n.* A lady's skimpy elasticated undergarment. *'Aw, the decorator's jizzed in me twatapult drawer again, Terry. You'd best have a word with him.'*

twat cap *n.* A flat or country cap when worn by a *scrote, pog* or ne'er-do-well.

twatch *n.* An oversized, gaudy timepiece of the sort worn by a professional footballer or Formula One racing driver. From twat + ch.

twat clap *n.* A *fanny fart, frampton* or *queef.*

twat hook *n.* Curved implement used to catch a *mackerel.* A chap's finger.

twatire *n.* Type of low level topical humour of the sort popularised by sour-faced Scottish comedians on programmes such as *Mock the Week.*

twat mallet *n.* A *fanny hammer. 'Need anything fetching from the shops, Mildred?' 'Just a loaf of bread and some new batteries for me twat mallet, George.'*

twatsuma *n.* Any annoying, bright orange celebrity, *eg.* Peter Andre, Katie Price, David Dickinson, Robert Kilroy-Silk, Robbie Savage, anyone from *TOWIE, Geordie Shore, Desperate Scousewives etc.*

twattachino *n.* Any one of the multitude of ridiculously overpriced, pretentiously-named variations on a cup of fucking coffee, as ostentatiously enjoyed by *man bag-toting arseholes* around the world. *'Could we take a latte macchiato, a mochaccino freddo, a double doppio Americano and a ristretto lungo please?' 'Right, I'll just check that order back. So, that's four twattachinos. That'll be twenty-eight pounds.'*

twat tractor *n.* Any large, black, four-wheel-drive vehicle of the type favoured by professional footballers and other *bellends. 'The new BMW X6 is as outstanding in performance as it is impressive in appearance. Powerful engines endow it with the dynamics of a sports car, while the chassis combines the athletic shapes of a coupé with the thirst for adventure of a thoroughbred twat tractor.'*

twatula *n.* A flat wooden paddle for spreading depilatory unguents on a *bird's clopper.*

twelve o'clock cock *n.* An erection which points straight upwards.

twenty-one gunt salute *euph.* A hen-night in Doncaster.

twhat *1. n.* Piece of self-consciously eccentric millinery sported by the sort of *cuntish* oik who thinks that such headgear marks them out as being someone special and wacky. Pete Doherty wears a *twhat. 2. n.* One of those tea-cosy-style *titfers* worn by Subaru drivers.

twig toothbrush *n.* A cock with enough bristles to fight plaque, dental caries and gingivitis.

TWIM/twim *acronym.* A lady who is sadly under-endowed in the *chesty substances* department. Tit Wank IMpossible.

two-bean salad *n.* A *lady golfer's* lunch.

2B2W *abbrev.* An internet or mobile telephone textual contraction, meaning "Too Busy To Wank". It is not thought that any male has ever actually been rushed off their feet to such an extent.

two-inch bather *n.* Descriptive of a *salad-dodger* who only needs to run the specified minimal depth of bath water before getting in to fill up the tub. *'Jesus, look at the back tits on that two-inch bather. I bet she can shit, your holiness.'*

two into ones *n.* Impossibly tight trousers, of the style into which an overly-optimistic *salad dodger* may attempt to squeeze their enormous *arse;* in flagrant contravention of the basic mathematical axiom that "two into one won't go". Even though it obviously does, because it's a half.

two little boys fighting under a blanket *n.* Alluringly unrestrained *fat rascals.* Also *two puppies fighting in a bag, dead heat in a Zeppelin race.*

two man sniff test *1. n. milit.* Following a chemical or biological incident, when contamination is no longer detectable, a standardised routine whereby two squaddies remove their safety equipment and alternately take shallow breaths in order to detect symptoms (vomiting, dilating pupils, muscle spasms, excessive salivation/drooling *etc.*) in each other caused by the latent presence of toxic airborne agents. *2. n.* A similar routine following a *two's up* in the back lane behind Cheeks nightclub, Aldershot.

two pint Tyson *n.* A bloke who goes all fighty after a minimal amount of ale. Also *two can Van Damme, tinny mallet, halfpint Harry, two pot screamer.*

two pit-stop strategy *1. n.* Something that Jeremy Hardy soundalike Formula 1 commentator Martin Brundle gets implausibly excited about during Grand Prix motor races. *2. n.* In a municipal *turdis*, breaking off a *copper bolt* mid-thread and moving to a different cubicle in order to prevent a blockage.

two shits behind *phr.* The situation of being so extraordinarily busy at work than one is forced to forego the traditional daily brace of trips to the *smallest room* during office hours. *'Sorry madam. I'm afraid the dentist won't be able to give you an appointment till Thursday week at the earliest. He's two shits behind as it is.'*

two slice toaster *n.* A person whose dishevelled appearance and evident social inadequacy leads one to conclude that they unlikely ever to find themselves preparing meals for anyone else.

two way teaser *1. n.* A well-known daily newspaper's coffee break crossword puzzle which offers both easy and difficult clues, both ending in the same result. *2. n.* A lady who, at the start of the evening, disingenuously implies that both an *easy pink* and a *difficult brown* may be on the cards.

tying down Gulliver *n.* The ineffably charming tableau of many men simultaneously *lobbing ropes* over one very lucky young lady.

ugly Betty *n.* A particularly unsightly *grimquim;* an unholy hybrid of *Terry Waite's allotment* and a *snatchmo*, with an odour redolent of Whitby when the tide's out. And not in a good way.

unable to find second gear *euph.* Being *sucked off* whilst driving, possibly to relieve the symptoms of chronic pancreatitis. *'Yes officer, I know I was only doing 10mph in the outside lane, but I was unable to find second gear. Wasn't I darling?'*

uncomfortable *adj.* Of shoes, having "fuck me" written all over them.

under starter's ordures *1. euph.* To squat like a jockey in the stirrups in an attempt to shift an obdurate *feeshee* lodged stubbornly in the *Enochs. 'Sorry I'm late. I'm afraid I had extra scrambled eggs for breakfast, and I was under starter's ordures in the crappers for an hour this lunchtime.' 'That's very interesting, Mr Forsyth. Now, do you want this fucking knighthood or not?' 2. euph.* Upon entering the office *Rick Witters* and finding all the stalls are occupied, to be left in an uncomfortable, defecatory limbo with one's *chocolate stallions* poised to gallop and champing at the bit.

under the Bush administration *1. adj.* Descriptive of the United States Senate between 2001 and 2009. *2. adj.* Descriptive of a lady who *knows her way around an engine.*

undie fudge *n. Miniature heroes, clinkers, winnets.*

unfuckcessful *adj.* Of an evening out, or a person, sexually fruitless.

unit counter *n.* Someone who is scared stiff of drinking to a respectable level.

unit move *1. n.* Film industry phrase describing the transfer of the crew and all their equipment to the next filming location. *2. n.* Toilet industry phrase describing a bowel *motion.*

unpacking a new memory foam mattress, like *sim.* Descriptive of the experience of removing tight clothing from a *lass* just before lights out, only to watch as she expands to three times her previous compact dimensions.

unpack your holiday luggage *v.* To unleash a gargantuan seven-day behemoth of a *Richard* when you get home from a week's all-inclusive. *'No, dear, we're not stopping on the way home to say home to your parents. I need to get home to unpack the holiday luggage.'*

unsinkable Molly Brown, the *1. n.* American socialite and philanthropist who survived the sinking of the *Titanic* and later became the subject of a Broadway musical. *2. n.* A buoyant *floater* left by the wife or a lady-friend, about which one would be unlikely to get backing for a sumptuously-staged theatrical production.

untertainment *n.* The opposite of entertainment, *eg.* That self-consciously highbrow *"Weakest Link* with A-Levels" telly quiz *Only Connect*, hosted by buxom gag-murderer Victoria Coren.

up and down like a jockey's bollocks *1. sim.* Descriptive of an act of *coitus* that makes up for what it lacks in technique with enthusiasm. *2. sim.* A colourful figure of speech. *'How many times has that fucking phone rang tonight? Honestly, I've been up and down like a jockey's bollocks, Lord Grantham.' 3. sim.* A poetic phrase used when referring to something that varies considerably and often above and below a comfortable median value. *'Have you seen them pictures of Kerry Katona on the beach in the Daily Mail? Christ, her weight's up and down like a jockey's bollocks, your holiness.'*

upload a file to the cloud *v.* To *blow off.*

up the Burway *euph. Up the wrong 'un.* Named after the eponymous narrow lane in the Shropshire Hills. *'I took the missus up the Burway for an anniversary treat.'*

urban jellyfish *n.* A rubbery, semi-translucent, parazoological beast typically found drifting in the stagnant canals and waterways of towns and cities. *Jubber ray, dunky, Coney Island whitefish.*

Usain Bolt *n.* That which is *shot* by a bloke with a tendency to be *out of the blocks* before the starter has fired his gun.

user friendly *1. adj.* Of an item of technology, such as a computer or similar, very easy to operate. *'Have you seen me new iPad? It's very user friendly. Even me grandad's had a go on it.' 2. adj.* Of a young lady, possessing the deeply attractive quality of requiring very little *end-user* input before satisfying a chap's beastly urges. *'Have you met me new bird? She's very user friendly. Even me grandad's had a go on her.'*

vadger farm *n.* An old folks' home.

vafrazzle *v.* To decorate one's ladyfriend's *vajayjay* with cheap, bacon-flavoured crisps. It could happen.

vafro *n.* A magnificently hairy 1970s *biffer.*

vag-a-bond *n.* An exceptionally adhesive *danny fishcharge.*

vagician *n.* One who uses *sleight of gland* to charm the ladies.

vagile *adj.* Of a female, unusually limber, supple or flexible about the nether regions.

vaginyl *n.* Classic, analogue *clopper,* much sought after by connoisseurs.

vagitas *n.* Tex-mex *snatches.* Hopefully served without salsa and cheese.

vag patch *n.* A wholesome, well-ploughed *ladygarden* which provides a chap with a fair percentage of his five-a-day.

vajizzle *v.* To improvise the decoration of a special friend's *vajayjay* when there are no Swarovski crystals immediately to hand.

valet your hoop *n.* To give one's *ringpiece* a bit of a wipe round.

valley of the deaf *n.* The cleavage of a generously-*top-bollocked* woman, wherein a fellow might hope to experience a temporary loss of hearing.

vandalised bus seat *n.* A well-*shagged minniemoo* which has been badly repaired using duct-tape.

vandaljism *n.* The wantom damage done to a lady's curtains, towels, bedsheets, cat *etc.,* when a chap elects to clean his pecker after an amorous assignation.

vank *n.* A *wank* in a van. From van + wank.

VAT fighters *n.* Larger-boned folk who perhaps, it could be argued, were wont to protest a tad too much over the recent proposed imposition of a 20% tax on sausage rolls and pasties.

vegan quiche *euph.* Something that is an entirely underwhelming example of its kind, *eg.* The Rover 75 CDT "Connoisseur".

vegan's fry-up *n.* Something that is extremely unsatisfying, *eg.* A *tit wank* off Tara Palmer-Tompkinson.

veinish blue *n. Hedam.*

veiny vuvuzela *n.* The latest addition to the *woodwind* ensemble, to be played alongside the *skin flute, one-eyed piccolo, American trombone, pink oboe, beef bugle, fleshy flugelhorn, ejaculating clarinet* and *purple-headed spam bassoon.*

velocipedophile *n.* A *snufty, snudger, shramper, quumfer, scrunger, pringle, snerger, snedger, snaffler, snarze, snerk, snerdler, shniffle-piffler, nurfer, moompher, barumpher, garboon, pooner, snarfer, snurdle* or *snurge.* A harmless fellow who takes his olfactory pleasures whilst in close proximity to young ladies' recently-vacated bicycle seats.

velvet parachute *1. n.* A new type of mushroom discovered recently in Madagascar. *2. n.* A *moss cottage* you could fry up for breakfast.

venison blinds *n.* Posh *mutton shutters,* sirloin *beef curtains.*

verse from the Old Testament, like a *sim.* Description of horrid sounds emanating from a *trap* during the exorcism of a particularly malevolent *copper bolt, viz.* "...much wailing and gnashing of teeth".

very tits off the Virgin Mary, thinks he's the *exclam.* Said of a person with a particularly high opinion of himself. *'Yeah, I met the tidy-bearded little shortarse at a helicopter show. Thinks he's the very tits off the Virgin Mary.'*

vesta *n.* A short, purple-ended length of *wood* that goes off when rubbed gently on the side of a *box.*

vested interests *n. Assets, competitive advantages, first impressions, qualifications, impressive CVs, leisure facilities.* An extensive *HR department* or splendid *set of references.*

Vesuvius sir! *1. exclam.* In the film *633 Squadron,* the radio signal sent to base to confirm that an overhanging rock has finally been bombed free. *2. exclam.* Said through the lavatory door to a concerned relative to announce that an over-baked *loaf* has successfully been extracted from the *mud oven*.

vext messaging *n.* Unreasonable, harshly-worded SMS communications sent by a chap's wife/girlfriend enquiring after his current location and status, *eg.* "For fuck's sake Baz where are you? You only popped out for some milk and that was 3 days ago. PS I gave birth to a baby boy. WTF LMFAO ... not."

VHS vixen *n.* A *stick vid* actress that one finds slightly less appealing on Blu-ray. A *low resolution fox.*

viagra falls *n.* A girl with such a *lovely personality* that she easily counteracts the stiffening effects of sildenafil citrate.

viagravation *n.* Discomfort and frustration experienced by a chap who has recently ingested a *Bongo Bill's banjo pill* only to learn that his life partner's immediate plans do not coincide with his own.

vice crispy *n.* A contagious wart, boil or scab, occasionally spotted whilst enjoying a *full English breakfast. 'Eurgh. What's this, love?' 'It's just a vice crispy. I've had it since that business trip to Amsterdam.'*

vicious circle *n.* An angry *ringpiece. 'Come for a night at the Rupali Restaurant, Bigg Market, Newcastle upon Tyne, and wake up with a vicious circle you'll have to take to A&E.'*

Vicks shit *n.* A *number two* of such olfactory potency that it manages to unblock your nose and make your eyes water at the same time. *Olbas soil.*

Vi-curious *adj.* Mildly intrigued at the prospect of a spot of *biddy-fiddling.*

vihagra *n.* Extra-powerful *bongo Bill's banjo pills.*

Viking funeral *n.* To tearfully flush a smoking *Bungle's finger* out to sea. The ancient Norse ceremony of *Up Helly Arse.*

vin blank *n.* A missing period of time caused by over-indulgence in certain grape-based beverages. *'SUE LAWLEY: Keith Floyd, you're one of Britain's most popular television celebrities, but you weren't always in the public eye, were you? Tell me about some of the formative experiences of your early life. KEITH FLOYD: Well Sue, I clearly remember going into the pub on my thirteenth birthday and I vaguely recall getting out of a taxi outside Broadcasting House about twenty minutes ago. Everything between those two events is pretty much a vin blank, I'm afraid.'* (Transcript of *Desert island Discs,* BBC Radio 4, broadcast on December 30th 1990).

vinegar dip *n.* A bout of penetrative affection with a lady who is sadly past her prime years of youthful ripeness, such that her *fanny* has went all wrong and caustic.

visit the graveyard *n.* To indulge in post break-up sexual shenanigans with a former girlfriend.

vitamin T *n.* Essential dietary supplement north of the border. Tennent's lager.

Voldemort *n.* Secret name for a chap's *thingie.* "Him who must not be named" or "you know who".

vombard *v.* To bombard with vomit from a high place. From vomit + bombard.

vomelch *v., n.* A lusty belch with an unexpected *yoff* follow-through that must then be swallowed back down, especially if one finds oneself amongst polite company. *Vurp, Monkhouse syndrome.*

vomelette *n.* A lumpy pile of yellow *chunder.* Mushrooms 60p extra.

vowel movement, have a *v.* To talk *shit*

V2 *1. n.* In aviation, the point at which a pilot is committed to completing a take-off. *2. n.* In *pooing,* the point at which there is no turning back, the *turtle's head* is fully engaged in the *dirt canal* and the *pooer* is committed to doing a *poo. 'Oh bollocks. I'm at V2 and my belt buckle has jammed. Mayday! Mayday!'*

vulvarine *n. Fanny batter* that spreads straight from the fridge.

WABOC/waboc *abbrev*. Shorthand terminology for a group of disagreeable people. What A Bunch Of Cunts.

wadding *n*. Poking a *Thora* down the plughole with one's toes following a natural delivery in the shower or bath.

wafty crank *n*. *One off the wrist knocked out* on the sly. *'Terry knew it would only take his missus ten minutes to pop the local corner shop to pick up her daily supplies of forty Embassy and eight cans of Natch, just enough time for a wafty crank. Or two.'*

wake up and smell the cocky *exclam*. Motivational phrase which can be used to encourage a wavering *vagitarian lezzer* to get *back onto solids*.

walking stick *n*. A long, knobbly *motion* that has bottomed out on the pan whilst still connected to your *arse*. A *neckbreaker, earthing cable.*

Wallace *n*. A disappointingly flaccid penis. From sweaty, egg-headed *Masterchef* host Gregg Wallace's catchphrase; "It doesn't get harder than this."

Wallsend trim *n*. A haircut so short that you lose three layers of skin off your scalp in the process. Administered by all barbers in the eponymous leafy Tyneside suburb, irrespective of the style requested by the customer. A *tuppenny all-off, Geordie affro.*

Walter *n*. A particularly verdant, luxurious, deep-pile *cunt-rug*. From "Walter Wall carpets". A *Judith*. *'Nice Walter you got there, your worship. You look like you've been hit between the legs with a bag of soot, look you.'*

Walters *n. rhym. slang*. Breasts. From the eponymous character in James Thurber's 1942 short story *The Secret Life of Walter Mockers.*

wang commander *n*. Temporary, transient rank enjoyed by a chap gripping his *joystick* in the *bogs* of an aeroplane.

wangle *v*. To *wank* oneself into an advantageous situation. Although it's not entirely clear under what circumstances this might be achieved.

wankameters *n*. Optimistic, self-administered moral, ethical and legal boundaries set and hopefully adhered to by single gentlemen, with the intention of precluding the development of undesirable habits and preoccupations.

wank and a cider *n*. A man's post-work plans for the evening. *'Doing anything tonight, Jeremy?' 'Yeah. After Newsnight, it's a wank and a cider for me.'*

wank chaser *n*. A swift *hand shandy* enjoyed during a brief lull in proceedings after *dropping the kids off at the pool. Icing the log.*

wankend *n*. A well-earned period of uninterrupted *relaxation* enjoyed by a gentleman between Friday teatime and *sparrowfart* the following Monday. Also *wank holiday, wristuntide.*

wanking glove *n*. A sexual partner to whom one feels no emotional attachment. *'Well, Martin, there were three of us in that marriage, so it was a bit crowded. To Charles I was no more than a wanking glove.'*

wanking gown *n*. A dressing robe made of absorbent towelling material, of the style favoured by bachelors at weekends, and those who are actively seeking work seven days every week. *'Aw, do I have to come down the morgue, Sarge? I'm in my wanking gown.'*

wanking sabbatical *n*. A three month tour of duty on a nuclear submarine.

wanking to the same jazz mag *phr*. Middle management jargon - a somewhat coarser variant of "singing from the same hymn sheet".

wanking wrench *n*. A gentleman's forearm. *'Posh, I'm thinking of having your name tattooed in Sanskrit along my wanking wrench, but spelled wrong.'*

wanklash *n*. A painful spinal injury sustained whilst *pulling off* without due care and attention.

wank nappy *n.* A small piece of tissue placed on the end of the *giggle stick* after a *solo session* in order to prevent tell-tale *slug trails* on the inside of the *dunghampers*.

wank side/bottom *n.* After a bedtime re-buff from one's somnolent significant other, the no doubt politically incorrect act of *bashing one out* over her lower back after she turns over and goes to sleep.

wank stamp *n.* A saucy thumbnail image saved to a smartphone device as an aid to *self help*.

wanktimonious *adj.* Descriptive of a person who denounces the practice of *self delight*.

wank wall *n.* The masturbatory equivalent of the marathon runner's "wall", whereby an over-achieving *self harmer* loses consciousness after biting off more than he can chew, if you will. *'Somehow, he must still have been in the porn warehouse when they locked up for the night. They reckon he must have hit his wank wall at about 3am. Anyway, ashes to ashes, dust to dust.'*

wanky panky *n.* Mutual masturbation. *'For crying out loud, Philip. If you suppose I'm going to get up to anything remotely athletic after that eight course state reception, you've got another think coming. A spot of wanky panky is the most you're getting, matey.'*

wanquet *n.* A magnificent spread in a *jazz mag*.

wap *n.* Afternoon shut-eye combined with a little light *relaxation*. From wank + nap. *'Look after the kids for a couple of hours, love. I'm off for a wap.'*

war and faece *n.* A substantial piece of *shiterature* taken into the *smallest room* to peruse during a lengthy *sit down adventure*.

war horse *n.* A "rearing steed" stance adopted whilst trying to pass an enormous *copper bolt* following two weeks of constipation. An ordeal that could possibly be ameliorated by imagining Benedict Cumberbatch shouting "Be brave! Be brave!"

warmhole *n.* A *hairy split* in the space-time continuum.

warm toilet seat, like sitting on a *sim.* Descriptive of the uncomfortable, dawning realisation that one may not be the exclusive beneficiary of one's current ladyfriend's affections.

war of the noses *n.* An uneasy, stenchsome armistice between two occupants of adjacent public lavatory cubicles, each one sitting over their *copper bolts* in silence and waiting for the other to make the first move, clean up and depart. A *Mexican shit-off.*

Warrington spa *n.* A quick blast of deodorant, a stick of chewing gum and a *wank*. The traditional preparations for a night out in the vibrant Mancunian suburb.

wasbian *n.* In the world of *grumbular* entertainment, a *carpet muncher* over the age of about thirty who should probably start thinking about earning a living in a manner that better befits her advanced years. Also *hasbian, lesbeen.*

waste buds *n.* Sensitive spice receptors located in and around the *rusty sheriff's badge*. *'Ooh, that prawn and Scotch bonnet vindaloo I had last night is really tickling my waste buds this morning, Rabbi.'*

waterboarding *n.* A brief drowning sensation experienced whilst *orally pleasuring* a *bird* who happens to be a profuse *squirter*.

Watkins *n.rhyming slang.* The *nipsy*. From the haulage company whose trucks are often to be seen along the A30 between the Clock House Roundabout and Hatton Cross; Watkins & Sole. *'Sit still will you, Prime Minister.' 'Sorry Nick, I've got an itchy Watkins.'*

wedgehog *n.* A *fuller-figured* lady who affects tight-fitting leggings, thus showing off her generously-proportioned *camel's toe* to great advantage.

wedgiemite *n. Aus.* Organic ooze *down under*

that collects in the *fairy hammock* on hot days. *Arse feta.*

welder's wife *n.* A spouse whose aesthetic attributes are best appreciated whilst afflicted with a severe case of photokeratitis.

well nourished *euph.* Descriptive of one who eschews salad.

welly full of custard *euph.* An over-full *cream pie*. *'She says she'll do the whole orchestra, string section first, then the woodwinds and finally the brass and percussion, which is fine as long as I can go first. After all, I'm the conductor and I don't want to stick my foot in a welly full of custard.'*

Wenlock *n.* A one-eyed monster of Olympian proportions. Named after the Shropshire town where all the trademark lawyers are hung like carthorses.

Wensleymale *n. Organzola, himula, felladelphia, veinish blue.*

wereminge *n.* A frighteningly hairy *twat*, occasionally glimpsed during a full moon.

werewolf whistle *n.* A two-part, audible signal of manly appreciation for a woman who appears attractive from behind but who, before the second note has been completed, turns round to reveal herself to be a monster, thus causing the finale to tail off pathetically.

west coast shit *n.* An *airburst*. Taken from the lyrics to the popular hit parade foot-tapper Xxplosive, *West Coast Shit* (feat. Hitman, Kurupt, Nate Dogg and Six-Two), during which Dr Dre (real name Andre Romelle Young PhD) also vouchsafes "my shit's the bomb".

West Indian 80s pace attack *n.* Another somewhat contrived cricketing analogy for toilet troubles to file alongside *Harmison loosener, viz.* An explosive early morning burst from the *Pavilion end*, consisting of several fierce *deliveries*, followed up almost immediately by a renewed and more dangerous onslaught. A *West Indian 80s pace attack* could end up with your nose bones lying shattered on the lavatory floor.

Wetherspoon wurzel *n.* A turnip-headed drinker who habitually lingers in branches of the eponymous public house chain, frightening off any *birds* who enter. A *pub scarecrow.*

wet Jeffrey *n.* Dubious sexual practice whereby a lady slowly lowers her *pissy fanny* onto a waiting gentleman's chin.

wet tea bags *n.* Small, saggy *tits*, usually found on the older woman. Or Willie Carson on *I'm a Celebrity.*

wetter than a window cleaner's cuff *sim.* Self explanatory description of a sexually-excited young lady's *parts of shame* that are *dripping like a fucked fridge.* Also *wetter than a cod's wetsuit, wetter than an otter's pocket, wetter than a fat bird's armpit, wetter than Meat Loaf's hankie, wetter than Lee Evans's suit, wetter than a turfer's knee* or *wetter than Whitney Houston's last joint.*

wetty *n.* The feminine version of a *stiffy.* A *wide-on.*

wet wipe *n.* The act of dabbing the *dewdrops* from one's damp *bellend* onto on a sleeping loved one's *aris* when returning to the *fart sack* after a nocturnal *slash.*

whackaday *n.* An early-morning *wallop* with the old *slug hammer.*

whack pack *n.* The essential equipment taken by a chap heading off on a solo self-catering break in a cheap hotel, *ie.* A holdall full of *seed catalogues*, five rolls of Andrex Extra Soft and a crate of Red Bull. *'Right then, mam. I'll be off.' 'Don't forget your whack pack, son.'*

whackult *n.* A yoghurty drink, full of *Vitamin S*, that plays an important role in the relief of Irritable Bollock Syndrome.

wheelspins *n.* The brown *skidmarks* on the *starting line at Brands Hatch* caused by the sudden acceleration of a *high arsepower shoebox special* when the flush is pulled.

where there's blame there's a claim *phr.* An up-to-date, topical version of the timeless poetic classic "He who smelt it dealt it".

whinge minge *n.* A disgracefully sexist and misogynistic expression for a woman's mouth that would never be acceptable for inclusion in a family publication such as this. *'This house has listened to the Shadow Secretary of State for Culture, Media and Sport at some length on this matter. However, Mr Speaker, she has equivocated for long enough. It is now time for my right honourable friend to shut her whinge minge and tell us which way her party intends to vote.'*

whippy shit *n.* A soft *Sir Douglas* that is whirled stylishly into the *crapper* and nipped off at the top end. Possibly with monkey blood and crushed nuts, although you would hope not.

Whitby kipper *n. rhym. slang.* Stripper. Possibly also a reference to the aroma released when an exotic early afternoon pub dancer cracks open her legs as the finale to her act.

Whitney Houston's last joint, wetter than *sim.* Offensively and disrespectfully descriptive of the moistness of a young lady in a state of excitement.

whopper with cheese *n.* A *buffet slayer* with a savoury fungal infection in her *club sandwich.*

whore DERV *1. n.* A shameless strumpet who works at the local petrol station. *2. n. Tart fuel, hen petrol, whore star* or *knicker oil.*

whorendous *adj.* Of time spent in the company of a *good time girl*, bad. *'Well, what a whorendous evening I've had. It's almost a relief to be going home.' 'That'll be two thousand pounds in a brown envelope please, Lord Archer.'*

whoregeous *adj.* Descriptive of a particularly comely *Covent Garden nun. 'Look at these photos of the pro I knobbed in Amsterdam. That's my cock in her mouth there.' 'Fuck me, well done mate, she's absolutely* whoregeous. *Anyway, I'm going to prescribe you a some penicillin for the syphilis, anti-virals for the genital herpes and a course of metronidazole for the trichomoniasis.'*

whorelage *n.* The stretch limo trade. *'I'm thinking of buying a 35-foot Hummer and going into the whorelage business.'*

whoreovirus *n. medic.* A dose of *cock rot* contracted from a lady of the night.

whoresome *adj.* Of a common *dollymop*, arousing wonderment in the trouser frontage.

whoretumnal *adj.* Descriptive of the latter years of a working girl's career, when her *foliage* begins to change colour and everything starts heading south.

whore wound *n.* Injury sustained when going into battle with a *good time girl*, usually in the form of grazed knees or a stabbed *arse.*

wife baiter *n.* Any borderline non-essential item purchased by a married man on the joint account he shares with his missus with the reasonable expectation that it might bring out the beast in her, *eg.* A new set of fancy, carbon fibre golf clubs to accompany the graphite-shafted ones he bought three months ago to replace the titanium ones he bought a couple of months before that.

wifeguard *n.* A computer system that prevents a man being killed by his missus, *eg.* The "Incognito" function on Google Chrome. *'My heart stopped when I saw her crank up the laptop, but then I remembered I was protected by the wifeguard.'*

wifer *n.* A fellow who is imprisoned in his marriage with no hope of escape, parole or remission.

wifey hotspot *n.* Any place that is a magnet for *bingo-winged*, middle-aged females, *eg.* Iceland, Mecca or the box office at any venue where Michael Bolton, Daniel O'Donnell or Take That are appearing.

WIFI/wifi *acronym. interrog.* Would I Fuck It?

Wiggins *n. Pubage* that carries on down the

insides of a young lady's thighs. Named after the trademark sideburns of yellow-jerseyed bicyclist Sir Bradley. Also *Rhodes Boysons, inside burns, thighbrows, judge's eyebrows* and *whack-os.*

Wilberforce *n.* An inoffensive term for one's *ladykiller.*

wild westing *n. Fingering* two women simultaneously, in a style reminiscent of a cowboy brandishing a couple of six-shooters.

Wilfred's bear, leave her like *n.* To liberally *bespangle* a lucky young lady. From the dirty, *spunk*-ridden ursine that is the object of the dog/man-in-a-dog-suit's affections in the eponymous television series.

willy welly *n.* A *jubber ray* that pulls your socks off.

WILSTAF/wilstaf *acronym.* A polite term for a particularly alluring female. Woman I'd Like to Shag To A Frazzle.

winching out the Chilean miners *euph.* The act of manually hoisting one's *tadpoles* up a narrow tube and out into daylight.

windaloo *n.* Following a piquantly spicesome *Ruby Murray* and finding oneself without access to a suitable water closet, violently voiding the *dirt bakery oven* through the nearest convenient casement.

wind chimes *n.* Soothingly melodic noises in the middle of the night.

wine flu *n. medic.* Short-lived virus typically caught from a drinking glass. Also *beer ache, rumbago, brewmonia, ginfluenza.*

wine-ker *n.* An aggravating and pretentious oenophile who can't glug a glass of Aldi screwtop without using words like "bouquet", "grape" and "nose".

Winkleman's fringe *euph.* An unkempt *mimsy.*

winners' podium *n.* Sir Chris standing proudly in the middle and the Brownlee boys on either side. The *fruit bowl.*

winter bone *1. n.* Title of an Oscar shoe-in movie starring newcomer Jennifer Law-rence. Never heard of it. *2. n.* An impressively robust *stonk-on* achieved on a particularly cold day.

winter warmer *n.* A particularly long, drawn out and stinky, hot *Miranda* emitted beneath the duvet at any time between October and February. *'That was quite a winter warmer, love. I think I'll turn down the electric blanket.'*

wipe your arse and call that a shit *exclam.* A witty retort to another person's foul *trouser cough.*

wise guy in concrete boots, go down like a *sim.* To embark on a marathon session of *cumulonimbus. 'You should have seen her face when she caught me strangling Kojak over her sister's holiday pics. I had to go down like a wise guy in concrete boots to get away with that one. And now here's Liam Dutton with the weather.'*

wishbone *n.* The often-pulled penile consequence of an aspirational sexual fantasy.

witches' knickers *n.* Thin plastic bags fluttering menacingly in the twigs of an urban tree. *Govan bunting.*

witch's leg, cock like a *sim.* A crooked, knobbly-kneed *giggle stick* with all blue varicose veins up the side.

WOAGST/woagst *acronym.* Said of a *yummy mummy.* Worthy Of A Good Seeing To. Also *hagst,* said of a *goer* who is *up the stick, viz.* Had A Good Seeing To.

wolverine wank *n.* An act of third party *manual relief* where the recipient is in fear of getting his *bell end* scratched by a lady with long, sharp nails.

womberang *n. Aus.* A randy length of *wood* that keeps coming back for more.

womb fruit *n.* A baby.

wombling *n.* When investigating a lady's *applecatchers,* the point when one's hand goes from exploring "overground" to exploring "underground", if you will.

women's game of pool, as long as a *sim.* Said of a particularly lengthsome member. *'And our final panel member tonight is Stephen Pound who has been MP for Ealing North since 1997. Prior to becoming an MP he worked as a bus conductor and hospital porter, in Tony Blair's government he was parliamentary private secretary to Hazel Blears, and he is well known in the House of Commons for having a charlie as long as a women's game of pool.'*

wonder how many calories are in that? *exclam.* A rhetorical exclamation in the wake of a particularly nourishing *air buffet.*

wonderlaps *n.* The impressive, swaying *headlamps* on an approaching lady cyclist wearing loose summer attire, which offer a pleasant diversion for gentleman road-users, providing them with a welcome respite from the dull business of observing the Highway Code, looking out for other traffic/pedestrians and steering.

wonga conga *n. A* Thursday night on the tiles funded by a payday loan.

Wonnacott wait, the *n.* When *working from home, one off the wrist* enjoyed in the no-man's-land between *Ken Bruce's Popmaster* and *Bargain Hunt.*

woo *1. v.* To charm someone with your romantic behaviour, perhaps by buying them flowers and chocolates and that. *2. v.* To *wee* and *poo* at the same time. From wee + poo. *3. v.* To charm a German by *weeing* and *pooing* at the same time.

wooden horse *n.* In a public *Rick Witter,* the act of releasing a noisy *chocolate hostage* at the exact moment when one's neighbour is flushing. Named after a famous Second World War prison escape which applied a similar subterfuginous stratagem.

wood glue *1. n.* Sticky white substance which is typically used for bonding timber. *2. n.* Sticky white substance which is not typically used for bonding timber, but might work in an emergency. *Population paste.* Also *cockidex, pyjama glue, sement, jazz glue, Aphrodite's evostick, gonad glue, prick stick, man mastic.*

wooden leg, draw the spunk from a *phr.* A somewhat hyperbolic assessment of a woman's attractiveness. *'Fuck me static, missus. You'd draw the spunk from a wooden leg, you would. Anyway, the reason I'm calling is to see if you have ever thought about joining the Church of Jesus Christ of Latter-day Saints.'*

woodwork chewer *n.* An arduous late night *dreadnought;* a laborious, supersized *moonlight flit.*

woolly scooter *n.* A very hairy, yet nonetheless tidy, *minge.* Perhaps with a load of mirrors sticking out the sides for good measure.

working on a dream *n.* Masturbating. From the lyrics to the Bruce Springsteen song of the same name, *viz.* "Out here the nights are long, the days are lonely / I think of you and I'm working on a dream ... / ... Rain pourin' down / I swing my hammer / My hands are rough from working on a dream".

working on his novel *euph.* Of a tortured artist, frittering away the limited time he has on this earth watching Jeremy Kyle, eating Quavers and *wanking* in his dressing gown.

worries about his clothes *euph.* Said of a chap who *makes a good quiche.*

worzel gummage *n. Horatio* off elderly, toothless ladies of Cornish origin. *Flo jobs.*

worzel rummage *n.* A wholesome, rural, bucolic outdoor *bum swizzle* in the bushes. *'You're late home, Terry' 'Yes, June. I've been at the police station. I got arrested having a worzel rummage in the rhododendrons by the bowling green steps.'*

wrestle with one's conscience *v.* To spend a sleepless night *tossing,* but not necessarily turning.

wring a kidney *v.* To pass urine. *'Where's the*

gurgler, your majesty? I've just got to wring a kidney before I get knighted. I don't want to piss meself when I kneel down.'

wristing the night away *n.* Standard evening's entertainment for the impecunious undergraduate.

wrist oil *n. Perseverance soup, guardsman's gloss, ball glaze, dew on the lily, balm before the storm, knuckle varnish, snake spit* or *French polish.*

writer's cock *n. psych.* Psychological condition whereby a man is unable to put pen to paper until he has had at least five *wanks*. A condition which is commonly suffered by journalists facing imminent deadlines, students with essays to complete and Ernest Hemingway. *'Ah, Herr Schubert. How is that Eighth Symphony of yours coming along?' 'Well, I was thinking of doing a nice scherzo section for it, and then maybe a big finale in B Minor in which all the themes of the earlier movements are brought together, only I've had terrible writer's cock for the last six years.'*

wronk *n. Self harm* performed in morally dubious circumstances.

wunch *n. coll.* Collective noun for a group of those hard-working, public-spirited heroes who toil for our benefit in the financial sector, *viz.* "A wunch of bankers".

XBox legs *n. medic.* Doughy, atrophied lower limbs, as sported by pasty-faced teenagers with unusually well-developed thumbs.

X-men *1. n.* A team of Marvel Comics superheroes; mutants who fight against Professor Magnus Pyke and the Brotherhood of Man. Or something like that. Ask that fat man in *spunk*-stained jogging bottoms lurking in the crisps aisle at the supermarket for more details. *2. n.* A member of an exclusive secret coterie of bachelor devotees of the sort of movies which are only available for viewing by a restricted audience. *'You know that bloke upstairs with the really thick glasses and extremely muscular right arm? Yeah? Well, keep it under your hat but I have it on very good authority that he's one of the X-men.'*

xmas tree light, weenie like a *sim.* An unnecessarily cutting reference to the diminutive dimensions of a fellow's *old chap*, as heard in kiddies' cartoon series *Family Guy*.

yawning goldfish *n.* A particularly wide *Jap's eye.*

yawning tabbycat *n.* Poetic term for the female *flangepiece*, particularly whilst in a state of post-coital relaxation.

yeast infection *n. medic.* A mild dose of *beer cancer.*

yeasty beasty *n.* A derogatory term for a lady with a dubious sexual hygiene regimen.

yellow Dick Turpin *n.* A speed camera.

yellow noise *n.* Diffuse and unsatisfactory pissing stream, which can only be tuned out by careful of adjustment of the *knob*. Possibly caused by interference from Hilversum. *'I was suffering from terrible yellow noise this morning, and now I've got Dutch brogues.'*

ye-stenders *n.* Dismissive epithet for any period soap opera, *eg. Cranford, Downton Abbey, Upstairs Downstairs.*

yoghurt weaver *n.* The sort of holistic, green, vegan, yurt-wearing right-on liberal who drives a G-Whizz.

you could hear a fly wank *exclam.* Literary phrase illustrating a scene of notable quietude. *''Twas the night before Christmas, and all through the house, not a creature was stirring, not even a mouse. The building lay silent, in fact to be frank, the house was so still, you could hear a fly wank.'*

you could make soup with her knickers *exclam.* Said of a woman who is not overly diligent about personal daintiness.

you got yourself a sandwich sir *exclam.* An advertising slogan used on commercials for Wendy's, an American burger restaurant, wittily pressed into service to describe a *bone-on* of notable length or girth, *ie.* A fat-filled half-pound of sweaty meat, preferably stuck between a couple of baps. With a cheesy topping.

youkakke *n.* The inadvertant practice of rendering oneself in one's own *nut butter.*

you shop, we drop 1. *phr.* Advertising slogan displayed on the sides of Tesco supermarket home delivery vans. 2. *n.* Tempting overture delivered by one or more *ladies of the night* through the rolled-down window of a Premiership footballer, or indeed his team manager's, motor car.

zasm *n*. The female equivalent of *jism*. *'Do you know where my other tie is, love? I can't read the Channel 4 News in this one, it's got all zasm down it.'*

zelebrity *n*. Somewhat oxymoronically, a Z-list celebrity. *'This Autumn on Living TV sees the return of Zelebrity Most Haunted Live. Some cunt off Hollyoaks, Becki from Big Brother 4 and the Duchess of York attempt to spend the night in a darkened room with Yvette Fielding, her fat mate and the bald bloke who looks like Uncle Fester.'* (from *TV Times*, August 2009).

zombie's fart *sim*. A poetic evocation of the potent morning-after breath of one who has eaten more than his fair share of kebab meat and chili sauce the previous evening. And then come home and opened the Doritos.

zopi clown *n*. A person comically attempting to carry out simple household tasks whilst slipping into a tranquilised state under the influence of the quick-acting prescription sleeping tablet zopiclone. *'Maw, maw! Come quick. Gran'paw's deein' a shite in the neighbours' garden the noo!' 'Don't worry, oor Wullie. The daft auld cunt's just playin' the zopi clown. I'll fetch ma brush.'*

zuffle cat *n*. An unfortunate pet that finds itself cornered in a curtainless bedroom.

ZZ Mott *n*. A badly overgrown *underbeard*. Also *Terry Waite's allotment, tank driver's hat, Taz, wookiee hole, yak, superfuzz big-muff deluxe edition, Judith, eskimo's glove, muff like your granny's hat, gruffalo, fanny like a guardsman's hat, busby berkeley, hairy knickers, Lord Winston's moustache, Paddy McGinty's goat, Percy Thrower's lawn, radar trap, barber's floor, beartrapper's hat, biffer, Bilbo Baggins's foot, wolf pussy, bushell, div-ot, Dougal* and *Mary Hinge*.

Z Zulu *euph*. A reference to a particular arrangement of nautical flags which means, variously, "I require a tug" and, apparently, "I am shooting nets". Also *flag zulu*.

ACKNOWLEDGEMENTS

Sir Roger Mellie OBE would like to thank the
following people, without whom this book
would not have been possible:

Caroline Addy, Russell Blackman,
Alex Morris and Charlie Brooker.
And a big thank you to all the Viz
readers who have so selflessly
sent in contributions.

Roger's Profanisaurus is updated
every five weeks in Viz Comic.

Submit your own favourite obscenities to
profanisaurus@viz.co.uk

www.viz.co.uk

If you thought this book was a waste of money, wait till you read THIS fucker...

- 12,000 entries
- 624 pages
- £13.99

Viz
DAS KRAPITAL
ROGER'S PROFANISAURUS

Dennis

THE REVOLUTIONARY DICTIONARY OF BAD LANGUAGE ★ NOW EVEN BIGGER